"*Sounds so good to me*"

Otis Rush   Photo by Amy O'Neal, Living Blues Collection

"Sounds so good to me"

The bluesman's story
Barry Lee Pearson

υ/ʌ UNIVERSITY OF PENNSYLVANIA PRESS • *Philadelphia*

To Elizabeth Pearson, wife and friend

Designed by Adrianne Onderdonk Dudden

Library of Congress Cataloging in Publication Data

Pearson, Barry Lee.
  "Sounds so good to me".

  Bibliography: p.
  Includes index.
  1. Blues (Songs, etc.)—United States—History and
criticism.   2. Musicians—United States—Interviews.
I. Title.
ML3521.P4   1984   784.5'3'00922 [B]   83-14764
ISBN 0-8122-1171-5

Printed in the United States of America

Third printing, 1985

The blues come from right here in America. That is your American music and if you don't appreciate it, it's like a child being born, don't appreciate his mother.

—*JOHNNY SHINES*

Contents

Illustrations

Frontispiece: Otis Rush

(following p. 72)

Preface

As the 1960s drew to a close, the first Ann Arbor Blues Festival attracted musicians from all over the United States. The biggest names in the blues business played to an enthusiastic audience. I was there as a blues fan first, but also as a graduate student intent on studying American music. Armed with a letter requesting that I be allowed backstage, I threaded my way through the crowd to the fenced-off performer's area. To my astonishment the letter worked, and I suddenly found myself in the company of some of America's finest blues musicians and my own personal heroes.

Having grown up in Chicago, I was no stranger to the music. I had even spent time with musicians like Big Joe Williams, Memphis Slim, and J. B. Lenoir. Big Davey Myers of the "Aces" taught me to play the bass from up on the bandstand of the now defunct club Big John's. Outside the same club, I witnessed back-alley arguments between the musicians and union representatives who were on their case for working below scale. Yet I never really considered blues musicians as union members— or as members of anything else for that matter. To my mind a blues singer was a loner, traveling life's rough road with only a guitar for company.

But backstage at Ann Arbor I was struck by the sense of community the artists projected. It shaped the way they spoke as well as the way they looked at the world around them. Friends and rivals exchanged greetings couched in a characteristic competitive banter. Old partners recalled their past adventures, introduced their new sidemen, and caught up on the latest gossip—who made it big, who quit, who moved back south, who died. Out front, the audience saw an exceptional blues show. Backstage, the musicians turned the event into their own family reunion.

At that point in my life I loved blues music. It had a special sound that combined evocative language and emotionally expressive music with some deeper human quality that spoke directly to me. But like most other young blues fans, I knew more about the recordings than I did about the artists who created and performed the songs I listened to. As I collected their records, I wanted to know more about the artists I admired.

In Ann Arbor it became apparent that I knew little about the blues artists. These were not the same individuals whose lives I thought I knew so much about from listening to their songs and reading the record jackets. As they talked to one another and to me, I caught the sound of their words against the backdrop of the stage show. Their voices and their music blended into a single soundtrack. Captivated by their words, I made up my mind to go back to Chicago and ask other musicians to tell me their stories.

In graduate school, my research became more and more centered on Afro-American music. In particular, I read critics and scholars who had been inspired to share their appreciation and interpretation of the blues tradition. It was, they agreed, a twelve-bar, three-chord, Afro-American song form played in four-four time with an AAB rhyme scheme. The blues became known by that name around the turn of the century, developing out of earlier forms variously known as reels, corn songs, railroad songs, free labor songs, one-verse songs, jump-up songs, and ditties. Musically, the blues stemmed from hollers, religious songs, ballads, and work songs, and employed vocal techniques characteristic of Afro-American song. Its arrival coincided with the increased popularity of the guitar, although it also represented a shift from earlier string-band traditions. Commercially successful almost from its beginning, the blues has remained a dominant force in American popular music.

Interpretations, however, often left me dissatisfied. Over the years, blues songs have been portrayed as the spirituals of the Negro underworld, songs of self-pity, spontaneous expressions of the singer's emotional life, and protest songs with hidden meanings. Blues artists, where the term "artist" was applicable, were shown to be thoughtless, natural musicians or items of sociological data. While these perceptions may have once been valid, none seemed applicable to the music I knew.

As a musician, I had intuitively begun to grasp some of the rules and values of the blues as an artistic system. Taking my cue from Sterling Brown, Ralph Ellison, and Albert Murray, I accepted the blues as an art form first and foremost. By extension I saw the artist as a master of his idiom and not as society's victim.

The bluesmen's art continues to be misinterpreted, and their contribution to American culture remains unrecognized. The confusion is doubly unfortunate because it not only denies them the recognition they are due, it prevents the public from appreciating and using what they have to offer. As much as these artists need recognition to enrich their lives, we need the blues to enrich ours.

But how can we begin to clear up the confusion? First, we can consider the sources of our information more carefully. Beyond what scholars, folklorists, poets, and critics have interpreted for us, our primary source of information is obviously the artists themselves, who give us information through their music as well as their comments on their lives and their art. While blues songs have received a great deal of attention in terms of content, composition, and performance, the bluesmen's story— what they tell us about themselves —has been taken for granted.

In writing this book, I wanted to take a hard look at the blues artist's story not only as a source of information about the speaker and blues musicians as a group but also as a creative document in its own right. Listening to the artists tell their stories, I was intrigued by certain threads that carried over from one artist's story to the next. Over the years, I continually encountered similar corresponding topics that appeared to be characteristic of the blues musicians' tale in general: their first instrument, their parents' response to their music, how they learned to play, who inspired them, first jobs, work-related experiences with alcohol, violence, and rip-offs, their relationship with other musicians, and their vision of the future.

I felt that these overlapping subjects, whether offered by the musician or solicited by the interviewer, provided a key to our understanding of the blues musician. I began to compare the artists' stories, paying special attention to repeated topics. I wanted to know what blues musicians generally say about themselves, what that means in relation to the blues tradition, and, to a certain degree, why they say what they say. I asked them simply to tell me their story, or life story. The musicians were familiar with the term "life story" and generally responded with some version of their life as a musician. I had intended to make my request and then keep silent, but I found that my vow of silence too often led to a dead silence that offended the musicians, who were affronted by what they perceived as rudeness. Besides, they were far too polite to exclude me, however passive I tried to be.

Most of the musicians I spoke with work at other jobs. Whether gravedigger or police officer, each considers himself primarily a blues musician and is proud of it. Each tells his story as a blues artist at the expense of his life's other aspects. I had no reason to probe the artists' private thoughts or to extract details of their personal lives— not that I didn't get this sort of information, just that I didn't seek it. In many cases there were already biographies available where such detail was a prime concern.

My interest was with the public figure. That is, I chose to look more deeply into the musicians' traditional mask and to use tradition as a way of approaching the art form. I wanted them to tell me the story they usually tell when they present themselves to the public.

The subjects of their stories—the images both concrete and metaphorical that a self-conscious group of artists use to portray their lives—form the nucleus of this book. My wish is to use the bluesman's story as a vehicle to celebrate the artists and to shed light on what they do so well.

The first two chapters provide examples of two bluesmen telling their stories. Chapters 3 and 9 consider the bluesman's story in general: the contexts in which it is told, the influence of the interview format, and the other forces that shape its content and provide its traditional subjects. Chapters 4 through 8 focus on these subjects, and, finally, Chapter 10 is about the musicians' view of their art form as well as their vision of their future.

As a folklorist, I am committed to the ideal of accurate transcription. The musicians speak for themselves, and their statements stand on their own merits. However, this procedure can be easily abused when the writer fails to reflect on how the speaker wishes himself to be seen in print. Print is not speech, and speech in print can improperly magnify rhetorical devices, such as repetition or dialect pronunciation, and make the speaker appear foolish. So, keeping in mind the goal of accurate transcription, I did not want to make these articulate men appear inarticulate. Print is limited when it comes to presenting oral expression. This is obvious in relation to blues songs, and the same problem of diminishing richness applies to the bluesman's story as well.

The interviews conducted over the past dozen years were a joy to me, and during them I found the musicians to be excellent spokesmen for the blues as well as gifted, empathetic teachers. (I especially recall James Thomas' concern that I appeared "worried," and I am grateful for the free psychoanalysis he provided.) Beginning in 1969, I spoke with bluesmen in Ann Arbor, Michigan; Chicago, Illinois; Indianapolis and Bloomington, Indiana; and the Washington, D.C., area. The interviews ranged from several minutes to several hours, depending on the time the artist was willing or able to spare. Correspondingly, transcripts ranged from several to seventy pages. Most of the interviews were one-shot situations, although I have spoken with several artists—James Thomas, Archie Edwards, John Cephas, and John Jackson—many times over the years. The interviews took place when and where the opportunity arose: in taverns and dressing rooms, at festivals, on college campuses, in the artist's home, at my home, on the street, and in a barbershop.

All the contributing artists originally came from the South, particularly Mississippi and the Delta region. These include Sam Chatmon, Lee Crisp, Jimmy Dawkins, David "Honeyboy" Edwards, Fred McDowell, Clyde Maxwell, Yank Rachel, Otis Rush, Johnny Shines, Sunnyland Slim, Byther Smith, Roosevelt Sykes, Eddie Taylor, James Thomas, Big Joe Williams, and Johnny Young. Wild Child Butler and Big Chief Ellis came from Alabama; Bob Lowery from Arkansas; John Cephas, Archie Edwards, and John Jackson from Virginia; and J. T. Adams from Kentucky.

I also interviewed white blues players Harmonica Frank Floyd and Bob Reidy, blues promoter Big Bill Hill, and *Living Blues* editors Jim and Amy O'Neal. Group conversations feature the off-the-cuff remarks of blueswoman Big Mama Thornton (the only woman blues singer I spoke with), Muddy Waters, Howling Wolf, Joe Willie Wilkins, Hubert Sumlin, and Babe Stovall. Finally, I occasionally employ corroborative statements from other artists interviewed by various outstanding researchers including David Evans, Bill Ferris, Paul Oliver, Jim O'Neal, Jeff Titon, and Pete Welding.

I wish to thank all the above for their time and cooperation. Thanks also are due my former students Susan Day, for the Chief Ellis material, and Cheryl Brauner, for supplemental John Jackson and John Cephas material; and the National Council for the Traditional Arts, the Smithsonian Institution, and *Living Blues*, for providing photographs. I also wish to thank my teachers: Stith Thompson, Richard Dorson, Alan Merriam, and, especially, my teacher and friend Henry Glassie, who has consistently provided moral support and direction. Further thanks to Bob Cochran, John McGuigan, John Vlach, and Ruth Zelenka for help with the manuscript. And a special thanks to Elizabeth Pearson, wife and friend, for every type of help along the way. Finally, a tip of the hat to my own blues brothers, Craig Jones, Bill McCulloch, Bill Lightfoot, and Rob Riley, who, whether they know it or not, goaded me into finishing.

"Sounds so good to me"

1
Johnny Young's story

Johnny Young had been in the blues business for forty years. The night we met, he was working as a front man for a predominantly white blues band at a Northside Chicago club, the Peanut Barrel. I recognized him from his records, a heavyset, round-faced man with sad eyes and a thin mustache.

What is known of his life comes primarily from what he chose to reveal in a number of interviews, tempered by the reminiscences of other musicians and of course his recordings. According to these sources, Johnny Young was born New Year's Day 1917 or 1918 in Vicksburg, Mississippi.[1] He grew up in a musical family, and his mother used to run suppers, a type of down home house-rent party where the guests would buy food and drink and dance to the blues. His Uncle Anthony, an accomplished musician on both guitar and violin as well as Johnny Young's major influence, often supplied the music for these events. Johnny Young soon followed in his footsteps: he was a professional musician by the age of twelve.

After moving to Rolling Fork, Mississippi, he picked up the mandolin, and by the 1930s he worked around Memphis with Houston Stackhouse and Robert Nighthawk and in Brownsville, Tennessee, with blues artists Sleepy John Estes and Sonny Boy Williamson. During the 1940s a developing market for transplanted Delta folk music served as a magnet drawing southern musicians to Chicago. Johnny Young also made the move and like the musicians who came before him sought out the artists he had worked with down home, eventually teaming up again with Sonny Boy Williamson. By 1947 he was working the streets of the Maxwell Street Market. Here, in the same year, he also cut his first record "Money Taking Woman," an energetic blues now considered a classic.[2] In 1948 he recorded again with Johnny Williams and Snooky Pryor, but then dropped out of the recording scene until the blues revival of the 1960s, when he recorded for Testament, Vanguard, Storyville, Arhoolie, and Milestone.[3]

In Chicago he was part of a raucous, new, and energetic sound—at first. But the Delta country breakdowns soon gave way to the electric blues and boogie that characterized the golden years of Chicago blues in the 1950s. Even though he gave up his mandolin to concentrate on guitar by the 1960s, Johnny Young's style of blues was decidedly old-fashioned, and he could not keep up with the progressive styles preferred by the dancers and drinkers in the South and West Side clubs.

For Johnny Young's generation of Chicago musicians these were hard times. They found themselves preachers without congregations. They encountered hostility from the younger generation and from the black media to whom they were an embarrassment. Money was bad—often below scale. The hours were long, the streets were dangerous, and a second job was mandatory. It is no wonder that a number of stars of the 1950s simply hung it up, tired of the hassle.

But even though it became harder for the veterans to find work, the blues tradition survived, perpetuated by younger, more progressive artists better adept at merging blues with contemporary trends in black popular music. Fewer clubs hired blues bands, but the blues musicians' audience never disappeared entirely. A small hard core of blues fans remained, either transplanted Southerners with a taste for down home things, or Chicago neighbors whose local bar happened to hire a blues band. The ethnic constituency that maintained the blues made up in enthusiasm for what they lacked in numbers. Despite the lack of attention from the media, blues performances in the small clubs were vital affairs where the people packed tight, close to the musicians and close to each other.

But even during the decline certain changes were in the air. A growing number of white patrons—students or fans or both—began to show up at the clubs. White musicians sat in more frequently, and following a common pattern in American music, they went on to form their own bands. These groups helped to sell the blues sound to a growing white audience, and for a time they overshadowed their teachers. Yet their success also called attention to their sources, and new opportunities began to open up for the blues veterans.

By the middle of the 1970s many established bluesmen began to move away from the low-paying jobs in the sometimes dangerous ethnic clubs where the critical demands of an audience familiar with the blues had forged the Chicago sound. Now the Chicago bluesmen worked Old Town, Rush Street, and other Northside bars that drew a young, white clientele. Mixed bands composed of older blues veterans and young white sidemen became common. One of these bands was run by Bob Reidy, a young piano player who worked hard to sell the blues to reluctant tavern owners and uninterested audiences. He had faith, however, and his energy kept the band afloat, providing work for a number of traditional bluesmen. The usual show consisted of several artists such as Johnny Young, Wild Child Butler, John Littlejohn, or Jimmy Rogers alternating sets, backed up by the Bob Reidy Band. The band's sound was tight, bright, up-tempo, modern. It reflected a new merging of black and white musical values. The innovations caused some tension, and egos clashed over musical differences and arguments over leadership.

The night I met Johnny Young, he had just finished a set and was not very happy with how it went. A blues veteran, he had his own idea about how his music should sound, yet he had to defer to the band, Bob Reidy's band. And so even though they were good friends, Johnny Young was defensive about working for the younger man and complained he wasn't being presented in his best light.

We tried to talk inside, but the jukebox made it impossible. Since it was an unusually warm spring night for Chicago and we had time to kill before his next set, we decided to go outside to my car. I drove to a nearby liquor store, where he went in to get a bit of scotch. The police ordered me to move along. "No double-parking." No use arguing. I sped around the block. Johnny Young was waiting outside when I drove up.

"You scared me to death, man," he said.

"I know. The police ran me off."

We drove back to the club and parked. Comfortably settled, we relaxed over our drinks and made conversation. He began by referring to my earlier interview with Bob Reidy.

"You see, Bob, you interviewed him. He wants to be a big star. He plays good, but my wife she come over here and didn't come back no more. She said, 'You don't need to be with that band.' Swear to God. Say, 'They ain't fitting your type of music. See, cause when you make a record you make it different than what you do singing with them.' Say, 'Your record sells and you know they do.' "

"When you make a record, you make it for you," I answered.

"That's right," he said. "Making it good for the public."

He looked over, so I responded. "Bob, he's got a good act, getting guys to play and sing, but the thing is, it's his act. It's not your act."

He nodded. "Please say it again. It's his act, not mine, cause he wants to be the boss. He is the boss. I do his act because that's what he wants, but I can do my act too.

"You know what he told me last night? Listen to me here, you know, honest to God. He said, 'Don't never leave me.' He said, 'I've got so many jobs from now till next May.' I said, 'What, Bob? You ain't got that many.'

"Cause Sammy Lay wanted me.[4] Sammy Lay say, 'That son of a bitch is dynamite.' I played with Sammy in Palatine, Illinois, last Sunday. You couldn't get in there for the people. They eat me up. See, he won't even let me play the mandolin too much. You know I play the mandolin. You know that I've got it sitting up there now."

"I know two people who play the mandolin," I said. "You and Yank Rachel."

Johnny Young nodded. "He's pretty good, but you know they told me in Europe they never heard nobody as good as me playing blues on the mandolin. I got a write-up, I want to show it to you, but it's wrote up in Dutch. Dutch is German—are you German?"

"No."

"Well, I was in— You know where I was? I was in Switzerland. Geneva, Switzerland. But it sure is pretty over there. Man, did you ever hear of those mountains? Pretty! And the people meet me at the airport, when I get off they say, 'Johnny Young.' They know me! By my picture on my record. I say, 'How you know me?' 'We know you better than you do.' They say, 'Johnny.' Oh those kids say, 'Sign here, sign it.' Lord. All night long in the dressing room. They makin me sign this, sign that, sign. I went all over. See, we had a worldwide tour. You know Jimmy Dawkins?"

I nodded.

"He was backing us up, him and his band. You know who they put behind me? Let me tell you. They put three pieces behind me. Drums, bass, [and guitar] and me. All my act. Every time I go up there they say, 'Listen.' I say, 'Please give me a guitar.' "

He shook his head. "Uh uh. Say, 'When you go down there, the guitar go down there, we don't know who's doing it, you or the guitar.' Say, 'We want you to play that goddamn mandolin and let them know who you is.'

"And I frailed that mother, man, I frailed it. And the little guy that used to set up the equipment, he say, 'Play, Johnny Young, play. Play, baby, play!' That son of a bitch be out in front of me doing—saying like that."

"I like your guitar-playing too, you know," I said.

"Everybody loves my guitar-playing. You know what the fellows told me with Sam Lay? The guitar player that was over there the other night, they say, 'Johnny, you know what I'm talking about.' Say, 'You a guitar player.' Say, 'Man you play guitar like Jimmy Reed.' 'What do you mean?' 'You play bass and lead all at the same time.' You know I do."

He acted out playing the guitar and sang a riff associated with Jimmy Reed, "Da Dow, Da Dow, Da Dow Da Dow."[5]

"I play bass and lead all at the same time cause me and Big Walter Horton used to play together with just a drum. We had them like that." He pressed his hands together. "You couldn't get in. Three pieces. We didn't have no six pieces like Bob. You couldn't get in, and we packed them in, and I was playing lead and bass. One fellow sat in front of me one night and he said, 'How in the hell can you do that with a guitar?'

"My wife thinks I'm the best guitar player in the world, you know. She said—but I mean with the type of music I play—she said, 'You a hell of a guitar player.' She likes the mandolin too, but I hate to tell you, she say, 'Get on the guitar!' I get mad with her. I say, 'goddamn it, white people like that mandolin.' She say, 'I'd rather you play that guitar, see, cause you can play both of them.' She say, 'But you know you can play the guitar.' I say, 'Can I?' She say, 'You goddamn right. You can make that guitar talk.' My wife loves me to play the guitar. I swear to God." He stopped, waiting for a cue.

"If you could just run down your background," I said, "like your life story."

He looked at the tape recorder. "You got it on?"

His story

"I'm Johnny Young. I'm from Vicksburg, Mississippi. My uncle was a professional musician. My mother blowed harmonica and my brother played harmonica, and I started when I was about eight years old. I made me a guitar out of a cigar box, and my mother say, 'He's got to be a musician because he done made himself a guitar.'

"She bought me a five-dollar guitar, honest to God, she bought me a guitar and we used to play at home. And every night we had people come to listen to me play—you know, neighbors. And my brother was blowin the harmonica, you see, I was playin the guitar—Pat, we called him Pat—and my other brother had a broom. Now this was the act we had. He would look in the fireplace and get some ashes just like you got ashes to throw out, put it on the floor. Whoop-de whoop-de, we had a bass goin.[6]

"So my mother said, 'I got to buy him a guitar!' She bought me a five-dollar guitar. And the people used to say, 'please let him play for my party tonight.' My mama say, 'He's too young, he's nothin, he's twelve years old.'

"I was twelve years old then, and I used to go up in to—they call them jukes, juke houses, juke joints, suppers, call them suppers. So I used to go play for the suppers. All I got was two dollars a night, hamburger, hot dog, and a pop, big strawberry pop."

I asked, "Why did you keep on doing it if you weren't getting paid that much?"

Irritated by the interruption, he cut me off. "Wait a minute—well we had to, we's in Mississippi, so at that time you could take two dollars and buy twenty dollars' worth of groceries, spend two dollars then like you spend twenty now. Things was cheap.

"Listen to me. My uncle used to practice. We call it practicing at home, not rehearsing. He had four guys sit on the porch at night and they practicing. The guitar was sounding so good, and violins, mandolins like I play. My uncle played a violin. So I used to sit and listen, and I said, 'God dog! That sure do sound good.' So when he go to work, my auntie would let me— I said, 'Could I come over?' 'Yeah,' she say. 'What you want, boy? Don't fool around with that guitar.' She would go in the kitchen. I'd hit one string . . . bong! It was hanging upside the wall. I'd get in the chair, lean up there, and I take it down and try to play.

"And so we moved from Vicksburg, Mississippi, to Rolling Fork, Mississippi, up in the Delta. So my mother bought me a mandolin. I had it tuned in Spanish—Sebastapol, they called it—you know, like Hound Dog plays the guitar and all the rest. Well, it wasn't tuned right.

"My uncle came up to play for a party for my mother. My mother used to give parties—suppers, we called them suppers. She had fish, hot dogs, all kinds of sandwiches to sell, pop, beer. And he said, 'Son, you're sounding good.' I play [sings a riff] any kind of way you know, then those fellows, uh, they didn't know what I was doin, see. And he said, 'You sound good, but you have to tune it in natural. See, cause you got it tuned cross key.'

"I said, 'Well, how do you do that?' He said [sings four notes] he said [simulates playing]. I looked at him so hard. I said, 'Do it again.' He did it. I said, 'Let me see.' I watched his fingers. I did it. He said, 'Good God a mighty, you gonna be a musician. You gonna be one of those high musicians, with a big band!' He said, 'Can you tune it?' I said, 'Tune it back like I had it.' I got the sound, honest to God, I tuned it just like he had it and that's just like I'm playing it now and ever since then I been tuning it just like that.

"I always was a musician. When I hear music I cry. I listen to it— Sarah Vaughan made me cry one night, really. She was at the Regal Theatre. She sang a song about Miss Julie [sings a riff]. It was just something so good that tears started rollin out my eye. I said, 'God give it to me. I know I'm a musician!'

"I used to sit on the porch and play and look up at the stars and play so good. I was playing that mandolin and I loved it, playing my guitar and I loved it.

"So then we moved up to a place called Swains, place in Mississippi out from Memphis, Tennessee. I met Robert Nighthawk. So when I met Robert Nighthawk I got with him, I was blowing harmonica. You know, I used to blow harmonica a little bit too. So I started blowing harp with him. He play—Nighthawk was a hell of a good musician—he play slide. He was so good he almost made me cry. So I had—we was wearing blue jeans, you know—had striping to here [he points] and big belts. I kept my pants pulled up like that, way up see, like I was a big shot musician. So I walked in and they say, 'There's a musician out there. Oh, here they are.' I met Robert Nighthawk, but Robert Nighthawk had a harp."

He suddenly asked, "You know Houston Stackhouse?"
"Yeah," I answered.

"We started together. Houston Stackhouse is a hell of a musician. Why, I hate to say it, man. So we, you know when that was, back in the thirties, '34, '35, all like that. And Sonny Boy Williamson was making records. I came up here and I played with him. I played with Memphis Slim. I played with Big Bill Broomless [Broonzy], Sunnyland Slim. I worked with everybody that's worth working with. I worked with Muddy, Howling Wolf, Hound Dog.

"First record I made was in '43, right when the war was goin on. 'Money Taking Woman.'

"You heard that record?"
"Yeah," I replied.
"You ain't even got it? I believe you got it. I made the tape. I had to borrow that record when I made it for Pete Welding."
"Yeah," I said. "I got the first one and the second one."

"Oh, come on, you gonna make me cry. Now I made the second one for Pete Welding so I made 'Money Taking Woman' for Arhoolie record company. Oh, I just cranked up.

"When I hit Europe, the first thing they want to know was 'Money Taking Woman.' I said, 'Oh, man, think of all the records I got out. You mean that's famous?' 'Money Taking Woman,' you know.

"They say, 'That made you famous.' I'm surprised they like it so good, you know. They went crazy wanting to hear 'Money Taking Woman.' You know what to do when you a musician, you make one hit. It made a hit for me because it's a good record, you know.

"She took my money and called me Jack
She holds her hands out and she never give it back.
She's a money taking woman."

He broke off and looked at me. "That's a good record, isn't it?"
"They don't make them like that anymore," I answered.
"Oh, come on. Now you jiving me." He looked at me and stopped,
then said, "Now what else do you want me to put on here?"

Before I could answer he went on. "I played with Muddy. I played
with Hound Dog Taylor. Howling Wolf—"

Suddenly we were jolted, almost spilling our drinks. "What is this?"
Johnny Young exclaimed.
"Somebody hit me," I said, climbing out of the car to a chorus of
Johnny Young's curses.
A very stoned Spanish-speaking gentleman got out of his car and
joined me in my appraisal, but there seemed to be no damage. After
several unsuccessful attempts at communicating, the gentleman
shrugged and got into his car and careened off into the spring night.
I got back in my car and explained what happened. After a bit I said,
"Look here, Johnny Young, you told me about your background. Let me
try to bring it up to the present. You worked with so many artists."
He nodded. "Sonny Boy Williams."
"Sonny Boy Williamson?" I asked.
He got angry.

"Not Williamson. Williamson and Williams—Sonny Boy. John Lee
Williams[7] is the one I worked with. 'Good Morning Little School Girl,'
'Sugar Mama,' 'Decoration Day,' 'Black Gal.' That's the man I worked
with. Me and Sleepy John Estes and Willie Nix and all them guys, we
were working together. I'm telling you, we was out of Brownsville, Tennessee, Jackson, Tennessee.
"I'm from all over parts of the world, man. See Bob Reidy and them
trying to bill this thing, I told them I'm from all over parts of the world,
man, I work everywhere.

He stopped to admire some young women who happened to walk by.
"Look at that shaky little brownskin chick."
He turned back to me. "What else you want to know? I know it's not
going to be too good, but you and me rapping now. We rapping."
I thought for a moment. "Well, people see you up on stage, they think
it's so easy to play. They don't think it's work."

"That's right. It look easy. Well, they don't think it is work, but it is
work. When you study from a kid up. I been playing forty-six years. I'm

fifty-seven now. Forty-six years playing music. Can you imagine that? And I had so many jobs. I shoveled coal, I washed dishes, I cut logs. I did everything to make a living, then I went back to music again."

"What kept you in music?" I asked.

"Because my heart's in it. My soul's in music. I wanted to quit. My wife, my other wife—yeah, buddy, I got a second wife now. She carried me to church every Sunday. She go out with me and ball and I said, 'You done had a drink. You want to go to church?' 'Yeah. I want to go to church.' That's what we did.

"Now she takes me to church. She wouldn't let me play. We both was working at a job together, me and my wife, and I said, 'Jesus Christ, I'm sick of working.' I got mad one day and throwed everything down. I said, 'I'm a musician. I know I'm one.' So I throwed everything down and I went back to playing music, you know.

"You know where I met Bob Reidy? One night in Old Town. Muddy was there. He had just got out of his accident and was walking on crutches. So they said, 'We got Johnny Young here tonight.' Chicago Slim—you know him? —Charlie Musslewhite, Paul Butterfield, have all played with me. I'm talking about fellows that I know. Paul Butterfield, Harvey Mandel, guitar player, and they all respect me. Just an old man, a man that tried to make it and is still trying to make it—and, oh God! give me enough power or give me enough luck, you dig me? Oh God! give me enough power to get me some money to make me a house or build me a house or buy me one, because I got too many years as a musician to be holding on like this."

He sat back wearily.
"Now playing with Bob Reidy is not Johnny Young. He pays me off."
I said, "I saw you working with the Aces down at the Wise Fool."
"No," he corrected, "the Aces was working with me. They was working with me. I was the star.

"You got another beer? No, I better not drink too much more cause I've got to do another set and my voice is kind of hoarse."

He looked at me intently. "Where did you say you saw me play—Ann Arbor?"

We went back into the club where he did another set—this time playing the mandolin. And he was right: nobody could play the blues as good as he could on the mandolin.

Less than three weeks later Johnny Young died. According to Bob Reidy, he suffered a heart attack while sitting on his front steps waiting for a ride to see his doctor.[8]

2
David "Honeyboy" Edwards' story

David "Honeyboy" Edwards was born several years earlier than Johnny Young, in 1915 in Shaw, Mississippi.[1] He began to play blues in 1930, after being inspired by the music of the legendary bluesman Tommy Johnson. By 1932 he was apprenticed to another popular Delta performer, Big Joe Williams, with whom he traveled and studied for about a year. He then worked with other Delta artists, including Tommy McClennan, Robert Petway, and the Memphis Jug Band.

In 1942 he was recorded by Alan Lomax for the Library of Congress. Following this session he continued his rambling throughout the South, performing off and on with such blues greats as Walter Horton and Sonny Boy Williamson. By the 1940s he had also made it to Chicago, where he alternately worked the open air Maxwell Street Market in the summer and returned south for the winter. Visiting Houston in 1951, he recorded his "hit" record "Build Myself a Cave" but then returned to Chicago to work the club scene with the likes of Junior Wells, Robert Nighthawk, Earl Hooker, Snooky Pryor, Sunnyland Slim, and Louis and Davey Myers of the Aces.[2]

But eventually his style of blues lost its popularity in the black clubs and his jobs dried up. After a number of lean years, he began to perform for white audiences, making the transition from rhythm and blues in black clubs to folk blues on the festival circuit. Today he continues to perform and is living in Chicago with his old partner Walter Horton.

I met him in Washington, D.C., five years after I spoke with Johnny Young. We talked briefly at a reception following his performance at the fiftieth anniversary of the Archives of Folksong at the Library of Congress.

Making small talk and drinking wine, he invited me to stay at his place the next time I visited Chicago.

That summer he was back in Washington as a participant in the Forty-second National Folk Festival. Since I was part of the festival staff, we were able to get together at a Virginia prep school that doubled as participant housing for the festival. Over dinner we chatted about the Chicago scene and later played some music together. I asked if we could do an interview before he returned to Chicago, and he agreed.

The next day we spent the morning together at the festival, where I introduced him at a workshop, after which we went to lunch. It was August in Washington, so it was uncomfortably hot even though we were out in the suburbs in bucolic Wolftrap Farm Park. We exhausted ourselves trudging up the hill to the meal tent. It was too hot to eat, so we sipped beer, grateful for the shade of the tent. By then we were somewhat at ease with each other's company. He knew me as a blues scholar, workshop leader, his personal host for the festival, and a former Chicagoan. Through our conversations we had established a frame of reference that included a number of mutual acquaintances and a working knowledge of the Chicago scene. The brief jam session the night before had established, without the need for words or further assurances, that I understood (at least to some degree) and valued what he did as an artist.

I asked if this was a good time for him to tell me about himself, and he agreed. I turned on the tape recorder I carried and asked him, "Tell me the Honeyboy Edwards Story," and sat back to listen.

His story

"I used to walk all through the country. And I would, I'd play a little town. I had it mapped out like I wouldn't play the same town every Saturday. I'd play on the street corners, you know, and people would give me quarters, nickels, and dimes and pennies to play different numbers. Like this weekend I'd be in Cleveland; next weekend I'd go to Leland— that's about twenty miles apart. I'd play in Leland and the next weekend I'd go over to Greenwood, that's twenty or thirty miles apart. I wouldn't be at the same town every weekend.

"I'd come back around every two or three weeks. I'd come back through there again, and the people would want to hear me play the blues again. I'd make the same amount of money. I wouldn't stay in no place too long—no place too long.

"Sometimes I would end up in my hometown on a Saturday, and they say, well, 'Honey's in town today.' 'Where is he?' 'I ain't seen him.' 'I'd like to see him.' When you walk up they say, 'Where you been, boy?' 'Where you been so long, boy?' 'Come on and have a drink on me.' You know, 'Have a drink on me.' " He smiled, holding on to the memory.

Interrupting his reverie, I asked, "Did people have more respect for musicians?"

"They did. And the people that you knew had seen you coming up for years in the neighborhood. They was crazy about you cause there wasn't, you see, in them times there wasn't too many Seeburgs.[3] There wasn't too many vendors, just a few nickel ones come out, put nickels in them. And musicians had a nice time down south cause there wasn't too much music in the little cities. All they had was some electric pianos when I was small that played by rolls. You go in the drugstore and listen at it play by rolls.

"And they had a string band in Shaw, Mississippi, my hometown. Alger Moore and his brother Tom Moore, Spencer, two brothers on guitar and Spencer on upright bass. I used to go up there in back of the drugstore and listen at them play, you know. It was a nice time.

"They had a better time then than they do now because people was more together and it looked like they enjoyed more what you were doing than they do now. And if they knew you played music they were nice to you, bought you drinks, talk to you, and have a nice time.

"But in the later years most women music lovers down south, they love the blues and the men would think the women loved the musicians most the time. And that's the reason the musicians didn't get along with some of the men. Some of the men thought that he wanted his woman, but all the time he wouldn't be at a woman—that woman would be at him. Woman come buy you a drink, sit down by you, laugh, and talk. Why, it's nothing to you all but the man's sitting rolling his eyes and he thinks that it might be something.

"So after I found all of that was happening, sometimes I'd, a woman come up say, 'Honeyboy, play me such and such a thing.' I'd get the request, tell them go on sit down and don't bother me cause I don't want no trouble. After the request tell em, well, 'Sit down.' "

He paused again.
"Did you ever get in any scrapes?" I asked.

"Every once in a while, guy come up, be drinking, say, 'That's my woman' or 'That's my old lady. Leave her alone.' I'd say, 'Man, I'm not talking.' You know that's always happening. At times like that I found it's better to play. They ask you to play it for them, you play them a couple of numbers, tell them, 'Go ahead and sit down. Leave me alone. You got an old man. I'll play it for you when you go back over yonder and I'm gonna stay over here. Go back over there.' "

"Was it worse in the South than in Chicago?"

"Well, it's not as bad in Chicago, cause when I first came to Chicago the men was a little jealous. Way back in the forties and fifties, cause some of them in Chicago, they had someone they had left south. Left south [then] brought them north, they still had that same thing in em about musicians. But now these days a man thinks if a woman wants him and he's taking care, putting up with her, if she's fool enough to want the musician, well, let her go on ahead with him. Cause everybody woke up on everything now.

"And at that time a man got a good job, got a good-looking woman. He knows he's ugly looking, funny man, he die about that woman. He knows there's not another one out there like that probably for him, and he don't want to lose that woman. At that time he'd kill you about her cause he don't want to lose that woman. You know he got a nice little woman and he feels 'I won't get nothin like this no more.' He'd kill you about her. It's true, It really is.

"I used to sit down at night, lay down and think about these things and map it out and I say, 'That's true. Leave those women alone if you want to live.'

"So if they sit down I say, 'Are you married?' They say 'No, but I got an old man, but we is on the bust.' I say, 'I'll see you later when you got yourself straightened out.' He already angry cause of me talking to her.

"A woman back then—see its the same thing happen to Robert Johnson, cause I knew him. Robert had been in Greenwood about three weeks before he got killed. I'll tell you what I know. The first week he came he was standing on Johnson Street playing. And I was twenty-two years old in 1937. Robert was about twenty-five. He was about along with me. Robert was playing on Johnson Street, playing the blues.

"Robert was brown skin, had a cataract over one eye, had one bad eye like this, half-closed and he had a keen voice. He could holler good. And one lady told him, she say, 'Can you play "Terraplane Blues"?' He just had made that record over in Texas, El Paso or somewhere, and then he come to Mississippi.

"See his home was in Robinsonville, up on Sixty-one Highway not too far from where Son House and Willie Brown's home was. They was all along together out of there, and he used to go with my first cousin, Willie Mae Powell. She's still in Tunica now. My cousin Willie Mae is about sixty-seven now. She's still living.

"And this particular Saturday he's playing on Johnson Street in the middle of the afternoon. She says, 'Can you play "Terraplane"?' He says, 'Miss, that's my record.' She says, 'I don't believe it. If you play it I'll give you fifteen cents.' At that time that was a lot of money. Robert Johnson started to play it—'Terraplane Blues'—and people started throwing quarters, nickels, and drinking white whiskey and running back in the alleys.

"So this guy had this roadhouse. He was between Greenwood and Itta Bena, a place called 'The Three Forks.' It was a joint sitting on three forks of a road near the highway. It was a store, but they had a juke in there. Closed the store and when they opened up it was a juke, a country juke, little old place, crackers and sardines. And this guy opened up a country juke house and Robert played for him that Saturday night. And the next Saturday night Robert played for him and Robert started going with his wife.

"In other words, that's how it started. Robert was playing for him, and then his wife she fell for him. Give him all the free whiskey he wanted, and some of his friends they told him that Robert was going with his wife.

"Robert didn't stay out there. Robert stayed in Greenwood, in [Baptist?] town on Johnson Street. So this woman, on a Monday she came to Greenwood where Robert was and laid around, she laid around. She came about two and a half miles to Greenwood. You could walk to town. She come in there and lived with Robert.

"Well, someone, her husband's friends, told him that she was laying out there with Robert. Robert was playing for him so that last night he played—and he was playing in town on the streets. So we all got in a truck and went to where he was playing. It was only about two or three miles.

"Twelve o'clock, no, Robert had been out there about nine-thirty or ten o'clock, cause the town closed up at eleven, because they didn't stay open all night like they do now. Close about eleven. And all the people stayed in the country had to go back home. Go out where the country juke is.

"So when Robert got out there he was feeling pretty good, was high. He played a few pieces, laid around and wait till the crowd would get there. And this man, this woman's husband—this is something I know and not nothing that people go around talking about what they hear, cause I was there. I had lived in Greenwood. I went to Greenwood High School. I went there '31 and '32. I went to Greenwood High School.

"And this Saturday night this man had a friend, a woman. The woman give Robert the whiskey, his friend, and she gave this man the poison. This man poisoned him. He give his whiskey poison cause, see, he was going with his wife. He didn't want it, see.

"It wasn't like it is now. A guy would kill you if he think you was doing something wrong with his wife. But this guy would do something underhanded where he can kill you, get you out of the way, and he think you don't know who done it. But you did. And he didn't go to the penitentiary, he didn't go to jail. But he got [you] to do it. But that's the kind of fellow he was.

"But she was a good-looking woman—brown skin, long hair that hung way down to there. About twelve-thirty, one o'clock the people started pouring out of Greenwood, pouring out of town coming out there. They had heard him playing on the streets. 'Come on, play me "Terraplane Blues." ' 'Play me "Kind Hearted Mama Blues." ' 'Play me "Hellhound on My Trail," ' you know.

"And Robert was beginning to get sick. That whiskey, he had it about a half hour, and it began to get to him. So he said, 'Naw, I'm sick.' He said, 'Naw.'

"Now the people was drunk and began to think he was bullshitting them. 'Aw, come on, come on.' But the man was sick. He was poisoned to death, but the other people out there, they didn't know it. Man's laying over the guitar, he's trying to play it, but he solid just can't. And the people, like everybody, got silent, dead. Walkin around cause the man was sick. And Robert died about one-thirty or two. He'd got sick and they stretched him out on a little old piece of cotton cloth and he died.

"And they didn't know where his people was, and they got in touch over there to a place called Hollywood, near Hollywood where his people were from. His mother wasn't up there and his sister was in Chicago, and the state, the county, buried Robert. The county buried him on Monday. They couldn't keep him around too long—and there wasn't any kin and his mother and them wasn't there.

"So they got a wooden box and nailed him up. Put him in his tomb. And his sister come that Monday night, and she got the telegram and dug him up and put him away. And I know that. This is no lie.

"But the man, at the time just like, it's something he learned. And that's the only thing he knew he could do for a living without work. And he didn't have no insurance, no nothing. No nothing.[4]

"Just like Charley Patton. He recorded those records for all them people, RCA Victor.[5] When he died, just had a marker on his grave. I know that too. Had a little thing on his grave made like this, like a cross. Stuck on here was his name, Charley Patton, had a little paper over it, you know.

"I came by there, that was on Tuesday. Never forgot it. On a Tuesday the last of March in '34. I come along walking there with a guitar on my shoulders. I was a youngster. I came to the Heaton store there and some boys were sittin at the store. The store had some benches nailed to the porch where you could sit on some benches, you know.

"And I walk in the store, get a nickel's worth of bologna and some crackers, and we got to talking, and the boy said, 'You know Charley?' I said, 'Yeah, I know him.' He said, 'That's his grave right out there.' I said, 'When did Charley die?' He said, 'Charley died about two days ago. See, that's Charley's grave.' I said, 'Oh.' I said, 'Sure enough.' And it just—the grave it was gumbo mud, black mud, it was just big hunks lying on top. You know, they couldn't spread it. They just dug it and you could see all the shovel prints.

"And his Uncle Sherman, he stayed across the field about two blocks from the store. Sherman stayed across the field. So I went over there to Sherman's house and he said, 'Oh well, Charley died.' I said, 'Yeah, I know. I just seen it.'

"So I stayed over there about a week with Sherman and he was giving country dances and Charley had been playing for him. And I played there a couple of Saturday nights and then I left. And Bertha was still over there, Charley's wife was still over there. I know about these things, I was lucky enough to be right around.

"Tommy Johnson,[6] Clarence, they all come to Wildwood in 1929. I was fourteen then. They come from Crystal Springs, Mississippi. They stayed in Crystal Springs. They had a old T-model Ford. They come up picking cotton by the hundred and they had a big double house they stayed in, a great big old house. And they'd pick cotton all through the day, and at night they'd sit around and play the guitars.

"We stayed on the farm, but they didn't come in. They were cotton pickers, day hands. Course in the hills there wasn't nothin to do, see they come out of the hills, around Crystal Springs, raise them truck patches and all that corn—wasn't no cotton in the brown hills. And they came up to the Mississippi Delta cause that's some flat country. They'd pick cotton, gather corn, make a little money, and go back to the hills later in the fall.

"So Tommy Johnson, Clarence, Mager—there were three brothers and Peg Leg Sam. Peg Leg died about seven years ago. He was in Chicago. He was playing with them too. I know them all.

"I was fourteen years old and I used to go over there. He was playing 'Canned Heat,' then before he made 'Canned Heat,' 'Big Road,' and he was playing 'Bye and Bye.' And I used to stand around in the house right around the corner here and every night I would listen at them play. Sounds so good to me—drinking that white whiskey, that moonshine. I'd just sit and look at them. I said, 'I wish I could play.'

"And then in '30 my daddy bought me a guitar, in 1930 from a fellow called Clarence McDaniel. He ordered that guitar in '29. I know when he got it. The same year Tommy and them were playing, he ordered it cause, see, we were living on the same plantation. He paid fourteen dollars for that guitar then. But that was a good guitar then, and my daddy gave him four dollars for it in 1930, and that's the first guitar I ever tried to play and just kept and strummed down on it. Didn't learn too much. Oh, I could play in Spanish a little bit.

"And in '31 we moved over by Greenwood. We was in Wildwood then, and me and some boys on a Christmas Day, I had the guitar on my shoulder with a little string about like that mike cord there, on my shoulder. We walking down Johnson Street, the same street that Robert was playing on when I met him, Johnson Street. That's the main street for colored peoples, sit around drinking and sit around and play music.

"And we got to tussling on Christmas Day, and one of them boys knocked the guitar off my shoulder and broke that little cord string and tore that guitar up. And I could have cried. I knew they couldn't pay me for it cause we didn't have no money then. I think I got seventy-five cents out of that boy.

"Then I didn't get me another guitar now until 1931, 1932. And my brother-in-law married my sister. He had a little old piece of guitar, the neck was broken on it, and half the finger board was off it down by the hole—broke from down the neck to up by the hole, so I just used the upper part of the finger board. And that's what I had when I went with Joe. I was playing that thing there. That's what I learned on."

He paused and looked at me.

"Was Joe the man who taught you most of what you have learned?" I asked.

"He was the first man ever taught me and carried me away from home, Joe Williams was.[7] Course I would just go around Greenwood and take a little peek at Robert, that is, Tommy McClennan and Robert Petway. And they didn't fool with me cause, see, I was young and they'd say, 'Yonder Honey comes,' and they'd run off and leave me cause it looked like they didn't want me to learn, cause I was so worrisome that every which way that they go, I was right behind them. I wanted to learn. Say, 'Yonder comes little Honey. Let's go.' They'd jump in the car and leave me. I'd just stand there looking at em and let em go, you know, like that.

"Well, what kicked me off was when I went with Joe Williams. And Joe Williams leaved me, and I went to Greenwood and Robert—I went back to Greenwood—and Robert and Tommy were surprised at my playing. They stand around and then they let me play with them then.

"I then left them and came to Memphis and started working with the jug band, the Memphis Jug Band with Son Brimmer, and I played there a year or two and then I went back. See, I'd go back and forth, home and back down there. I was good then, boy!

"Me and Tommy played together then. I had tightened up then. I knew some things that he didn't know cause Tommy, all he played in one key and holler a hundred different songs. See, I know Tommy just like a book. He played, well, he played in the key of G a lot, but he played mostly in E. He played some numbers in C, but he didn't play like I say, what we playing now. He just play the blues. Play straight blues. There wasn't nothin betwixt nothin. Just straight go. But he was good and people liked what he was playing and everybody said Robert Petway could beat him playing but Tommy could beat him singing. But they was the same size. Look like midgets when they played together."

Again he stopped and waited.

I asked him, "Did you make money right away?"

"The first job I got some money for, we was playing in a store. That was in '32. We played in a man's store they called Mr. Russel in Greenwood.

"Well, the kind of store he had, he had a big grocery store, and he would let the people from the country come and take up groceries until the next month. Like you buy groceries and then you come back in the middle of the month and take him some of the check. And in the back of the store we'd had sacks of beans and we'd sit on those sacks and we'd play. Sit on the beans for a seat and the people be in the front of the store buying cheese, sausage, and drinking white whiskey. Anyhow, we were paid a dollar and a half, a dollar apiece, and that was the first money I ever made.

"Joe Williams got the money and give me what he wanted to give, but that's the first time I thought I could make some money playing guitar. And from then on, Joe had learned me the ropes, he go stand on the corner play collecting, nickels, dimes, quarters, put it in his pocket. When I get hungry he give me a quarter, fifteen cents, and let me go eat. I get sleepy, he rent a room, but he didn't give me too much money cause I'd be out shootin mouth with the boys whilst he be chasing the women.

"But I see how he was doing it. I said, 'Hell, I can do the same thing,' so when I started to play I put that harp on that rack, go up on the corner and ask for them nickels and dimes too. And I made it.

"And in '42, I recorded. I was playing in '41, '42 around Coahoma, Mississippi, at them country dances and things and one Monday morning Alan Lomax drove up. One Monday morning. I don't know where he heard of me, but he was looking for musicians and somebody told him my name. Honeyboy, they always called me Honey. And I had been playing that Saturday night about three miles out from Coahoma and while I was there, about a mile and a half from Coahoma, it was the first town between the two.

"I was living with a woman about thirty-five years old then. I was around twenty something. Minnie, her name was Minnie. And I was laying up asleep that Monday morning cause I didn't never get tired with no crop. She done makin a crop with her aunties. Farming, but I didn't never get tired at it as I would always stay free to go. And he drove up in the yard that Monday morning in a 1941 Hudson, Commodore, green, four door, and my auntie was scared. He asked for Honey. 'Do Honey live here, fellow play guitar?'

"My aunt say, 'I don't know.' I guess she was scared. She come in say, 'This old white man out there got a Washington license plate on his car.' I said, 'What's he say?'

"He says, 'I'm Mr. Alan Lomax,' say, 'I'm from the Library of Congress of Washington, D.C., and I want to do some recording. I want to record him.' And she come back in and I said, 'Well, tell him to come on in.'

"So we talking for a while and I jumps in the car with him. We went on to Clarksdale and went to a place out on Forty-nine highway—Forty-nine goes to Clarksdale, and Sixty-one goes straight on down to my hometown. Forty-nine goes over toward Tutwiler, Drew Ruleville, Parchman.

"This place was sort of like a Holiday Inn, where they rent. He rented him and me a room, fed me, took care of me, so we got in the car and went about three miles in the country, in a school. And we recorded there that day, and in the middle of the recording session, there come a big storm. I mean a big storm. They had to quit recording me in the middle of the storm till it was over, then they started back in again and finished recording.

"He give me twenty dollars. That was a whole lot of money then. Twenty dollars, man, was a whole lot of money. You worked all day long for a dollar a day down there, a dollar a day. He went on down to Rolling Fork and recorded Muddy, then, the same year. Muddy wasn't in Chicago.

"And, uh, when that recording business come on with Lester Melrose, and all of them down through the South, with Vocalion, making them records, those seventy-eight rpm. They were looking for me. And Bluebird, RCA Victor, Vocalion were recording. And that's when Tommy and them made their first numbers. They looked for me everywhere, but I was just like a dog, I wouldn't stay nowhere long enough to amount to nothing. If I couldn't make me a quarter in a city I was gone.

"They went to Yazoo City lookin, look for me, they went to Florida, went to Jackson. Everywhere, they go, they say, 'Honey have just left.' 'Well, we just as well go back to Chicago.' Well, that's where I missed that bloom, that recording bloom. I missed it.

"And I found out Tommy had recorded, Robert Petway had recorded. I missed all that, and it throwed me way back. But I jumped and went on over to Houston then, and I recorded for Miss Collum, Artist Recording Company, and I did 'Build Myself a Cave.' And I come and jumped back and I recorded for old man Bill Quinn, Gold Medal. And I think he sold some of that material to Chris Strachwitz, but I know 'Build Myself a Cave' Chris got it cause I got royalties on it.

"I've done a lot of gettin about, you know. After I got up and got older I learned a little better and I sees where I made a mistake. I missed a lot of things by going too fast, that's why I missed out, I was going too fast. I wasn't settling for anybody to find me, nobody to pick up on me. I knowed them, but they couldn't catch up with me.

"And I missed some recording sessions in 1937, '38. I missed a recording session in Jackson, Mississippi, for H. C. Speir, Old Man H. C. Speir, he's on Ferris Street there, he run a furniture store. Me, Sonny Boy[8] and Big Walter Horton went down there and he sent us to Camden, New Jersey, over to New Jersey to record in Camden. But it was so close to Christmas that he couldn't get us in there.

"So we left and went over to Monroe, Louisiana. Me and Walter and Sonny Boy went on to Monroe, [over] Christmas now, playing. And Old Big Walter was playing so much harp—he was young then—till Sonny Boy left us. He got mad and cut out. See, I had two harp blowers with me and Big Walter, he was playing all his life. Big Walter was playing so much harmonica that Sonny Boy got mad and slipped on away.

"So we got over there to Shreveport and Joe Morris out of Memphis, he's a harmonica player, I don't know if you ever heard talk of him. Joe Morris was broadcastin then out of Shreveport on the radio, Joe Morris was. He had left Memphis and went to Shreveport, a harmonica player.

"So when he come to Memphis, to town, me and Walter left and went over to Sibley, Louisiana, around Ravenswood, Louisiana. We start to playing over there. Well, I played all over Monroe, Shreveport, Alexandria, Winfield—that's in Louisiana. I played all over. I played in Leesville, a soldier camp.

"I played there for Mr. Scott, he had the Roof Gardens out on the highway, the Roof Gardens. He just had a big P.A. system, me and Little Walter playing then. We play over the P.A. system and we had a crowded house every night. That was my job. That's what I was doing. If I couldn't make no money I'd go somewhere else, I wasn't married.

"I really didn't marry till 1952, but I stayed with the woman from the last of '47 up till '52, married her then. That's the one I got them kids by,

Bassie. She stayed with me until she passed. And I got hung up with her, I wouldn't get rid of her. I just kept on, kept hanging on to her."

Here he stopped again deep into the memory. I waited a moment, then asked, "What was it like in the South, back in the early days?"

"Well, I'm gonna tell you, the white people down south really didn't care much for the blues, back in that time. They were the old-time white people way back in the eighteen hundreds there, on the farm, used to have the Negroes for their slave, work for nothin. And they found out before the Negro found out that if a Negro learned how to play the guitar or learned how to make him a little quarter or two, he wouldn't work. What happened, the white man found out that if the Negro learned how to play blues good enough to make him a quarter, he wouldn't work for fifty cents a day. Would you?

"So when he see one coming with a guitar on his shoulder, he get madder than hell. He get mad, that's them old farmers then.

"And they have always been two type of people, and you take some young white boys coming up, they had cars and girlfriends, give country dances. They'd take me out and I'd play for them and they'd take care of me. But them old farmers, they'd rather see a dog than to see you coming down the street with a guitar. You got that machine on your back, 'He won't work.' Sometimes they pick you up and try to put you on a county farm, anything, you had to dodge that bullshit.

"And later they just throwed that out of their mind, you know what I mean. Music got kind of proper and then they started playing in theaters, on the streets in town, picture shows, anything. (That's coming right on out of the gutter, you know.)

"But when I first started playing, on a Monday morning, you better not be out there with no guitar, on the plantation, staying all day, all night long. You better get away from there or stay in all day long. That night you leave out when everybody come out of the fields.

"And then the towns, the little cities like you stay in, they had something like they call the 'Hog Law.' Like, if you was a farmer and you didn't have enough labor on your plantation, keep your farm cleaned out, a lot of people living in these towns. If you say, 'I'll give you a dollar a day,' they'd strike, they wouldn't go out for that dollar a day. Say, 'You got to give us a dollar and a quarter, dollar and a half.' Well them people sit down and strike. Well, that farmer go to the city hall and pretty soon one of them come out—say, 'We'll get them niggers out the city, they ain't doin' us . . . force them out.' Then they put on something like the 'Hog Law.' If they caught you any time that day they'd lock you up. You supposed to be working somewhere. You understand?

"So the days when I wouldn't work, I had a girlfriend, she cooked for white people, come home with my dinner in her hand. All this stuff the white people left from dinner. The white people down south have always eat good. They had steaks, chicken, and stuff and throw away more food than we could get cause they was gettin all of it, you know what I mean? And so she would bring home the meal and say, 'Honey, here's your dinner.'

"I'm layin in the house, see, I wouldn't come out until six o'clock cause they might pick me up and arrest me, cause I ain't choppin no cotton or pickin cotton. I wasn't going out there. I stay in the house, put a fan on, stay in the house all day long. Stay until six o'clock when I come out, they don't know if I had been in the country or not.

"And sometimes when the water level, when the levee break, high water break, they'd pick the boys up out of the streets and they wouldn't ask you nothin. 'Come on, go to work,' stacking them there sacks down at the levee, stop the water from comin in the city. They wouldn't say how much they give you or nothin—just 'Come on, get on the levee, get them sacks and stack them up over there.' 'Yes, sir.' And after you get through they might give you a couple of dollars, but you got to do that. That was a rough time down there, rough time."

"But folks didn't try to stop you from being a musician?" I asked.

"Oh no, they didn't put no penalty on it, because they couldn't, but they just have such a hatred against what you was doin. Look like you learn something to keep from helpin him. He wants you to work for him for nothin, that's what that was. He didn't mind you learned something, but you learn something to keep from working for him, you know, you learn how to make a living, or halfway living and eat. You learn how to eat out of something, he say you making a living out of it, cause you eat and sleep about it, he say, figure, you won't work for that fifty cents a day then. So that's how that was. It was rough, it was.

"I been pretty busy for the last four years. See, now I get about four hundred dollars a month. I don't do nothin. I draw my security, about four hundred seventy dollars a month, and my old lady she gets a check. She's young—ain't but twenty-eight years old. I ain't got no old woman. Me and Big Walter. Big Walter got the mama and I got the daughter. Big Walter Horton. She's named Fanny and her daughter's name is Jean.

"And then me and Walter, Big Walter, had some hard times. But we used to go down on Front Street in Memphis—that's where all the hustling women lived. The gals out of Arkansas and the hilly part of Tennessee come up on Front Street. That's next to the river, that's Front Street. That's where the women on the river were hustling.

"And we come along playing the blues late at night, you know, hitting the blues, just me and him— 'Come on in here, come on play us some blues. Why, here's a quarter, I'm gonna give him a quarter, you give him a quarter.' And we started playing and the women would bring us a big pint of white whiskey. We'd play there and get drunk and go on downtown on Beale Street to one of them cafes, sit in there all night and drink that nickel mug of beer. It was a rough time, but we made it good.

"Course things was so cheap, you make two or three dollars, you could live. You know then you could take six cents and get two pounds of neck bones, three cents a pound. And you take three pounds of neck bones, give you a pot full like this, put in a couple boxes of spaghetti. Hell, that's enough to feed four or five people. See what I mean? And mixed pork sausage, that was seven cents a pound. You got yourself three or four dollars and you had some money.

"And I knowed the time when I was young, woman was turning tricks was fifty cents or a quarter, right there on Beale Street. Turning tricks, hustling. When I first start— This old big woman down the street, everytime I get a quarter she know it somehow and try to shit me, 'Come on, little boy.' It was a hell of a time then.

"And after that Depression raised up a little bit, 1937 it started to, it wasn't gone but you could feel the difference. See, when Roosevelt got in there, he ended that bullshit. Thirty-six was a little rough, still straining, but in thirty-seven he passed that law—he started to pay us two dollars a day, two dollars picking cotton on a hundred of cotton. Some guy could pick three hundred pounds of cotton, he made him six dollars. That was a hell of a lot of money. More than he been making.

"See, he had been picking cotton for fifty cents a hundred. If he picked three hundred pounds, he didn't have but a dollar and a half. See what I mean? Things were coming along back there, '38, '39 do all right. And then '40 jumped down, the war started, and the blues jumped up. See—it had been on a level up until now.

"Except there's something, some shit, trying to start now. You know it's rougher in a lot of places now. I'm gonna tell you the only thing that's holding this thing on now is the people. See, back in '35 there wasn't no old-age pension, wasn't no security, wasn't no disability, wasn't no charity, there wasn't nothing. The Red Cross give the people a little split beans and rice and they come around later with the P.W. and A. That's a job, like a defense job. P.W.A. work you all the week and give you twenty dollars a week and the rest of it they give you a month in groceries. Twenty dollars in cash and the rest in groceries. We work five, six days for that. Then when the war broke out boys were in the army, defense jobs opened up, and then all the steel mills opened up and they started raising salaries so you stayed up there until a few years ago. But you take right now, like it is now, if it wasn't for them two things goin it would be a slight depression now. Because the workin people, if it wasn't for them checks coming in from the government, the workin people don't make enough money to support the other people. You work from week to week, you could not keep up with your living from week to week, and what you got to give the other person? You understand, you got to give him nothin.

"Today a dollar ain't worth nothin. You got a hundred dollars, you ain't got nothin. You used to take a hundred dollars, a hundred dollars rattled and talked shit a long time, but it ain't nothin now. I made a thousand dollars since the fourth, spent all of it. I played two festivals, five hundred dollars a festival. That money's gone."

"I know what you mean," I said.

He resumed.

"I was playing a lot of Elmo James stuff, it was at Fifty-ninth and State, right on the el there, sell barbecue on one side and chicken on the other side. And Magic Sam, he was right opposite the el on the west side of the street, and I went in there and we played. He called me up and I played a couple numbers.

"Magic Sam was going off on the road that summer lots of times, and his band liked my playing, so he left me with the band till he come back. He said, 'Man, I like your style. I want you to play with them till I come back.' So that's where I stayed with them till he come back.

"Yeah, I knowed him, he died young, like Junior Parker. I sure did like to hear that boy sing. I loved to hear him sing. That boy had the sweetest voice I ever heard, and he could hold it right where he put it and wouldn't bend a bit. I liked to hear him sing those blues—I play a few of his numbers. I play a lot of things when it comes to me if someone speaks the name, but I know so many.

"Jimmy Rogers, before he made them numbers he used to live on Newberry in Jewtown.[9] When he came out of the army around '46, he hadn't done nothin then. Jimmy, he couldn't play that good then, he was playin harp then. Jimmy playin harp then. He stayed with a little old yellow girl in the basement. He had one suit and an old hard-top straw hat.

"Him and me and Little Walter used to play together on Maxwell Street everyday or around there. Stovepipe, John Henry Barbee, Porkchop, Peg Leg Sam, Big Fat; he would play the banjo, play it on the street. And Earl Hooker, Zeb, we all called him Zeb, me and him we all played together, I knew all of them.

"We used to meet up there and have a big jam session there. Sometimes Robert Nighthawk come through there and stay with us, sometimes Floyd Jones, Snooky Pryor, Baby Face Leroy, we always be around together.

"See that's something. Most all the blues players or players around there know each other, cause every one of them lookin for somewherc they can make some money. And I'd run into you, you run into me, sometime you like each other and you team together and try to make some moncy together. That's the way they work it then.

"Floyd Jones was workin in the steel mill and making forty-six dollars a week, and Big Walter he had up and left and went back South, last of '46. And Little Walter was playing there and so Floyd was working at the steel mill. So him and Floyd started playing together a little while, so Walter asked Floyd, 'Say, what you making a week, Floyd?' Floyd say, 'I'm making forty-six dollars a week pouring steel, man.' So Little Walter say, 'Let's make us some money.' So they went to playing in Jewtown on the street and Floyd was making forty dollars a day. Had to give that job up. Floyd say, 'To hell with that job.' Floyd done quit that steel mill job. He did. Then on a Sunday, they made more than that on a Sunday."

We laughed. It was a good blues story.
Hc began another one.

"And it's a funny thing. When Walter stai ted playing with Muddy, Walter was fractious. I mean he was quick tempered. I knowed him, fight quick but he was good if you let him be good, quick tempered.

"And Muddy and him went down to Clarksdale. Muddy had a gig at Clarksdale, and they got to fighting down there. And Walter, he had made a few numbers with Muddy at Chess, but he hadn't done nothin. So Chess knowed he was a good harp player. Chess knowed that but didn't have nothin of him. So Muddy thought he was everything. Meanwhile he put him out of his car and come on back to Chicago and Walter, hitchhiked and caught a ride back to Chicago.

"That's when Chess recorded Walter. And Walter made 'Juke' and that was at the top of the jukebox then. Walter told Muddy, he say, 'I don't need you no more.' Muddy, he gets hot and goes on back to Memphis and picks up Big Walter."

We laughed again.
As the tape recorder clicked to a halt, Honeyboy looked at his watch. My daughter came over and asked me for a Coke, so Honeyboy gave her some change. We had been sitting there for quite a while, and it was suddenly time for the next workshop.

As we walked down to the stage I thought about the Little Walter bit again—put out, down and out in Mississippi—then turning around and making a smash hit record, turning the tables on big Muddy Waters. It reminded me of so many blues songs about someday, baby, you'll be sorry you treated me this way and someday, baby, I won't need you any more.

At the workshop, Honeyboy Edwards performed to a large, receptive audience. He played a fine set shifting back and forth between his own songs and those of Robert Johnson, Charley Patton, and Tommy McClennan, keeping their musical memory alive.

3
"You know what you're going to get now? Interviews!"

Since the 1920s, bluesmen have been asked to explain the blues. Many have done so, and in the process told their own story.[1] A few outstanding spokesmen—Leadbelly, W. C. Handy, Jelly Roll Morton, and Big Bill Broonzy—all justifiably remembered for their storytelling as well as for their songs, provided full autobiographies published in book form. These essentially collaborative efforts described their lives and their music and provided a glimpse into the bluesman's world.[2]

Since the publication of these pioneering efforts, hundreds of blues musicians have had their stories published in books, popular magazines, and specialized blues and jazz journals.[3] We encounter their stories in print format, but the bluesman's story comes in spoken form and depends on the techniques and conditions of oral expression.

The artist tells his story to someone else in the context of an interview, or less often as part of his onstage act, and his tale reflects the presence of an audience. The interviewer brings his own set of assumptions to the interview and his own reason for being there, just as the artist has his assumptions and his reason for consenting to tell his story. Furthermore, both parties are influenced by previous interviews or even a tradition of the interview with its own unwritten rules regarding appropriate questions and answers.

These factors—the oral format, the interviewer's presence, the artist's goals, and the interview tradition—conspire to make interviews rather formalized exchanges between the bluesman and the outside world. Still, the musician's story is an artistic narrative, the result of the bluesman's creative effort.

Basically autobiographical, it may include historical commentary, philosophical speculation, and straightforward self-promotion. On the one hand it works like a business card or resumé announcing who the man is and listing what he has done: his training and accomplishments, where he's been, and who he knows. Like a resumé, it focuses on a specific area, blues-playing, presenting information that portrays the speaker as he wishes to be seen. It authenticates his background and justifies his claim to the bluesman's role.

But that is the businessman's side of the story. On the other hand, when told by Big Bill Broonzy or Honeyboy Edwards, it also becomes an artistic narrative. Since the speakers are artists, professional entertainers, poets, musicians, storytellers in song, their performance experience— their command of oral techniques and their artistic perspective—has often honed their tale-telling skills to a cutting edge.[4] While their stories remain the most important source of what the world knows about the blues—excluding blues recordings—they also deserve appreciation for their artistry. Through sequences of sometimes brilliant episodes, their stories portray the adventures of a remarkable group of individuals collectively called bluesmen.[5] However, before looking at the substance of the bluesman's story, we need to consider the context in which he tells it—the interview.

One reason they have a story to tell is that they are asked to tell their stories. Blues musicians are unusual people, celebrities who have been sought out to talk about themselves. As the "blues revival"[6] hit its stride, the chances of being interviewed increased dramatically. Some type of interview experience became more the rule than the exception. Most well-known artists grew accustomed to talking about their lives and their art, having been interviewed several times, sometimes more than once too often. Artists like Johnny Young and Honeyboy Edwards, already men of words, gifted in the techniques of an oral culture, fashioned their own accounts of their lives as blues musicians which they call their story.[7]

Beginning with our two examples, let us think for a moment about how the bluesmen approach the interview, what they bring to it, and how much they know about it. Then we need to consider the overall effect of interviews in general on the major themes of the bluesman's story.

On break between sets, sitting in a car with a stranger, Johnny Young sipped his scotch and talked about his talent. After our brief liquor store separation and with another set before him, he was slightly nervous and so was I. He knew nothing about me except that I was interested in him and had a tape recorder. It took time for us both to loosen up, so we made conversation, searching out a common frame of reference.

Having been through the same routine before, he was not at all fazed by my request for his story. Taking his cue like a seasoned veteran, he picked up the microphone, but first asked, "Is it on?" After all, why waste a good performance on a rookie who forgets to turn on the tape recorder? Although he paid attention to the quality and continuity of his story, the distractions of street-corner nightlife broke into his act enough to worry him: "This isn't going to be too good." But then he rationalized the effort: "But we rapping, we rapping."

He knew what he wanted to say and appeared irritated by interruptions, yet he acknowledged my needs by asking, "Now what else do you want me to put on there?"

An emotional, even passionate man, his story dealt with feelings, how he felt and how others felt about him. They loved him, and they loved his music. His characters, his mother and uncle, serve primarily to testify to his special talent. And even during the interview, he demanded affirmation from me, but if I overdid it, he cut me off with a curt "That's right." Then he would be off again, energetic at first, acting every part, but then he would wind down, tired out by the effort of his busy performance.

Oaths, curses, voices, dialogue, musical bits, even snatches of song punctuated his excited account. Starting, stopping, jumping from subject to subject, the events he described were brief flashes of his brilliance interspersed with testimonials. Throughout he maintained a tight focus on musical subjects: his homemade guitar, the family band, playing suppers, listening to his uncle, taking the guitar down from upside the wall, learning to tune, crying at the sound of music, making records, and his musician associates. Other subjects show his dedication: how he quit music at this wife's insistence only to return to the blues, convinced of his own talent, and how he had to work other jobs to support his music. The entire story keeps to the point of promoting his musical skill and dedication to his art form—the single major exception being his plea for a home, which is the only time his positive self-projection really slips, allowing a brief glimpse at the man behind the mask.

As his own agent, he was a salesman for his talent, and his story provided his credentials by listing his references and establishing his authenticity. He emphasized his ability as a sure-fire crowd pleaser and an attractive person to hire. With this in mind, he downplayed his current job as a temporary marriage of convenience which did not do his talent justice.

Honeyboy Edwards knew me better, and more important, he had some idea of what I already knew about his life and work. Unlike Johnny Young, he did not have to stop to see that I followed his story. Nor did he

have to worry about time, since we were both scheduled at his next
workshop, and he knew from past experience that I would make sure we
got there.

Showing more confidence in my tape recorder know-how, he took his
cue and launched into what amounted to a monologue, confident that I
could follow his story. This allowed me to sit back and listen in accord
with my avowed goal of silent nonparticipation. Yet every so often, out of
politeness, he would pause and look to me for a question.

Like Johnny Young, he had done interviews before and had a clear
picture of what he wanted to say, certain that people with tape recorders
appreciated his firsthand information about Robert Johnson and Charley
Patton. If Johnny Young resembled a salesman, Honeyboy Edwards
seemed to be a teacher lecturing an appreciative student. First he established his credibility as a witness, a man who was on the scene. Then he
tried to show me the meaning of the events he had witnessed and ana-
lyzed, and to this end provided examples or illustrations to drive his lesson home. In contrast to Johnny Young's staccato rap, he spoke slowly
and deliberately, supporting his account with detail that further emphasized his participation. And by filling in the historical background he
placed his subjects in a more meaningful historical and social context.

Where Johnny Young's story had more or less a single subject—himself—Honeyboy Edwards' account was far more expansive, balancing his
own experiences with the history and traditions of the blues. His story
gives us a sense of blues musicians as a mutually supportive self-conscious group who work together, travel together, drink together, and in
Honeyboy Edwards' case even live together. He gives examples of what it
is like to be a bluesman, and his anecdotes about other artists emphasize
the values of the blues community. He provides an introduction to blues
musicians as a subculture and to playing the blues as a life-style.
Whereas Johnny Young referred to some of the same characters—in fact
at times the cast of characters appears terrifically inbred—he did not
take the time to develop the relationship that binds them together as co-
workers and fellow artists, as Honeyboy Edwards did.

While the characters of Johnny Young's story were witnesses for his
achievements, Honeyboy Edwards was himself the witness to the events
of his time, lending his account the feel of being a lesson in blues history
and the sociology of the blues musician as well as an autobiography.

Both his story as a whole, and the individual episodes that compose
it, were much longer and more descriptive than those in Johnny Young's
account. Showing little concern with chronology, he skips the standard "I
was born" and begins his story as a walking musician. He often ties his
story together by theme or shared subject, moving, for example, from

how much people liked music to the dangers posed by admiring women to an illustration in the stunning legend of the death of Robert Johnson. Robert Johnson's grave, or lack of it, leads to Charley Patton's grave, to playing music for Charley Patton's uncle, back in time to his own inspiration listening to Tommy Johnson.[8]

He continues to stress other famous musicians as he tells of learning, and unlike Johnny Young, he portrays himself learning through determination rather than from some mystical gift. In general he speaks of people—including famous folksong collectors—and conditions rather than music; his observations range from white attitudes toward the bluesman to working conditions, the depression, forced labor, economics past and present, and even government programs.

Throughout he looks for motives, reasons to make past events more sensible, such as why women can be dangerous, why bluesmen have a bad reputation, and why musicians hang out together. These are lessons he has learned, sometimes the hard way, but now that he has them mapped out, he wants to pass them on. This attitude sets the tone of his story; he was there, he knows about these things, and he knows he's willing to teach someone else how it really was.

Yet in spite of the range of his story and his tendency to go outside himself, Honeyboy Edwards' story consistently shows him in blues-related situations. He portrays himself playing music down on the corner, avoiding farm labor, lying in the house all day long, hitting the road with other bluesmen, hanging out with the hustling women on Beale Street, drinking white whiskey, drinking beer all night, and working taverns. His anecdotes of other artists also stick with blues-related subjects, and generally his entire story deals with subjects that are easily tied to the bluesman and in some cases can be found in blues songs. The major exception is his reference to attending Greenwood High School, which is not unusual yet contradicts the bluesman stereotype.

Still, both these similar yet different stories portray the speaker-subject as a consistent character employed in blues-related activities not too far at odds with the expected or stereotypical blues life.

While Johnny Young and Honeyboy Edwards had a story they were willing to tell to a relative stranger, other artists had no story to tell. Otis Rush, twenty years younger than our two examples, also came from Mississippi. Handsome, urbane, he remains one of Chicago's greatest contemporary blues stylists with an instantly recognizable sound. We spoke one night at a Northside Chicago pub where his band was working. Although we had set up the appointment the night before, he seemed surprised when I showed up, tape recorder in hand. We sat away from the jukebox next to the stage. There was about an hour to show time, and

Otis Rush seemed relaxed and slightly amused by the interview. He definitely was interested in the tape recorder and asked if I would sell it.

After several false starts he asked, "What do you want to know?" I gulped, "Well, uh . . . your capsule life story." He laughed, "That'll take forever."

But he continued: "Like anyway, I was born and raised in Mississippi, Philadelphia, Mississippi. Came to Chicago in '49 and have been here ever since."

Again he stopped, so I asked, "Did you get into playing in Mississippi or did you get into it here?"

"Here."[9]

Though he had no patented life story, he did discuss his work, responding only to specific questions with well thought out answers. An articulate man, he offered almost nothing on his own and quite simply did not especially care to talk about himself—a trait other interviewers also noted.[10]

Primarily a matter of individual personality, his response also reflects the younger generation's attitude toward the blues business. Unwilling, and possibly unable, to tell a story in the manner of the older artists, some younger musicians consider the bluesman image old-fashioned and somewhat degrading. Wishing to be accepted for their musical performance alone, they refuse to act the part on stage or off. Rejecting older performance techniques they scornfully refer to as "clowning," their attitude toward their art is progressive and they see the bluesman stereotype as holding them back, preventing them from being recognized as artists.

Jimmy Dawkins, also from Mississippi and two years Otis Rush's junior, was also willing to play the blues and talk about the blues, but not to play the blues musician; as far as he is concerned, those times are past and gone, and his own approach to the blues parallels the scholar's or the critic's. His interest in the history of his art form involved him with British blues magazine *Blues Unlimited*, for which he prepared a column featuring his own taped interviews with his fellow bluesmen. Asking as well as answering the questions, Jimmy Dawkins combines playing the blues with studying its artists and its history. And in his own case he uses the interview to promote Chicago's West Side sound, which he feels has not been recognized for its own stylistic integrity.

I think the new, modern type of blues ought to be out. A new thing away from the B.B. King and Muddy Waters type of thing. Because B.B. is growing in popularity to the white peoples and too much. He's always overexposed as being such a big influence on all the blues artists because B.B. King's got the biggest name. He's not the biggest influence on us. He learned his runs from

T-Bone Walker and we learn ours from more modern techniques. When B.B. started it wasn't much, they didn't know much about guitars. They was using a clamp and so forth, now we use more modern techniques. We throwed the clamps away.

Now we're not trying to play like B.B., Luther, or Freddie King. They identify Albert King with B.B. Totally untrue, not that at all. It's a totally new thing. And we playing from our hearts ourselves. But every time you always hear this, every story that's written it's something about B.B. or something about Muddy or Wolf. These guys got their own thing and that's a prewar thing. And we in a new era now, and this is why I work hard with *Blues Unlimited* and so forth trying to, uh, not create but let people know about a new thing that's been created.

I mean I was in Mississippi in '51 and '49 hearing about these guys and I come to Chicago in '55. And I wanted to do more than just learn to play the blues, I wanted to learn something about it. You know. And about the artists. So I'm not just interested in it up on the bandstand. I'm interested in the story, and the life of the musicians because you got a lot of potential musicians that's very good that don't get the breaks because they clouded out by Wolf and Muddy and B.B. And this is just a lie, it's not that at all. We sit up in our living room and do our jobs and gig and things. And we the ones that have it hard and don't get paid and things.[11]

A variety of factors— age, region, personality, competition, the availability of models, whether or not the artist has something to push, and finally experience —all influence the way the bluesman approaches the interview and telling his story, if he tells one at all. Since interviews have become part of the public relations side of the blues business, most but not all musicians do—or at least did—cooperate with what they call "the press." They respect the impact a write-up in *Living Blues* or *Rolling Stone* can have on their career, so they use the interview to present their public profile, fully aware that their words may end up in print.

For example, white blues player Harmonica Frank Floyd stopped in the middle of his story and noted:

"Now they've got a book, a write-up in it about me in the *Mystery Train*."

"Yeah, I saw that," I responded.

"Did you see that book? Did you read about me there?" he asked.

"Yeah."

"Well, you know I'm telling the truth."[12]

Harmonica Frank's apparent faith in the power of the printed word to act as evidence reflects his continuing struggle for the recognition he thinks he deserved. On the large scale, he wants his place in history. Closer to home, he wants the money he is owed and is searching for help, so he takes the time to tell his story to a stranger.

Recently I spoke with Virginia bluesman John Cephas, an especially perceptive and articulate man. Asked if he considered interviews to be part of the blues business, he responded:

"Yeah. Absolutely. I'm very enthusiastic about interviews, especially where people will get exposed to the conversations that we have and maybe get a better insight into the blues and the blues musicians themselves. And I'm always eager to tell people what it's all about, how I learned, and what the blues is all about, and probably create more interest in the blues, cause a lot of people don't really know, you know. So much of our history has been suppressed or just hasn't been paid attention to."[13]

Sometimes looking to a wider audience, musicians use the interview in their own manner to suit their own purpose. John Cephas wants to promote the blues to see that it gets proper credit, Harmonica Frank wants his own credit and his money, Otis Rush prefers to talk about the blues business, Jimmy Dawkins promotes the new sound and did the interviewing himself, Honeyboy Edwards speaks of the history and traditions of his occupational group, and Johnny Young promotes his own act. And other blues artists will have their own reasons for consenting to do the interview and taking the time to tell their story.

A third-hand story attributed to Dick Shurman and told to me by Jim O'Neal of *Living Blues* concerns a conversation overheard between Chicago artists Hound Dog Taylor and Louis Myers of the Aces:

"Hound Dog and Louis Myers were overheard talking. Hound Dog by that time was a pretty big name on the college circuit with white fans because he had that album out and things and Louis Myers told him that he had just made an album which was for Vogue in France and Hound Dog said, 'Oh, oh. You know what you're going to get now? Interviews! People gonna ask you about your grandfather and grandmother and when you were born and when did this happen and all that.' "[14]

While musicians joke about the predictability of interviews, Hound Dog's warning shows that musicians talk among themselves about interviews and may even learn what to expect from other musicians.

I asked John Cephas if he could remember the first time he was interviewed. He thought a moment, then smiled.

"Yeah, I was at a festival at North Carolina and they had a workshop. And at the workshop they had some reporters there and all the people just want to ask questions about, you know, where you came from, how you learned to play blues. And at that time I was a little nervous. I would always depend on— People would say something to me, I would turn say 'Chief?' [Chief Ellis, an older piano player]. We laughed. But little by little I just got kind of used to it. But I think that was the first time somebody really asked me, 'Where did you learn to play blues?' and 'How did you and Chief get hooked together?' and 'What is it about your playing?' and stuff like that."[15]

First relying on his older partner, John Cephas eventually picked up the routine through observation and plenty of practice. Musicians learn this part of their business as part of the "whole ropes" of being a bluesman. And as with most of their lore, they learn from other artists and from actually doing it.

Both Hound Dog Taylor and John Cephas alluded to the types of autobiographical questions the musician encounters. Because a tradition of the interview has led over the years to the same questions and to a certain degree the same answers, they develop a predictive awareness of what to expect. Consciously or unconsciously, interviews depend on earlier models, which provide a frame of reference of sorts for both the artist and the interviewer. Knowing what to say or what to ask does not necessarily detract from the meaning of the exchange, but it does indicate that the interview has become a formal and at times almost ritualized exchange.

Speaking from great experience, Jim O'Neal commented on interviews:

"Most of the interviews I've done pretty much go the same way, have the same kind of pattern. People like to talk about how they learned music and the people that they know. Some people like to talk more about the music itself—the technique—and others would rather talk about the history, you know, their own history. Some people like to dwell on themselves, you know, about how good they are, what part they played in this, where other people, like, can just talk forever about the people they worked with."[16]

Jim O'Neal's description roughly applies to our two examples and may help explain the similarities between the two accounts. Beyond the fact that blues musicians often lead similar lives, the similarities in their stories become even more pronounced when interviews follow a similar pattern. Once the artist becomes at home with the format, he can anticipate questions with his own prepared statements or set pieces, which among other things allows him to control the interview. But even though his story reflects his own decision with regard to how he wants to present himself, specific questions and the interview tradition influence the range of his choices.

This applies especially to natural questions such as how did you learn, which both John Cephas and Jim O'Neal mentioned. From the former's perspective, people ask how he learned; from the latter's perspective, people like to talk about how they learned. Both are correct because one leads to the other, and whether offered or requested, the topic is predictable, a useful, comfortable focus for an interchange.

Knowing what to expect, the bluesman can put together a generalized response as a part of his story. For example, slide guitar stylist Mississippi Fred McDowell responded to questions about his way of playing with a powerful statement:

"Well, I was a little bitty boy, my uncle, we living, my home, everybody calls me Mississippi Fred McDowell, but that's not my home. I was born and raised in Rossville, Tennessee. That's about thirty-five miles from Memphis.

"My uncle used to play for us. He had a beef bone, reamed it out, fine tooled, really fine. He wore his here, on his ring finger. He play blues with it sometimes just like I do. I would stand there in the corner just like you standing there, you understand. I said, 'If I ever get grown, I'm gonna learn to play a guitar.' Boy, it sounded so good to me, so if I ever get grown and learn to play a guitar, gonna play with a bone.

"After I learned one tune. First piece I ever played was 'Big Fat Mama with the Meat Shaking on Your Bone.' I learned that—I took that bone, I took part of that and put it between my fingers here. But you can't make a chord worth a plug nickel, but it sounds good if you know how to turn it loose.

"Well, I broke off a bottle about that long. It was too long, you understand. I found, drove me a piece of iron in the ground—about like that. Broke this bottle off down at the shoulders and this one, you know, this bottleneck and me, they been to Bonn, Germany, yeah."[17]

Fred McDowell's account satisfies the reporter's who, what, when, and where, but also achieves an artistic or dramatic quality that goes far beyond answering a question. The story compresses his musical career from the instant of inspiration to the present day, taking him from Rossville, his real home, to Bonn, Germany. The magic of the sound brings on his own dramatic declaration of intent, and the "how to" aspect of his technological improvements teaches his audience exactly how he did it.

On another occasion, asked a similar question, he responded:

"This here bar, this slide part, my uncle, I was a little boy then, I would sit in the corner [jook (sic) sat]—He had a beef bone, you know, a bone cut out of a steak, and he had that bone smooth as I got this ring. And he played it on his little finger. Boy, I'm telling you I thought it was the prettiest sound I ever heard in my life. I said, 'If I ever get grown and learn how to play the guitar, I'm gonna get me one of those bones.' But I didn't start with no bone. I started with a pocket knife. You gotta play with the guitar laying flat across your lap. Cause I was playing with it between my fingers like that, well, you see, you can't make a chord with the other fingers. And so I studied, I tried a bottle after I learned and I been headed up ever since."[18]

In spite of the differences, the piece has become set and corresponds to what Amy O'Neal, co-editor of *Living Blues*, termed a "standard rap." Standard raps can be used from interview to interview as a formula response to more or less predictable questions.

Although the bluesman as an observer and social critic can improvise and comment on a remarkable variety of subjects—and in a more casual context usually does—the special formality of the interview lends itself to relatively set responses constructed along the same lines or using the same dramatic imagery from interview to interview. And the more he tells his story the more polished it becomes, until he has a fully developed narrative or episode at his disposal, which he knows has worked before. He is then free to concentrate on making an effective performance.

Through selection and repetition, the bluesman creates an artistic version of his past. But the artistry does not negate the story's validity or meaning. Yet because "standard raps" have a stylized quality—too dramatic or too entertaining for some tastes—they have at times been misjudged as "jive." While it is true that set responses can be used mechanically to fill up interview space, they still represent the artist's choice of how he wants to represent himself. It does not mean he has reached his limits with regard to his ability to explain about his art form or his life. Instead, we see the artist taking control of his story by applying his artistic skill. Nor does repetition mean the story cannot be changed. Even standard raps evolve to suit the needs of the bluesman storyteller.

Virginia bluesman Archie Edwards provides a lengthy set of examples that demonstrate how a story changes and allows him to display his storytelling skills. We first met at the Maryland Folklife Festival in 1976. At that time, he combined police work, cab-driving, and barbering to make ends meet, viewing his music as a hobby and a means of self-expression. One summer night in 1978 I went out to his barbershop to ask him about blues in Maryland. In passing, he spoke of blues in Virginia and how his father's friends would come over for country jam sessions. They did this most Saturday nights, but one night stood out.

"My father and my uncle sat inside playing. My uncle laid his guitar on the bed and went out. I took it up and played one thing that was in my head [plays a riff]. They holler, 'Who's that playing on the guitar?' Say, 'Well, Uncle Roy that's your boy Archie.' So that's what I played and it was professional.'"[19]

Since that time he quit police work to devote more time to his musical ambitions, and I have been fortunate to be able to watch his skills develop. Along the way I've seen him rearrange his account of how he learned to play, adding and subtracting detail, shifting the emphasis, bringing in the audience, and even improvising a parallel anecdote. A fine storyteller as well as a gifted song composer, he has had ample opportunity to make the story more effective. While working at folk festivals, workshops, concerts, and classroom demonstrations, he generally would field a few questions between songs. One day at the University of Maryland a student asked, "How did you learn to play?"

"My father had a buddy. His name was Boyd Maddox. Now, he played real good guitar. So he would come to our house on Saturday nights. He'd stay till Monday morning sometimes. So one night this guy and my daddy was sitting in the house playing the guitar. So my mother fixed dinner, so they put the guitar on the bed. You know, in the country the bedroom— the bed—is in the living room you know. So he put the guitar on the bed. We all sitting around the fire there.

"So there was one note that the man made on the guitar that I said that I just had to make that note. If I could make that one note on the guitar, then I knew I would be able to play the guitar. So this is the note that he was making [plays a riff]. That was the old 'Red River Blues,' and I made that note. From then on I been playing that guitar.

"So the funny part about it, my father say, 'Who in the world is that there in the house playing the guitar?' That man said, 'Uncle Roy, that's your boy playing that guitar.' Sure enough, it was Uncle Roy's boy. Uncle Roy's boy been playing it ever since." [Laughter.][20]

On another occasion the large audience included members of a local historical society, the media, and even a few of his acquaintances from his police work. In reply to the same question, Archie answered:

"It's very simple, because I know my dad, he played the guitar a little bit and the harmonica and what not. So he had a buddy named Boyd Maddox, a young fellow that was really good on the guitar. He used to come to my father's house on Saturday nights. They'd sit up, drink whiskey, and play guitar all night. So one night, it was very cold in March, real cold and windy. So my mother fixed dinner. So my father and this fella went in to eat dinner. The man lays the guitar on the bed. They were playin a song. It really started something buzzing in my ear. I would strike a note—but a kid wasn't allowed to touch anything, unless somebody give you permission. So something kept telling me: 'Pick that guitar up and make that one note I heard that rang in my ear before. If you can just make that one note you'll be okay.' I finally got the nerve and the courage to sneak up to the guitar. So I made that note. My father [said], 'Who's out there playing that guitar?' 'Roy, that's your boy playing that guitar.' Sure enough, it was true. Roy's boy was playin that guitar. Roy's boy has been playing ever since. But first thing I played . . . this was the note I played. Something called the old 'Red River Blues.' [Plays.] Damn! I can play guitar now—I love that note, you know. If there was just one note that I had to make— It was just so easy, when I made that one note everything was over and I've been playin ever since. [Plays notes.] Still sounds good, doesn't it?"[21]

Here Archie added whiskey to the performance—which always brings the bluesman a response—and included a reference to the weather. He also emphasized childhood rule-breaking reminiscent of Johnny Young's taking the guitar down from the wall. Furthermore, he played the riff twice and then included the audience by asking, "It still sounds good, doesn't it?" With everyone laughing, he looked over at the emcee and said, "Shoot me another one."

A week later in a college classroom a student asked, "How did you get started?"

"I started playing when I was six or seven years old. See, I—my father played when I was a kid you know. He had some friends that played the guitar and on Saturday night back in those days people didn't have nothin to do but walk five or ten miles and come by his house, you know, and eat dinner, drink whiskey, and play the guitar. So my father had a buddy that would do that quite often.

"So one Saturday night in March of I reckon around the early thirties—I was a little child. So my father and this fellow was playing the guitar and my mother fixed dinner, so when they went in to eat dinner the fellow left the guitar on the bed there in the living room.

"So there was one note that was ringing like crazy in my mind, in my head, you know. So in those days, you know, children were taught not to touch anything that belonged to anyone else. If you did you just got torn up. But this note that this guy had made on the guitar it sounded so pretty and one mind told me, 'Say, man, if you can just get over there to that bed and make that note just one time real low you'll have it made.' So I finally got the courage to sneak over there to the bed and I picked up the guitar and I made the note. [Plays.] I think I dropped down a little too heavy with that and my daddy hear it.

"He says, 'Who's that in there playing that guitar?' and that fellow said, 'Uncle Roy, that's your boy playing that guitar.' Says, well, he's right it was Uncle Roy's boy and Uncle Roy been playing, Uncle Roy's boy been playing ever since. But I just knew if I could just make that one note I could do it. So that's when I started. When I was about six or seven years old. But I knew if I could just get that one note I'd have it. That's what you call the old 'Red River Blues,' but when I dropped down, uh oh, I got it now, but I didn't get the whipping either. That's one thing I did my father did not whip me for: 'Now, wait a minute as young as he is he done made that note like that.'

"That was almost like the same thing happened to me one day when my son was at the barbershop with me. He was about three years old, three or four, and I had bought an old pellet gun, you know. So all around the barbershop on the walls they had mirrors hanging up there. So I walked outside one day to wash the car or do something. When I came back that boy had taken that BB gun. Man he had shot one of those mirrors to death. I said, 'Boy, you done ruined my mirror,' and I grabbed him, you know, about getting ready to spank him. He said, 'Wait a minute, Daddy. Wait, Daddy.' Say, 'Look up there at that good shooting.'

"So I looked and say, 'Dog if that isn't good shooting.' Now he had made a straight line from the bottom of that mirror all the way to the top and in a space, you know. I couldn't have done it to save my life—six inches apart, bottom to the top. I looked at that and said, 'Son, that is good shootin.'

"This is so true, I had to laugh. And sometimes I'm sitting in that barbershop and I look at that mirror and I think, man, that guy he was smart, man, from the time he came into the world, because he knew I was gonna tear him down but he knew that was good shooting too."[22]

Beside the addition of the extra detail, the tale now turns on the whipping he didn't get, which then provides the inspiration for the secondary account of his son's shooting. A generation later, the roles reversed, his son recreates his cleverness by being bad but being so good at it.

Although an extreme example, it illustrates the malleability of even set pieces. While other artists tell of learning by breaking a rule or of having their childhood accomplishments witnessed by established musicians, few approach the sheer complexity of Archie Edwards' tale. Through shaping and reshaping the episode, adding detail, and finally improvising a suitable parallel experience, he shows he can excel in prose as well as in song composition.[23]

How a musician tells his story depends on the artist and the circumstances. Some, like Otis Rush, prefer a "just the facts" question-and-answer approach. Others, like Archie Edwards, following in the tradition of Leadbelly and Big Bill Broonzy, use the interview to display their narrative skill. Searching for an anecdote where a word would do, they explain their art and their lives with illustrations drawn from their past experience or the lore of their fellow bluesmen.

For example, Eddie Taylor was asked, "Do people dance to the blues?"

"Yeah, whoo! Break the house down. I was under the house one night and the snakes, cats, dogs, chickens came out from under the house with me, running, POW! I didn't know what it was, a bomb or something, but it was the house broke down, right in the middle of the floor. You know, the truth is the truth. The only thing saved me, I was sitting over in the chimney corner, right up under the piano. Roosevelt Sykes was playing that night. Roosevelt Sykes and Brother Montgomery, a whole lot more— There was a guitar player, Yank Rachel, I think. They had a big time that night."[24]

The tendency to draw on personal experience or to use anecdotes in order to make a point is by no means confined to blues artists. Nor is the tendency to present a life story as a sequence of such workable episodes. John Dollard criticized what he termed the average life history for its tendency to present "events separately identified like beads on a string."[25] Although far from average, the musician's story benefits from the analogy. Think of it as a string of beads with some beads brightly polished through repetitions, others still in the rough. In a sense, the entire string should show polish if the artist has told his story before, but as we have seen, new materials may be added at each telling. Yet some materials noticeably stand out as more stylized, more artistically contrived, and more dramatically presented. While the entire narrative demands a certain degree of selection and creative reshaping, these episodes show an even greater development, perhaps because they are used on stage or told as isolated anecdotes outside the interview.

So far our examples show that the most polished beads bear repeating because they work either by answering predictable questions (as in the case of Fred McDowell's rap) or by drawing a laugh (as with Archie Edwards' tale) or even by eliciting awe (as with Honeyboy Edwards' legend of the death of Robert Johnson). But these extremely stylized accounts are unusual. More often the episodes simply show the author in a situation appropriate to the bluesman, in effect proving him to be a musician, as in Johnny Young's brief account of making a guitar.

With or without dramatic emphasis, scenes of this sort make up the core of the bluesman's story and take care of the business of presenting him as a musician. More artistic than extensive, his story does not attempt to describe the gamut of his experience but concentrates on blues-related subjects. But what types of subjects seem appropriate for the bluesman? A brief comparison of Johnny Young's and Honeyboy Edwards' stories offers some clues.

Looking back at our two examples, we can see certain similarities, which of course indicate similar lives. Yet the fact of shared experience does not fully explain why certain subjects were chosen and others were left out. Nor does it explain why other musicians describe similar subjects in their stories. Of course, as we have already noted, some topics are formed in response to the interviewers' questions, but even so we are left to ponder why these questions are asked in the first place.

Interviewers ask questions based on what the musicians do and on the signs or symbols through which they are known. One such symbol is the guitar. Johnny Young and Honeyboy Edwards spoke of guitars: homemade guitars, broken guitars, makeshift guitars, and guitars hanging "upside the wall." Both also spoke of how people reacted to their music, how they were appreciated, and how their parents allowed them to play—the exception being Johnny Young's first wife, who pulled him away from music. Each told of learning through traditional methods and being taught by older, established artists—one stressing his gift, the other his determination. They both told how they became professionals at an early age, playing suppers and jukes. Both talked about working, playing down south with other musicians, then coming to Chicago to work Maxwell Street and then taverns. Both spoke of making records and of hanging out with much the same set of musician friends. Finally, each commented on current tours and festivals and today's hard times.

In the following chapters, I will focus on the same topics: instruments, community opposition and support, learning the blues, making money, working the blues, and finally the future. I have devoted a chapter to each. Before the final chapter, which discusses the future of the bluesman and the blues, I will briefly restring the beads in order to consider the factors that shape the artist's story.

But first I will unstring the narrative, taking episodes out of the greater context of the transcribed interview. Dismembering individual stories makes me uncomfortable, but countless examples of the bluesman's story are already available; in fact, their existence not only makes my study possible, it makes it necessary. Right now the need for a better understanding of what we already have outweighs the need for another collection of autobiographies.

Before proceeding, I should make my own organizational role clear. While the topics derive from the musicians' stories either offered by the artist or elicited by the interviewer, I am responsible for the book's organization. Since musicians often talk about several subjects in the same account, taking an episode out of context and placing it in one chapter or another may appear arbitrary. The sequence of the chapters implies a pattern of growth that also reflects my editorial presence. However, since lives are being described, a sense of chronology is inherent, and most musicians adhere to it in some degree. Yet as we have seen, the musician's approach to his story is flexible, allowing him to jump ahead, flash back, or move thematically from subject to similar subject, or otherwise address whatever topic is currently on his mind.

Although the following subjects are those commonly talked about by musicians, they in no way represent the extent of what bluesmen have to say. Nor do all musicians touch on all the subjects, whether asked about them or not.

All this considered, the fact remains that bluesmen use these topics, drawing from the Southern folk beliefs, music traditions, popular stereotypes, and the special lore that musicians share with one another. Each will be explored in relation to the reality of Afro-American folklife and as a metaphor that a special group of American artists use to explain their lives and to define themselves. Whatever the source—black folk tradition or the interviewers' preconceptions—these subjects tie the musician's world to our own and have by unspoken mutual consent become the means by which we know him.

4
"I'm gonna get me a guitar if it's the last thing I do"

Byther Smith, known to his fellow musicians as Smitty, worked the house band at Theresa's, a small Chicago club that is now an internationally known blues landmark. Here, during the summer of 1974, he backed up Junior Wells and Muddy Waters Jr.,[1] as well as taking his own turn in the spotlight as lead vocalist.

His background exemplifies the diversity of American music. Born in Monticello, Mississippi, Byther Smith attempted to learn guitar as a teenager but put it aside to work with a gospel group. Later he traveled west, joining a country and western band as a bass player. Finally he moved to Chicago, where his uncle J. B. Lenoir was an established blues star. Here he went back to the guitar, sitting in with his neighbor Robert Junior Lockwood and other blues veterans. To keep up with other Chicago musicians, he took music lessons at Lyon and Healy, a local music company, and credits much of his guitar-playing style to his teacher there, rock guitarist Roy Buchanan.

Unlike Johnny Young's or Honeyboy Edwards' generation of transplanted country musicians, Smitty learned his music in an urban context that included the likes of Otis Rush and Jimmy Dawkins. Along with these younger artists, his approach to blues is serious and progressive. Scorning what he considers unnecessary showmanship or clowning, he concentrates instead on the music, which he plays with great feeling.

Modest about his considerable musical skill, he takes pride in his reputation for dependability, a trait not traditionally associated with the blues musician. His manner is businesslike both on stage and off, and from his point of view, playing blues is a job, but a job he chooses to do. So he works at it with dedication and determination.

Smitty does not lay claim to any special gift for music, nor has he had any real breaks, yet he stubbornly works the music business, confident that his work ethic will eventually enable him to make it. I witnessed this determination one evening when he played with his chording hand completely wrapped in a bandage, his fingertips poking through. A lawn mower accident had nearly severed his fingers, but still he played his Fender Telecaster with his own uniquely pure tone.

Several nights later I drove down from the Northside to the far South-side suburbs. When I arrived, he was out in front of a beautiful brick house mowing the lawn and waiting for me. Standing in his front yard, he told me how he found his home:

"When I came out here the first time, I was looking around and this white guy came out, a policeman. He was selling the house. He kind of looked at me, and he said, 'Well, we don't have any colored people around here.' So I said to him, 'That's all right, I don't want to buy any colored people, I want to buy a house.' "

And so he did.[2]

Inside we sat at his dining room table, his children in the living room listening to the latest soul hits, his wife in the bedroom resting. I tested the tape recorder, and after a few awkward moments he began to speak about his life and music.

Like Otis Rush and Jimmy Dawkins, Smitty did not have a set story to tell in the manner of Johnny Young or Honeyboy Edwards. Relatively new to interviews, his story was still evolving, and despite my attempt to force him into a monologue, he was far too polite to leave me out of the conversation. Even so, he did offer a number of episodes characteristic of the bluesman's story. First and foremost he told how he got his first guitar.

"I really got interested in playing the guitar when my cousin started playing the organ, and he was smaller than I was. That's when I really got interested, but I couldn't learn to play that organ. And I really got interested in playing by all those boys right around me.

"I was more interested in playing—so that's when I didn't have no money to buy a guitar with, cause my brothers and sisters, like I said, my mother and father were dead by then. So I steal this corn out of the corncrib and go trade it to a white boy and get a guitar. So he give it. His father come and take the guitar away, but he didn't bring the corn back [laughter]. This was the greatest part about it, he gets the guitar but he didn't bring the corn back, which wasn't very much.

"So later, my brother buys a twenty-two rifle and I steal the rifle out of the house and go and trade it and get me a guitar. My brother makes

me take the guitar back. I had to take the guitar back to return the rifle.
So I, after that, I get mad and tell him I'm gonna get me a guitar if it's
the last thing I do. I was gonna get me a guitar, and he says, 'If you do,
you gonna have to buy it. You don't steal nothin to get and trade.'

"So I worked for a white fellow fixing up a fence, you know, something like a hog pasture, calf pasture. I work for him, I don't know how
long, seem like to me that it was a month, but I don't think it was more
than three weeks. But he finally just up and give me an old guitar he had
lying around there."[3]

Byther Smith's involved account of transgression and persistence,
complete with threefold repetition, portrays his getting that guitar to be
the sole purpose in his life. In retrospect, the reason for this choice is
obvious. As we have seen with Fred McDowell and Archie Edwards, an
instrument is needed to begin life as a musician; likewise, the musician's
story often begins with an instrument.

Like members of any occupational group, blues players are concerned
with the tools of their trade. But an instrument can be more than a meal
ticket. As well as a vehicle through which the artist can express his soul,
it may be a work of art in its own right. Personal, even loving, relationships develop between musicians and their instruments, and like the
weapons of great heroes, some guitars have their own names: B.B. King's
famous "Lucille," Albert King's "Lucy," and Drink Small's "Geraldine."

Ideally, an artist should feel rapport with his instrument so that it
becomes an extension of himself, or, as Johnny Shines intimates, a second
voice:

"I don't talk myself. If my guitar don't talk to me then we don't have
a conversation between each other. That guitar you see down there, we
learned to understand each other. I love that guitar. That guitar, you say,
don't have any life, or any feelings, but it responds to me. So there *is* a
feeling between me and that guitar. We're very much in tune together."[4]

Central to the musician's livelihood, instruments are also the artist's
single most important prop. They speak for him both as a second voice
and as a calling card, the symbol of the bluesman's role.

Musical instruments from the most rudimentary to the most sophisticated serve as boundary markers in the musician's life. Beyond the facts
of birth date and place, the musician's story begins with a musical encounter, usually a reference to a musical instrument. On the other side of
the coin, quitting the music scene can include the symbolic act of selling
or even giving away one's guitar. For example, Byther Smith told me of
amateurs who, failing to make it on stage, signify their defeat by selling

their new three-hundred-dollar guitar to the first buyer for twenty dollars.

Musicians are connected to instruments all their musical life and can even organize an autobiography chronologically around the different guitars they have owned. But of all the instruments a musician runs through, none is so frequently or so reverently spoken of as the first, which, like a first love, is idealized.

Driven by what is portrayed as an inner need, the true born bluesman makes, begs, borrows, or steals something capable of making music. Whether the artist builds a guitar, breaks a rule to get it, receives it as a gift, works for it, or simply buys one, he includes it in his story, often as the opening scene.

People familiar with the bluesman's story, like Jim O'Neal, recognize these topics:

"Yeah, usually the first instrument is some kind of makeshift guitar, or something their parents bought for them, or something they got at the secondhand store—Sears Roebuck. Yeah, all remember their first instrument very well. They could give you a big story about that."[5]

The homemade guitar ranks as the most popular piece in the musician's story. Fortunately it is also the best documented.[6] Handmade or improvised instruments, often with West African precedents,[7] persisted from the days of slavery well into the twentieth century.[8] Even after commercially produced guitars became commonplace, children continued to put together their own instruments and form makeshift bands. For example, blues publicist W. C. Handy described a children's band with combs, bones, and a broom bass in his 1941 autobiography,[9] and Big Bill Broonzy, the major blues spokesman of the 1950s, described his uncle's "barnyard band," composed of washtub, plow points, and the omnipresent broom, as well as his own handmade guitar and fiddle.[10]

Today blues musicians continue to recall handmade instruments as coexisting with and usually inspired by a real guitar too valuable for children to play with. One of my former students and Mississippi neighbor of Ike Turner explained: "Children would make their own guitars, see, cause their daddies didn't want them to mess with theirs. So they were hung up out of reach so the kids couldn't get to them."[11] Nor were homemade instruments confined to the Delta. Bluesman John Cephas recalled growing up in the late 1930s and early 1940s in rural Virginia:

"Well, we used to take a wooden crate, like a box, a small wooden crate or a box—now I did this many times—and we'd put sticks on them and stuff like that, play a one-string guitar, or if we could get two strings of some kind attached to that. And we had all kinds of contraptions where you'd bend the neck to change the key or just slide something up and down it to change the note. Yeah, I used to do that."[12]

Brooms, buckets, boxes, and baling wire provided means for the common end of making music—or at least trying to.

It is difficult to determine the extent of the tradition or how many children went on to play music. Mississippian Clyde "Judas" Maxwell considered homemade instruments incapable of producing real music. He recalled their construction as common practice but downplayed their importance to becoming a musician.

"A lot of em done that. But they didn't learn to play any music on it. Didn't play no music on it. Just some kind of noise. Now let's see, I used to have five, used to have seven friends, but I got five friends over there now, and they make some kind of guitar out of them old buckets. They hit on an old bucket, puts tops on them and cuts holes in them—get strings. Put some strings on it and wind it up. But they never really learned how to play it. They plunk it, everything else. But you think it sounds good, just plunk it and think you got a guitar. But it's not like a real one."[13]

Yet for other artists, homemade instruments suggest a special gift or talent. Here, rather than stressing rural poverty, the makeshift instrument implies destiny. K. C. Douglas of Canton, Mississippi, claims he used to beat on a water bucket until his fingers bled, trying to make it sound like a guitar. In retrospect, he considers his actions a sign that he was born to be a musician.[14]

Instrument construction takes on special importance in a traditional belief system of signs and special inborn gifts or talents. For example, Johnny Young begins his story by telling how he made a guitar. His mother saw it as a sign, declared him a musician, and went out and bought him a guitar. Blues legend Sleepy John Estes spoke of a similar experience:

"Then I went and made me a cigar box with one string on it and started to playing it. The string come from a broom. You know, on a broom you had a wire wrapped around it to hold it. My mother told my father, said, 'That boy goin to be a musician, might as well buy him a guitar.' He said, 'Wait till fall and I'll buy you one.' So he worked and bought me that guitar."[15]

Details of instrument construction—references to brooms, how the construction was viewed as a sign by his parents, their acceptance of the sign, and their willingness to sacrifice for his future—emphasize John's inherent gift for music. He claims that even before this a seer determined he was to be a musician. "When I was born, a man from Texas told my mother I was going to be a musician, said it was a talent."[16] Eddie Taylor also spoke of instrument construction, like Sleepy John Estes opting for the broom:[17]

"I used to take my mama's broom and tear the wire off it and make me a guitar upside the wall—boom-boom-boom. The first real guitar I got was in 1936. My mother ordered it from Sears Roebuck for twelve dollars."[18]

The inclusion of facts, dates, and exact price for the gift guitar point out the importance of the event as something worthy of memory as well as to authenticate the gift event.[19]

Wild Child Butler, a short, stocky harmonica player from Alabama, told me about himself in a car parked outside a tavern. His account inverts the homemade instrument to real instrument sequence:

"I was small. I stand and watch em. So I used to beg them, 'Let me blow some, let me blow the harp.' They let me blow and you know, I'd strike a little tune or something on it. So they told me, 'Say, you going to be a big man blowing this harp one day.' They gave me an old harp. So I kept that old harp for a long time. I blowed on it and I blowed till the harp went bad. I took me a Prince Albert Tobacco can and beat, put some rocks on it and closed up the mouth where it made some holes in the back of it and I used to hum, hum!—and sing and stomp my feet."[20]

As with Johnny Young, he emphasizes the recognition of his talent. The younger artist observes his elders, then amazes them with his prodigious talent. The musician is marked as a potential artist—"a big man blowin harp"—and he is encouraged by the older musicians who help convert him to their camp by giving him an instrument.

Homemade instruments, while a very real folk tradition, loom larger than life in the bluesman's story. They show the artist interested in music at an early age in the rural South and resourceful enough to do something about it. Furthermore, instrument construction may be seen as a sign of musical destiny. Finally it can be used as a dues-paying reference, as when Chicago guitarist/drummer Mickey Martin told my class in Indianapolis: "You see, when we were kids we couldn't afford no instruments, guitars. So we had to make our own instruments to play on."[21]

From Johnny Young's perspective, making a guitar sets him apart, yet considering bluesmen's stories in general it may be the rule rather than the exception. This is not to say that everyone tells the same story, but blues musicians recognize the story as part of the collective lore of the blues. Enough artists include some reference to instrument-making in their stories that it has become a cliché of the musician's story.[22] And artists who did not make an instrument, who perhaps now feel they should have, can at least construct a story about it.

Similar stories are told of nonblues performers, such as Chet Atkins, who allegedly used strings from a front porch screen. Although not unique to black folk culture, most contemporary one-string players are black; and the homemade guitar has become tied to the bluesman image and is a recognized and at times even a suspect motif of the bluesman's story. What began as a black folk tradition now is part of the bluesman stereotype and, as a stock item of record liner notes and folk festival programs, now serves to authenticate the artist for an essentially white audience.

However, the theme of improvisation and of making do with whatever is at hand runs through the musician's story. Whether the bluesman made an instrument or not, the recurring image is that of the youngster determined to make music through any available means and whatever the risk. For James Thomas it meant playing his uncle's guitar on the sly:

"I didn't make one, but I used to go around with these boys and they would have that hay baling wire up and mess with that. But my uncle had a guitar as far as I could remember, and when he'd go to work—he wouldn't let me play it, you know—but when he went out to work I could get in and play it."[23]

Breaking rules and risking punishment also show the youngster to be single-minded. And, as exemplified by Johnny Young and Archie Edwards, it is a common theme. Tempted by that forbidden guitar left untended or hung just out of reach "upside the wall," the young man is determined to play it whatever the cost. While he often gets a licking, he proves his sincerity by a willingness to consistently disobey. And sometimes the sheer nuisance of it all can work to the artist's advantage.

During a "Voice of America" interview, I spoke with Virginia bluesman John Cephas. I asked him, "I heard that your father played. Is this where you first ran into a guitar?"

"No. No. Uh, my father— You know this is the kind of story that I tell a lot. This is a very true story. When my father first bought a guitar he was an adult man and he was kind of fascinated with a guitar and he had aspirations of playing the guitar, of being a blues musician.

"So at that time, I had already been exposed to the blues. I was actually playing a little bit of open key stuff and slide that he didn't know anything about. So he went out and bought himself a guitar. I didn't have a guitar. He went out and bought himself a guitar and he used to hide his guitar in the closet. And he would not allow me to play his guitar, wouldn't allow me to touch it.

"Well, when he wasn't home I would go and get his guitar and I would play his guitar. And almost every time he would catch me. He would come home and catch me and I got many a licking because of his guitar.

"And finally, he never did learn how to play the guitar. So when he just finally got disgusted with his efforts to play the guitar he just told me, he say, 'Well, you—I can't stop you.' He said. 'There's the guitar if you want to play it. There it is.' Said, 'You can have it, you can play it.' So then I was kind of home free with the guitar then, and that really gave me a chance to play it as much as I wanted after he almost killed me trying to keep me from playing it."[24]

As the "type of story he tells a lot," the account rates validation as a true story. Its staying power is justified by the way it shows the speaker winning his father's guitar, earning the gift as a tribute to his talent. By beating his father playing music after his father had literally beaten him for playing music, he proves himself worthy by learning when his father could not, and he pays his dues suffering for his art.

Junior Wells tells an elaborate narrative of his own overwhelming need for a harmonica. In this version, taken from a record jacket liner, several elements stand out, primarily the gift of the instrument as earned by the individual's obvious talent, followed by the need for the instrument and the amount of work or trouble put forth to obtain it, and finally the inclusion of price in the story:

"I went to this pawnshop downtown and the man had a harmonica priced at two dollars. I got a job on a soda truck, played hookey from school, worked all week, and on Saturday the man gave me a dollar and a half. For a whole week of work. I went to the pawnshop and the man said the price was two dollars. I told him I had to have the harp. He walked away from the counter, left the harp there. So I laid my dollar and a half on the counter and picked up the harp. When the trial came up, the judge asked me why I did it. I told him I had to have the harp. The judge asked me to play it and when I did, he gave the man fifty cents and hollered, "Case dismissed."[25]

Exploited of wages, playing hookey, and finally yielding to temptation, Wells points toward his own fate. He would become a musician because he *had* to have it. The humor and irony implicit in the quick transition "when my trial came up" adds another level of ethnic drama to the story, culminating in official judgment that he was a musician and had to have the harp, even if the judge had to pay. "Case dismissed," without stretching a point, not only proclaims the young man innocent of being a thief, it authorizes him as a musician: the verdict is "Guilty of being a musician with talent." That the fifty cents as a token gift came from as high authority as the judge, notorious in black tradition for the intolerance for black offenders, places this anecdote in the category of "bragging exaggeration." The shape of the brag is: How good was I? Well, this is how good I was.

Narratives about an instrument given as a gift, as a reward for or simple acknowledgment of special musical ability, while less frequent than homemade instrument stories, are still noteworthy. While the gift, just as the making of an instrument, may function within the life story as proof of special ability, as with Wild Child Butler it does not always do so. Often the tale of the gift simply involves parents acquiescing to the wishes of their children.[26]

For the lucky novice whose family was affluent enough, a guitar could be acquired from a number of mail order houses. Archie Edwards and his brothers managed to purchase a guitar as a family project. The source of their income derived from their peripheral participation in the local moonshine business, a romantic enough way for a youngster to earn a little money. Their collective acquisition, "that old Gene Autry guitar with Gene Autry and his dog and horse on it," launched Archie's career:

"Gene Autry was somethin else—they had a little Gene Autry guitar cost five dollars. So me and my four brothers had to get the money by selling moonshine, selling a little whiskey. So me and my four brothers figures to get it together, that's only a dollar and a quarter a piece, so we sent up there and got it brand new, guitar, case, instruction book, and everything, and brother, we took off from there. Started off with a Gene Autry guitar in the thirties— I learned to tune before that but the Gene Autry five-dollar guitar was the first one that I ever really learned to play and carry it out and win the public with it."[27]

Arkansas-born Bob Lowery also spoke of a mail-order guitar as well as a gift instrument:

"We ordered it from a little company in Houston, Tennessee—uh, Nashville, Tennessee. They call it National—you never heard tell of that? We ordered that guitar, and that was an expensive guitar. I think we paid eleven dollars for that. Now after we got that guitar out of the box—we couldn't wait till we got it out. We got it out. My old man he tuned it up, worked with it for a while, and it sounded real good. Look like wire strings were on it or something. Well, about three weeks, four weeks, one, the neck on that thing, it looked like a bow and arrow. Something you couldn't hardly play, so that's where I started playing a little slide, you know, that's just about the only way you could play that guitar. Until, you know, one of my white friends gave me some kind of guitar. I wish I had that guitar right now—great big guitar and it sure sounded good. And I messed around and pawned that guitar and I never did get it out of pawn. It was a guitar too. He got that guitar out of the loft and told me I could have it. Boy, that guitar. Boy, it would mean something now if I had it. I mean I just can't forget it."

"Why did he give it to you?" I asked.

"Well, he knew I liked to play and I'm always around him so he just say, 'Boy, you can have this one right here.' Cracked just a little bit, but all the sound was still there. Yeah, it was a bad guitar."[30]

Even in retrospect the sense of excitement is evident. Musicians remember details such as the price, an important feature distinguishing those days from today. The narrative also points out the tendency for guitars to warp. There seldom were cases for the instruments, and they hung "upside the wall," fully exposed to the heat and humidity. As we have noted in so many young artists' stories, a warped or broken guitar did not prevent the amateur from playing, but it often altered the style in which it was played. The bottleneck, or slide style, reported from the turn of the century on, can be seen as partially determined by the condition of the instrument, which often precluded any but a slide approach.

Note also the transition from first to second instrument, a gift from a white friend, as noteworthy as the first shared instrument. This guitar, lost but still loved even after all these years, went to that graveyard of instruments, the pawnshop.

Virginia songster John Jackson also tells of purchasing a guitar as a family project:

"I was picking apples in the orchards, I may have been twelve or thirteen years old. Some man came down there in the woods with this big guitar on his back. It wasn't quite as big as this [points to his guitar], but it had a big steel shiny plate in the front of it. And me and my brother was picking apples, and he just kept standing and talking to us.

"And finally he said, 'I'd like to sell you this guitar.' And we looked at the guitar said, 'We ain't got enough money to buy that guitar.' And he said, 'I don't know. I'd like to sell it to you.' And we asked how much that he wanted for it. Said, 'Ten dollars.' And our boss was in the orchard and we told him we needed ten dollars and he gives us ten dollars and that's the first guitar we bought."[29]

The mysterious stranger and the amenable boss add a touch of destiny to his often repeated account.

Yet it is misleading to imply that every blues singer is a master storyteller with an expansive anecdote concerning his first instrument. Mississippian Babe Stovall stuck to the facts:

"I taught my own self. I sold a little old white shoat, about that high. I sold it, that shoat, and got me a guitar. Yeah, I had a mind for it. I had a mind to play it, and that's what I done. After I bought that little box, I commence to play it."[30]

Lee Crisp, called the Tennessee Blues Boy, was even more terse when I asked him for his life story:

"The way I got started, my grandmother bought me a harmonica from a rolling store and she taught me 'The Saints Go Marchin In.' "[31]

Regardless of length, complexity, or artistry, musicians generally have a story of their first instrument.

Musicians have many instruments in their lives. Several of these may show up in their story either in a sequence or because of something interesting about the instrument or how it was acquired. Examples of sequence are provided by Bob Lowery, John Jackson, and Honeyboy Edwards (whose valuable gift guitar gets broken and is later replaced by an old, beat-up guitar). Johnny Young moved from homemade guitar to gift guitar and in another interview spoke of his teacher, Uncle Anthony, giving him one. Eddie Taylor moved from a homemade guitar to a gift to his first electric guitar.

Artists can jump from one instrument to the next as a way of ordering their stories. Sam Chatmon mentions a three-dollar Stella and a mail-order instrument but focuses on the guitar he played most of his life:

"The first guitar I ever owned was a Stella. I paid me three dollars for it. I picked on it and I picked on it then after a while I got a— What is that company's name? It wasn't no National, there wasn't no Nationals in them days. It was a Montgomery Wards. That was the next guitar I had, and I got rid of that and the next guitar I got was a Washburn. And I kept that Washburn until I got this guitar here. That Washburn is in California now. The fingerboard is plumb worn out cause I done played it so much. It's better than this. I got it in 1910 and it was old when I got it, second-handed. I tell you it was one of the finest Washburns made. He said, 'Let me have it and I'll keep it for a souvenir.' I said, 'Well, I'm not giving it to you, but you can keep it here.' He wanted the old strings on it just like it was and he wants the folks to look at it, how I wore the neck off playing it. It's hanging upside his music room right now."[32]

That guitar, Sam's partner for so many years, now hangs retired "upside the wall," an object of reverence—like Sam, a survivor and a well-worn beauty.

Other artists, rather than impress the interviewers with their need to be a musician or their talent, use the instrument narrative to relate a humorous anecdote. Along these lines, utilizing a lost-lover theme, so popular within the blues genre, Hogman Maxey told Harry Oster:

"Really what caused me to get it on my mind was me and another man was sittin down with one lady between us all night long. So just before day, she reached back in the window and picked up a guitar and set it down between us both. So she spoke, 'So now this is you all choice. Is either one of you all kin play?' Well, I couldn't play but the other boy could. Well, the minute I walked away, I says, 'I'm got to learn to play the blues.' "[33]

BoBo Jenkins also learned to play later in life because of a woman:

"One day I went to the dark room to develop my pictures and left my girl outside whose name was Elizabeth Thomas. When I come out, Percy, the guitar player, had stole my girl and taken her away. I discovered he had left his guitar— It was then Johnny Lee Hooker told me, 'He got your girl so take his guitar,' but I didn't know how to play guitar. The next morning I went down to the Wurlitzer Music Company and bought me a guitar and amplifier— My purpose for learning to play the guitar was to get revenge."[34]

James Thomas also utilizes a revenge motif, in his case to pay back a stingy uncle:

"So after I got large enough to play, I wasn't able to buy no guitar at the time, and I had learned to play two songs. So my uncle, he wouldn't let me play when I got ready. I had to give him fifty cents, a dollar, to play his guitar and I couldn't keep it too long. So I got a chance to pay him back when I got me— I bought me a brand new Gene Autry guitar, and he didn't have a guitar then, you know. I started playing for the teenagers. He was runnin all up and down the road looking for me to borrow the guitar to go play for some grown-up people. I said, 'Well, we busy now.' "[35]

In several narratives, James Thomas sets up his uncle as a competitor and beats him in music-oriented contests, such as who can draw the most people to a party.

Musicians also spoke of how instruments were lost or ruined. Both Byther Smith and John Jackson had their brothers break their guitars. Honeyboy Edwards told an especially sad account of breaking his first guitar. Bob Lowery referred to the neck warping on his first guitar, and guitarist Hubert Sumlin told me that his first guitar warped so badly you could pass your body between the neck and the strings.[36]

Hanging on to a guitar or other instrument has never been an easy proposition for a traveling bluesman. When the wolf is at the door, the temptation of the pawnshop looms. Traveling in fast company or dealing with tough customers can result in the loss or destruction of instruments as well. Big Joe Williams, for example, is famous for the guitars he left behind while jumping out of windows to save his skin. Theft too is a constant source of anxiety.

James Thomas spoke of the theft, recovery, and yet another theft of his guitar:

"This fellow stole this guitar from me when it was new, and I drew a picture of it and give it to the sheriff, and in about a week or so he had found it. I was scared I would never get it no more. He tried to sell it, he tried to sell it for two dollars and a half—enough to get him some whiskey with it. Doubt if he could have got some whiskey with it.

"He got so hot with it he went and carried it, put it up in a barn. Well, when I first drawed this picture a boy said he knew who had it. He knew but he didn't want the man to know that he told cause he lived on the same place. He told the sheriff, so he went up and got it. When he got it he carried it, went and got it, brought it back.

"So I supposed to go to Jackson and play—my guitar was all tied up down at the police station. They didn't want to let me have it till they had a trial. So I told them I said, 'Man, look.' I said, 'I got to have my guitar because that's how I make me some money.' I didn't have no steady job then. I worked at the funeral home part-time, so he let me have it.

"And I been scared ever since. You can't trust people now. Like the other day we had been playing at a nightclub, and when we got out of the car at another little place to get a sandwich—they didn't have no sandwiches, I got a boiled egg and come right back out and they had done got the guitar that quick! Got it and gone! Didn't miss it till I got home ready to unload."[37]

It is not surprising that musicians should talk about instruments. They do this among themselves, comparing the virtues and faults of various brands of equipment. But I have never heard them entertain each other with stories about homemade instruments. These they reserve for the interviewer. The variety of instrument references and their frequency in the musician's story demonstrate the musical instruments' symbolic value as well as their central position in the artist's life.

The musician's story begins with an instrument, however acquired— handmade, gift, or as a result of trials and tribulations. While the acquisition of a guitar, harmonica, or piano initiates the youngster into the world of music, it is only the first step on the road to becoming a blues musician. Other obstacles to be overcome begin with the musician's own family. And then the young bluesman needs to find other musicians to teach him how to play the blues and how to live the blues life.

5

"They used to say it was the devil's music"

Albert Luandrew, a.k.a. Sunnyland Slim, was born in Vance or Lambert, Mississippi, in 1907.[1] More than seventy years later we met in a Washington night spot called the Childe Harold. He readily agreed to talk to me, so we went upstairs to what passed for the performers' lounge. Sitting back in a threadbare armchair, he immediately took over. Tall, distinguished, self-assured, he spoke slowly and steadily. Since his story was a more-or-less prepared statement, I sat back after my lead question and listened. We were interrupted once by his protégé, Big Time Sarah, who apologized, "Oh, I didn't know you were interviewing."

He spoke of his life, how he ran away from home to play music in theaters and lumber camps, and how he came to Chicago in 1932 but turned around and went back south. To his mind, Chicago was not yet ready for the blues. But in 1939 he returned for good, becoming a fixture of the Chicago scene during its "golden age." In Chicago he worked with all the major artists from Big Bill Broonzy to Muddy Waters and recorded steadily from 1947 on. Today, an elder statesman, he continues to be an active force in Chicago blues, recording, performing, and producing records.

I asked him, "Tell me the Sunnyland Slim story."

"The story of it, well I could say, started in the early twenties, not Sunnyland Slim, but I was a country boy, a farmer, loved guitar, loved music, but my people were Christians. I didn't play nothing. I never thought when I was six or seven years old that I would ever play anything. But I could hear the guitar that some of them played.

"My mother, she lived till I was about six. Then my grandfather was beautiful to my grandmother. I had it so nice comin up. They had a little place in Vance where I was born, and my father, he married, he married then.

"We had a little place, about a hundred and sixty acres of land. We was round in that little neighborhood, and there was a piano there in Vance, an organ, them old organs you pump. So I'd go with the girls to people's houses for a little bit, hear just a little bit.

"And my peoples didn't go for blues. My father was a Christian. Grandfather and grandmother were Christians—didn't go for that. Called them 'corn songs.'[2] That was around 1912.

"Well, after my father married this stepmother, I must have been about six or seven, she was mean to me. My grandfather had another place about six miles out from Vance. Up there, that's where my father went and that's where I started to catch the devil, seven years old—eight years old. And at the same time these people that had the organ moved from Vance up to another little old place with a fellow called Blaines. He worked a lot of land, chopped cotton, picked cotton—people pay him.

"I was growing up. So my stepmother was mean. My cousin worked with my father, my father raised him—Spense and another fellow, we called Monahan. And I was still— What I did, I could go around these girls and play one little piece on the organ that would stay in my head all night. And while the boys be around the girls, I'd be trying to put that to the organ, you know.

"Till I got about eight or nine I was scared. I was so scared of my father and peoples, my stepmother, till I couldn't concentrate on the organ too much like Brother could when he was young. Little Brother Montgomery, he started playing about five or six years old. And what I did, I'd play, I tried to play when it would rain. You couldn't work, so you go down and play. 'I want to play this. I want to hear this.'

"So when I got about eleven years old I run off from home. My father kept on preachin. Now he got me that time, and I come back and they put me back out working. And when it would rain I'd go over to another lady's mother's church. My father was a pastor. She had a beautiful organ and Jeff Morris would be over there.

"And this next time I got to be about thirteen. I run off to Crenshaw. They found me again, and me and her got into it again. I run off and went to a logging camp. That's where I lost him at. And I stayed there awhile and this fellow had an old piano and I'd stay around that."[3]

Sunnyland Slim's narrative echoes a traditional theme common to the musician's story. For many bluesmen, trouble begins at home, and they describe their childhood in terms of facing up to, running away from, or just outgrowing their parents' hostility to their musical goals.

For Sunnyland Slim—just a "country boy"—family intolerance and the burden of agricultural chores stood in the way of learning music. Unlike his hero, Little Brother Montgomery, the formidable combination of a preacher father and mean stepmother forced him to break away, to escape in order to pursue his ambitions. Three repeated attempts emphasize his determination to get away. Finally, on the third try, he was free to seek a sanctuary where his values would be tolerated, crossing over to a world sympathetic to the blues. But he made it himself, the hard way, thus earning the right to a musician's name.[4]

Even though some artists—Johnny Young, Archie Edwards, and Sam Chatmon, to name a few—grew up surrounded by instruments and musicians, the standard motif, as Sunnyland Slim recounted, portrays the artist struggling against family opposition.

Including the threat of supernatural punishment to intimidate aspiring musicians, the church supplied the moral authority for family opposition.[5] Grandparents and parents warned that singing reels and blues guaranteed a quick road to hell. Closer to home, the warning was accompanied by physical punishment, and many musicians complained of being spanked for their musical leanings. Having suffered from the church's attempts to malign musicians, blues players sometimes returned the hostility. But more often they questioned the church's right to monopolize music. Because of the musical similarities between church-approved music and the blues, church opposition seemed somewhat hypocritical.[6]

Music affirming church values and performed in church-controlled contexts was acceptable, but blues, reels, or other dance music was frowned on. Dance music, after all, took place at suppers, juke houses, or taverns—all institutions that competed with the church for the community's allegiance, dollars as well as souls.[7]

The church's intention to exclude the secular musician is summed up in the proverb "You can't serve two." One could not play blues and remain a church member—better to concentrate on sin.[8] Despite musical similarities, social distinction between the forms of expression was very real and forced a choice between the two. Big Bill Broonzy tried to preach and play music at the same time, but his uncle warned him he was straddling the fence and urged him to get on one side or the other. Fortunately he chose the blues.[9]

Forced to make similar decisions, other artists encountered the wrath of God in the form of a preacher-father. At the very mention of the word "blues," this patriarch of a Christian family became the strong right arm

of the church and the musician's nemesis. W. C. Handy recalled his father's reaction to his decision to become a musician:

" 'Son,' he said, 'I'd rather see you in a hearse. I'd rather follow you to
the graveyard than to hear that you had become a musician.'

"I did not answer. My father was a preacher, and he was bent on
shaping me for the ministry. Becoming a musician would be like selling
my soul to the devil."[10]

As Handy and other artists tell it, parents, teachers, white folks, and
preachers stood aligned against secular music. Although music was one
of the few avenues open to blacks, parents generally disapproved of musical careers as undependable, dangerous, and morally unsound. Playing
dance music was a suspicious hobby and certainly no way for a talented
youngster to waste his life. As far as respectable people were concerned,
blues threatened the community's moral fiber; hence sermons con-
demned the blues along with dancing, gambling, drinking, snuff-
dipping, and keeping company with loose women. In the face of such
attitudes, young musicians had to play in secret and learn on their own.
Chief Ellis went to his sister's house:

"My parents were very religious, and they didn't allow blues to be
played around the house. I really learned on my own, cause I always
loved the blues and the sound would always stay with me. After a while I
used to go over there to practice on Saturdays. She used to let me practice over there for about fifteen minutes every Saturday."[11]

Jimmy Rogers faced the same predicament:

"My grandmother, she raised me and she was a Christian-type,
church-type woman, and man, they's really against music, blues, period.
I just taken it up on my own and by chances I would go over to a friend's
house that had a guitar, piano, something like that."[12]

Jimmy Rogers' childhood friend Snooky Pryor told a similar tale,
stressing how he taught himself because his minister father wouldn't
allow blues in the house.[13]

Recently I encountered an intriguing Ghanian parallel when I spoke
with E. T. Mensah, known as the King of Highlife. He attended a blues
workshop in Accra, Ghana, where I asked him how his parents felt about
his interest in music.

He laughed.

"It's very interesting. I was living in a house where there was a native
fetish and the fetish does not like flute or fife music. So any time I blow

the flute or clarinet, I was hushed by the chief priest because I was disturbing the fetish."

He laughed again. "So I was clashing with him all the time."[14]

These diverse examples point toward a typical pattern of younger musicians banding together beyond the control of their parents. Seeking out the company and the support of fellow musicians or music-lovers, they began their lifelong association with the blues community.

Sunnyland Slim ran away from home, but musicians had other options. Chief Ellis, for example, learned away from home but eventually won his parent's grudging approval:

"The weirdest thing that ever happened to me was when my parents found I could play. This white guy from Siluria, Alabama, he came to Birmingham looking for Price Laneir. Price Laneir was out of town playing, and the kids on the corner told him that I could play the piano. And then he came down to my house, and my parents didn't even know I could play the piano.

"So when he asked my mother could he take me to Siluria to play for this party, mother said, 'Well, my son doesn't play a piano.' And so I said, 'Yes, I do, Ma.' So they carried me up the street to where a piano was, and my mother heard me play and this guy heard me play.

"Well, she was so astonished. 'Where did you learn to play like this?' She still couldn't give me permission to go until my father came home. And so, after my father came home, this guy waited till my father came home, and then my father said, 'Well, he can't play no piano.' So my mother said, 'Yes he can, and you should hear him.' And so my father heard me play and my father gave me permission to go."[15]

In a rite of passage parallel to earning the gift of an instrument, Chief Ellis earned family acceptance of his musical career and avoided the trauma of an unhappy parting.

Other artists simply outwaited the opposition. For example, Bob Lowery outgrew his parent's ability to dictate his life:

"We all had to go to church whether we liked it or not, you see. The trouble was your grandmother went, so you had to go along with her. But you a certain age, you had to go to church. You couldn't be caught dancin or nothin like that. We used to go over in the house and do our dancin and some of the little children—brothers, sisters, around there go back and tell them. You in trouble then. But once you get up, alone, you know you're free, you know. You're not bound by none of this stuff. None of this tradition, you know, rules like they have like that. But they don't have those rules no more."[16]

John Cephas also kept his music hidden until he was old enough to face up to his mother:

"I used to keep that kind of secret because of the type of music I wanted to play—but like I said, my mother had us in church all the time, but I was leaning toward the blues, so I had to kind of keep that hid for a long time. See, cause they didn't want the young people playing the blues because they were round the houses where people were drinking and—you know, where they had these fly women and places like that. They'd try to lead us way from that and lean us more toward religion, but, you know, I was more impressed by the blues. They used to say it was the devil's music, and even today my mother's still living now and she always asks me that I should give some time to the church and stop singing blues. She still says that, you know."[17]

While the musician outgrows parental domination, he may continue to encounter church and family pressure to rejoin the flock. Fred McDowell confided:

"I went to church. You see, I got religion. And I quit playing. My mother, she asked me to before she died to quit. So I quit about six years. I wouldn't pick up a guitar."[18]

I have heard other bluesmen laugh about their fellows who get religion and quit. Yet many of these artists share in the belief system and may also repent some day.

Just how many potential sinners were kept in the fold by the anti-blues propaganda is impossible to determine. But in listening to the bluesman tell his story, it is apparent that opposition did not stop him from following his star, though it did make life harder. Like the home-made guitar, church-blues tension is a cliché rooted in reality, accurately portraying black life in rural America as the artists remember it.[19] But accounts of family opposition may be emphasized for their dramatic potential by providing a convenient dichotomy dividing the world into two hostile camps. In retrospect, early experience can be recast in relation to this set of opposing forces. Key phrases—"I couldn't concentrate," "I really learned on my own," and "I had to get out of there"—highlight the obstacles the musician encountered and the transition from one camp to the other. The budding artist, ego emerging, exchanges the warmth and security of home for the adventure of being a musician. Through self-sacrifice the protagonist shifts from dependence to independence and from family to other musicians.

Still other objections to the blues focused on the nature of the job, the contexts in which musicians worked, and the alleged character of the musician. Blues-playing alone could seldom support a family, and it involved travel and long, late hours. Furthermore, where you found blues you also were likely to find drinking, gambling, whoring, and fighting—at least according to stereotype. These associations affected the musician's reputation to the point of being ingrained parts of the bluesman's character. The image of musicians as idlers and dissipated characters coincides with beliefs common to Africa as well as Europe.[20] Although musicians complain of being considered lazy, they often went out of their way to foster this aspect of their image. On the one hand, the stereotype was most unfair, but on the other hand, the image of being too talented and beautiful to have to work was consciously projected. But whether the stereotype was true or not, musicians were branded as lazy, and parents feared their children would develop these traits and neglect their chores.

From the parents' side, music interfered with necessary work: from the musicians' side, work interfered with learning. Finding time to practice was sometimes as hard as finding a place to practice. Byther Smith neglected his chores to fool with a guitar, much to his brother's irritation:

"Then I wouldn't help my brother around the house. My brother come in from work. I wouldn't have went to the barn and taken care of the stock out in the barn. I wouldn't have done anything. I'm just sitting up there plucking along on the guitar. I wasn't playing nothin. So my brother, he got mad about that, and he just steps on the guitar and breaks the keyboard on that. And that really got next to me."[21]

Positive recollections of early life did not extend to farm labor, especially when it stood between the artist and what he wanted to do. As a dues-paying reference, musicians talk about how hard they had to work, but according to folk belief the successful artist avoided labor or at least tried to give that appearance. Honeyboy Edwards' boast "I never did make no crop" represents a posture that elicited both admiration and jealousy from the common laborers. On the one hand, the itinerant musician presented the image of being footloose and fancy free—a romantic alternative to the drudgery of sharecropping. On the other hand, they were resented as parasites and potential troublemakers who hung around the house while the menfolk went off to work.

More than a youngster rebelling against his parents, the blues musician represented a way of beating the system and was therefore an affront to the paternalistic white power structure. Again, Johnny Shines looks to the white man as the ringleader in a conspiracy to malign the musician:

"A black man, if he didn't work out in the fields, he was called lazy, no good. But who was he working for? You ever figure out who the lazy one was?

"Well, lots of blues musicians or musicians as a whole, now there are good musicians. You can't be a good musician and a field hand at the same time. You got to be one or the other, and if you are a musician, the white man taught the black man he was no good. Keep him away from your house because he's after your wife. He's after your daughter. You understand what I mean? And some of it was true, see. I mean, just because he's a musician, I don't say that he's thorough, . . . he's cleansed, he's holy. You got some dirty people in all walks of life. Look at the politicians and people like that. Look at the things they have to cover up and sweep under the rug, and why in the hell should a musician be any better?"[22]

Even if Honeyboy Edwards' contention that the old farmers would rather see a dog than a guitar player is overstated, the musician's ability to survive—and at times thrive—did not go unnoticed. The bluesman's life represented an option to breaking your back and your heart working in the fields. And the apparent attractiveness of the blues life-style—wine, women, and song—called for all the counterpropaganda the community could bring to bear.

Yet the public image of the man of leisure was probably more ideal than real, despite some musicians' claims that they never worked. For example, Sonny Boy Williamson (Rice Miller) bragged that he never worked, but his old partner Arthur Crudup debunked that claim:

"If Sonny Boy say he never work in his life, he's a damn liar. I lived in Mississippi all my life, and there's no colored people that don't work. He didn't play no music but on the weekend, Sonny Boy had to work. He had an old lady to keep."[23]

When it came to image, Sonny Boy, like Honeyboy, preferred to be seen as being kept by his old lady instead of the other way around. Byther Smith, in debunking the stereotype of laziness, spoke of the folk traditions of signs:

"The older used to say all the peoples round had the sign, but all the white peoples had the money. And I found out that all that was just an idea, you know, they was talking bout the sign, the sign if you learn to play, you going to be lazy, you not going to work. I think that is just backwards [laughter]. I've been working hard."[24]

In light of this belief, youngsters had to cope with parental outrage. Fooling with a guitar when chores were left undone not only was vanity and foolishness but put an extra burden on some other family member. Why, if everyone who wanted to be a musician stopped doing his chores in order to practice, then who would do the work? But when the musician began to bring a little money home to contribute to the family livelihood, music became more acceptable.

Images of opposition, no matter how much a part of the bluesman's story, present a one-sided picture of the bluesman's early life. The other side shows a community eager for music and crazy about musicians. Countering the forces aligned against the blues, a loose network of informal institutions supported the musician and encouraged young performers. These included family bands and such local events as suppers and country breakdowns, which provided opportunities for the bluesman to earn food, drink, prestige, and even money.

In contrast to the intolerant preacher-father, musicians recall parents, aunts, uncles, brothers, sisters, or neighbors who played or at least knew someone who did. Those artists who came up in musical families had obvious advantages and could participate in musical activities without leaving home. Instruments were available, as were teachers, and the artist had the family's blessing to learn music if not pursue it as a career.

On rare occasions, family groups like Sam Chatmon's family even played professionally. Indianapolis bluesman J. T. Adams also formed a commercial family band after learning from the preceding generation:

"I played ever since I was a kid. My dad played. My mother played. Yeah, I fell in love with it. My dad was a banjo picker . . . it was just a hobby. All of them— He had about four or five—three uncles: Uncle John, and Charlie, Uncle Jim. All of them was banjo players, could play banjo and guitar, play some darn good music too. Just about like me and my brothers—we played for dances like that. Hell, we played all over down there in Kentucky. You know, different places.[25]

Guitar players and piano men pounded out blues at work camps, and people even sang blues on break in the fields. While work songs had generally gone out of fashion, music still filled leisure time. Wild Child Butler, whose mother was musical and who still gets together with his kin for music parties, recalls how music was part of his life:

"I was raised up with it. Matter of fact, the people who I was raised up [around]—my parents and their neighbors, Moe and Sloan and them—used to work in the fields when I was young. And they would bring they guitars to the field with them and on their lunch, when they would come off at dinner (they call it dinner down there) they would play, play and sing blues and drink corn liquor and have a good time and then go back to work. And I was raised up around that and it became a part of me."[26]

Archie Edwards found the opportunity to play at a logging camp:

"Then I started working at the sawmill when I was about sixteen. I did a little sawmilling and a lot of the farm-working, you know. And someone had guitars, you know. We had this little camp out there in the bushes, you know, not too far from the sawmill, and we would go out into the woods and cut logs—and cut logs and haul them down to the mill and saw lumber all day.

"At night we'd go back to the camp and we would sit around. Some of the boys would play poker and some would pitch horseshoes and do this and that. But I would sit around and pick the guitar and listen to other guys play. So I got to the point where I was pretty popular at the sawmill camp with the guitar."[27]

The popularity he achieved at the lumber camp, reminiscent of Sunnyland Slim's lumber camp experience, illustrates how music could be a vehicle for recognition and self-esteem. Artists appreciated their popularity—especially with the opposite sex—and even spoke of learning to play primarily for this reason.

While working contexts sometimes included music, blues thrived during leisure time, especially at parties. Most of the artists I spoke with, including Archie Edwards, began to play before the public at country parties. These community events ranged from picnics to country breakdowns, house parties, suppers, or even jukes and provided a chance for the aspiring artist to get into the public eye; later jobs in cafes, taverns, nightclubs or concert halls seem to pale in comparison to the homegrown institutions. People wanted musicians at their parties and treated them well with food and drink. And if the musician was good enough, he not only had fun matching his skill against other guitar players, but became a star even as young man.

Wild Child Butler refers to these down home events at the outset of his story:

"Well, I'll start from where I was born. I was born in a small, little, old— It was a small town, but it was a big plantation in Autauga, Alabama. Me and Wilson Pickett and all of us came up together. And I used to play at them all-night jukes. They— My people called them suppers. They call them suppers. We call them all-night jukes cause we call my blues juke blues."[28]

His interchangeable terms match Johnny Young's reference: "I used to

go up to—they call them jukes, juke houses, juke joints, call them suppers. I used to play for suppers."

While "juke" connotes a more permanent commercial venture, both
juke and "supper" refer to events where food and drink were sold. Suppers, like their urban parallel, "house-rent parties," were significant institutions in the black community. Considering the limited avenues toward
economic independence and the paucity of social events beyond the
church, these small-time operations take on even greater importance. As
a sort of cottage industry, owned, operated, and patronized by the people, they demanded little investment—food, drink, and guitar or piano
players, yet they returned so much. James Thomas recalls Mississippi
house parties:

"My uncle, he played music; also my granddaddy, he played some too.
And they sit around home and play a lot. People would come around
[and] sit on Sundays and Saturday nights. Sometimes they would give a
party. Well, that's a big gang of them comin in there Saturday night.
They spend their money there. Next time someone else give one and they
all would go down there to the next house."[29]

Shifting from one house to the next, the parties brought in a little
cash money for the hosts and hostesses as well as providing a place for
the people to gather and enjoy themselves. If their success threatened the
church, they provided nonetheless a healthy option reminiscent of Ralph
Ellison's description of Kansas City dances:

"Jazz and the blues did not fit into the scheme of things as spelled out
by our two main institutions, the church and the school, but they gave
expression to attitudes which found no place in these and helped to give
our lives some semblance of wholeness. Jazz and the public dance was a
third institution in our lives."[30]

Virginian John Cephas extends Ellison's image in his warm description of rural "country breakdowns":

"Well, in the early beginnings of my incline toward blues, like in the
country, we had nothing much else to do on the weekends—you know,
after a hard week's work. I was just a kid, you know. Everybody, they
would gather around different family members and friends' houses, and
we played guitars and whatever other instruments we'd have. And we'd
all get together and drink corn liquor and play guitars and have a real
good time, you know, like a country breakdown, we used to call them
country breakdowns.

"We used to travel around together when I got a little older on that house-to-house circuit, playing for house parties or just about any affair. It was like a community type of a thing. It wouldn't necessarily be a gig, you know, if somebody be having a party or you would just sit around and have a few drinks.

"You kind of have to understand, music was a kind of outlet for black folk and a lot of people couldn't play, but they enjoyed the music. And weekends, well, during these early days we didn't have no place else to go. We were mostly poor. We didn't have no money to really go no place, and a lot of places we couldn't go at all because we were black. So this was an outlet for us. This was something enjoyable that we used to do and we really had a good time."[31]

Music in itself, while a means to recognition and social reward, did not develop in isolation but rather in conjunction with other institutions that developed a constituency of their own in defiance of church, parental, or other antiblues mandates. If these segments of the community despised the musician, a third institution of suppers and jukes accepted his leadership. Appreciative audiences eventually replaced disapproving parents. Here the musician was the center, the focus of attention, the galvanizer of the action, and the person who set the tempo for the good times.

Accounts of early life detail both opposition and support, the hard times and the good times. Family attitudes, however, seldom stopped the musician. Whether forced to leave home to find other musicians or benefiting from a musical family, the artist himself decides to play and having made the decision commits himself to learning his craft.

6

"Sounds so good to me"

Sam Chatmon found his musical inspiration at home. His father—a prominent local musician—his brothers, even the legendary Charley Patton, an adopted member of the musical Chatmon clan, all played as a family venture for fun and profit. Born in Bolton, Mississippi, in 1899, Sam, along with his brothers Lonnie Chatmon and Bo Carter, formed an influential string band known as the Mississippi Sheiks.

The Sheiks achieved great success in their day, and were popular with both black and white audiences. As well as blues, their repertoire included hillbilly tunes and the popular hits of the day, and their records sold well for many years. The group carved out its own niche in American music history, and in his own right Sam Chatmon had a long and successful career.[1]

We met at the 1976 Smithsonian Folk Festival in Washington, D.C. Following several conversations, I brought up the question of an interview, but at first he declined, owning he "didn't feel too sporty." He blamed the festival food. Later, however, I returned to find him in better spirits holding court in back of one of the stages. Entertaining a small group of festival staff, he cracked jokes and passed on health tips, including "When you're tired, go to bed, and when you wake up, get up." These common-sense habits had kept him young and handsome some seventy-seven years.

He cut quite an imposing figure with his full white flowing beard, expressive eyes, and outsized checkered cap, and because of his great looks he was easily persuaded to pose for a photographer representing a festival sponsor. In fact, he participated too enthusiastically, striking numerous dramatic poses, none of which suited the photographer. He was after a more natural picture and asked Sam Chatmon to just keep talk-

Big Joe Williams, 1976 Smithsonian Folklife Festival
Smithsonian Institution

Johnny Shines, National Folk Festival
Photo by Earl Dotter, National Council for the Traditional Arts Collection

Otis Rush
Photo by Amy O'Neal,
Living Blues Collection

George Wild Child Butler
Jewel Records, Living Blues Collection

Fred McDowell
Photo by Andrew Souttront, Living Blues Collection

**Bob Lowery,
California 1978**
*Photo by Bill Mead,
Living Blues Collection*

James Thomas, Forty-Second National Folk Festival
Photo by Margo Rosenbaum, National Council for the Traditional Arts Collection

Sam Chatmon, 1976 Smithsonian Folklife Festival
Smithsonian Institution

Johnny Young, Sweden
Photo by Charley Nilsson, Living Blues Collection

**Big Chief Ellis,
Washington, D.C.**
*National Council for the
Traditional Arts Collection*

**Archie Edwards,
University of
Maryland**
Photo by Cheryl Brauner

James Thomas
Photo by Carl Fleischhauer

Dyther "Smitty" Smith
Photo by Jim O'Neal,
Living Blues Collection

Jimmy Dawkins
Photo by Amy O'Neal
Living Blues Collection

Lee Crisp in Europe
Photo by Rien Wisse,
Living Blues Collection

Archie Edwards and Author, University of Maryland
Photo by Cheryl Brauner

David "Honeyboy" Edwards at the Fiftieth Anniversary of the Archive of Folksong, American Folklife Center
Photo by Carl Fleischhauer

Eddie Taylor
Photo by Charley Nilsson, Living Blues Collection

**Yank Rachel,
1976 Smithsonian
Folklife Festival**
Smithsonian Institution

John Cephas   *Photo courtesy of the United States Information Agency*

John Jackson
Photo by Carl Fleischhauer

ing. Because of my proximity, I became designated straight man. Seeing
the chance, I asked him, "Since we're already talking, do you mind if I
tape what you say? Looking over my shoulder at the photographer, he
agreed.

In the confusion of the moment, I varied my usual opener and mum-
bled, "I heard you were there when it first started."

Despite the vagueness of the question, he knew what I meant, yet
shifted his response to the direction he wanted.

"No. I wasn't there when it first started. I was there directly after it
started. People ask places I learned how to pick the guitar. They ask and
I told the truth, told them I learned to play by lying. I— Soon as I would
pull that guitar off the wall—see there wasn't no cases in them days—
I'd get that guitar off the wall and I'd wind it until I broke a string and
I'd slip back in and I'd put it back up there. They come in and say, 'Who
had my guitar?' And I'd say, 'I didn't.' So you see I had lied and that's the
way I learned to pick."[2]

As Sam Chatmon, John Cephas, and Archie Edwards indicated, people ask, "How did you learn?" So the bluesman, anticipating the question, tells them. But while the musicians I spoke with could go into great
detail about music, their story calls for something more economical and
more artistically sound. Instead of trying to put into words techniques
that have become second nature from a lifetime of practice, artists usually select one or two events to represent or encapsulate how they
learned. These accounts may focus on learning a necessary but rudimentary skill, hearing an inspirational musician or piece of music, learning
from recordings or a legendary teacher, or in the case of Sam Chatmon,
Archie Edwards, Johnny Young, James Thomas, and Lightning Hopkins,
learning by breaking a rule.

But whether an informative descriptive sequence or a single dramatic
or entertaining event, these accounts feature powerful images: the guitar
"hung upside the wall," the old-fashioned victrola with a horn, the sound
of musicians playing on the porch, and the older professional musician in
all his romantic glory. These pictures still convey a sense of magic and
give the listener a taste of how the young musician felt. They are likely to
be set pieces like Sam Chatmon's bit, obviously intended for entertainment. While his story has numerous parallels in the stories of other musicians, Sam Chatmon's version of learning by breaking a rule—and in his
case a string as well—is suitable for a stage performance and sure to
draw a laugh. Archie Edwards also tells of a single event to explain how
he learned. He is a guitar teacher, fully aware of the need for practice
and able to talk theory for hours, but in his story he picks up the forbid-

den guitar and plays as if by magic. Established musicians witness this act and testify in his behalf—and he has been playing ever since.[3]

As a professional entertainer, paid for his work, the bluesman understands that most people prefer entertainment to a lengthy treatise on traditional techniques. Rather than frustrate himself by rationalizing his music and method to an audience unfamiliar with traditional values or oral techniques, he offers an anecdote—which in its turn may frustrate the academic or critic.

On another occasion, faced with the incredible question "Why did you learn?" Archie Edwards chose another type of traditional response: "I don't know. It's just a gift."

The idea of gift, talent, or mark refers to a special inborn skill that implies fate or destiny.[4] Johnny Shines, for example, described his partner Walter Horton, saying, "You see, this harmonica blowing is really a mark for Walter. It's not something he picked up. He was born to do it."[5]

Detroit bluesman Baby Boy Warren, in a now familiar tale, tells of taking his brother's guitar down from the wall and—"Before you know it, I could tune a guitar as good as he could. It was a gift to me. It was in me to learn how to play guitar."[6] Johnny Young's likewise uncanny knack for tuning a guitar was read as a sign of his gift, and so was his ability to make a guitar. Gift anecdotes complement other accounts of learning and often can be seen as examples or proof of the artist's inborn talent for music. While part of the bluesman's rhetoric and a means of deflecting a thorny question, the gift narrative embodies a belief in gifts and signs shared by the musicians as part of the Southern milieu in which they grew up. Having a recognized gift—especially when it's confirmed by other musicians—boosts self-confidence and brings a supernatural validation into the story.

The idea that some people have greater musical potential than others is not unique to the blues or, for that matter, to folk music. But the bluesman uses it, as do other traditional musicians, to represent traditional skills in opposition to formal education. Johnny Young told Pete Welding, "I've been able to go through life on mother wit, and I always did have the gift for music."[7]

Without negating the magical aspects of the gift, it is important to keep in mind that, like mother wit, it may cover a variety of traditional skills developed over a long period of time. Artists who learned within an oral tradition are aware that they are looked down on by those who can read music. Reading music, like literacy in general, is a valued skill, so one encounters ambivalent feelings toward traditional methods. Often a line such as "I don't know how I do it, I just do it" is used to avoid complications.

Blues great Eddie Taylor confessed his inability to read music:

"No, I can't do it. I really can't. You think I'm lyin? If somebody else was playin in front of me, I could do it and I would do it. But me by myself, I can't, really. No. Cause I can't read music. I went to New York in 1953 and I played at the Apollo Theatre; me and Jimmy Reed, and Count Basie was playing behind us. And I was playing some things and he said, 'How do you play that? You can't read music.' And I told him, 'I don't know, it's just a gift, I guess.' "[8]

Both men represent the blues tradition, but the former knows the language of formal music, while the latter does not and is forced to fall back on the traditional statement "It's a gift"—part apology, part boast.

While blues remains essentially an oral form demanding much more than playing the correct notes, bluesmen today learn to read music and synthesize tradition and formal training. Byther Smith referred to both gift and school when comparing himself to other musicians:

"I have to keep pace with it, and I like to play it with feeling. You take Matt Murphy and guys like that: I know I'll never be able to match it with those guys playing guitar because it was more of a gift for them. It was more of a gift, and they had time to go to school for it."[9]

But Smitty also went to school, in keeping with his consistent pattern of hard work and self-improvement, but the idea of the blues artist going to school runs counter to the stereotype of the bluesman as lazy and spontaneous and of the blues as a natural outpouring of emotion. The public obviously prefers the notion of a gift. But musicians, though they flaunt their gift, know it is only one side of the coin. The other side involves determination, hard work, and study, whether at a Chicago music school or at the knees of Big Joe Williams. Ability, coupled with the will to make it and the willingness to work, separates the bluesman from those who fell by the wayside.

Despite the stereotype of the bluesman as an untutored natural musician, becoming a blues artist is similar to becoming an artist in other mediums. One must first learn the fundamental skills and the basic techniques of the art form. For the blues player, these include learning the notes, traditional phrases, chords, a picking style, and time—which means knowing when to change chords, how to keep the beat, how to match singing and playing together, and even how to learn other artists' styles.

Given the right circumstances, time, place, and audience, the bluesman does a remarkable job of explaining how he learned. But the task involves selecting appropriate events to describe, compressing the event into a workable narrative (often focusing on the instant of success at the expense of the weeks of practice, giving the impression of a sudden jump from can't to can), and finally translating from one idiom to another: traditional to mainstream, musician to academic. (If only the listener put in as much effort trying to understand.)

Beyond gift or talent, learning involves inspiration, study, and perhaps patterning—that is, learning another musician's style. But in the beginning there was the sound. Sound, while it remains a major concern throughout the musician's story, dominates references to early musical experience.

Exposure to music at suppers, jam sessions, jukes, or clubs allowed the youngster to hear and internalize the blues. Musicians speak of listening from bed or from under the house or from outside the window. They watch, they listen, and they pick up the sound.

At some point an inspirational event—the appearance of a great musician or a certain style of playing—suddenly sharpens their interest, and observation becomes more conscious. In the musician's story such an occurrence receives extra emphasis as a turning point. Having listened to and caught the sound, the youngster looks for a means to recreate what he has heard, from thought to sound, even if he has to make a guitar.[10]

Usually we simply say the artist learned to play by ear, a cliché that adequately suggests learning by listening and firsthand participation. Listening to a phrase until it is memorized, hearing and holding a sound, the artist learns through observation and imitation. But the simple and naturalistic implication that the budding artist hears a song and then immediately plays it ignores the important fact that the musician studies the sound and practices it in his mind until given the opportunity to recreate it on an instrument. Even then, further practice is necessary for accurate phrasing, but at least the sound itself has already been internalized. Alabama-born piano man Big Chief Ellis caught the sound:

"I listened to a lot of blues players. In fact, there was a club about two doors from my house, and they used to play blues all the time, and I used to listen to the blues players, and the sound used to stay with me. In school, during recess, I used to play in the auditorium and practice playing with one finger—keeping the sound. I kept it in my head, all the time."[11]

Fellow piano player Sunnyland Slim provides a far more detailed account:

"I can remember the first key I played in, F, and he [Jeff Morris] tried to show me. He'd put— The way I do— I drawed the organ with my pencil, and the white keys and the black keys and where he had his hand. I'd put a print there. And when I see it was the same thing just below, I'd make it get the sound. Some of the sound would stay in my ear.

"And by me running around there, I cut wood and stayed with a lady in Corton. Her husband gambled. He didn't like to do nothin but gamble, sit around and drink all the time, and go around where they gambled. That's the organ I first learned how to play 'Tramp, Tramp, the Boys Are Marchin.' That's a song, a march in school. And I learned 'If I Could Hear My Mother Pray Again,' and it sounded pretty good.

"I wasn't doin much. I used to, much of my time, do all kinds of things. Play a little bit. And I got in love with a girl. This guy take her from me. Mostly all the girls go with him. He had an old T-Model Ford, and that's where I changed 'If I Could Hear Mother Pray,' some of it, into blues. And in that blues I seen another key.

"Jeff showed me a little bit. He'd say, 'That's C.' So I'd just play [he would] play that, and I'd do the same thing. And I fooled around and got by. Directly they wanted to give me fifty cents playing around little old parties. Fourteen years old, and I played around there."[12]

Sunnyland Slim's development as a musician illustrates an ongoing improvisational, learning process, a continuous recasting of available materials drawn from whatever sources he could find. The sound of his lesson was captured and abstracted into a makeshift keyboard drawing. And then within an almost classic blues mold, a religious song was merged with the experience of a broken heart and became blues—which then led to the awareness of another key.

Sunnyland Slim attempts to tell how he learned, step by step. And conjuring up the image of Claude Lévi Strauss' *bricoleur*, he provides an extreme example of the bluesman's characteristic method of learning any way he can.

Eddie Taylor also speaks of the sound and being driven to play, but his statement also shows how easily categories overlap, as he combines the gift and single-mindedness with the parental opposition and home-made guitar theme:

"See, that's something born with you. Your mother and father can whip you to make you do what they want you to do. But you still are going to do what you want to do. Certain numbers they would play would stay in my mind. I used to go under the house and listen through the floor and hear that ringing in my head, and it wouldn't come out, and then I'd go and make me a guitar, with a cigar box and some broom wire. When a sound sticks in your head like that you can do it."[13]

Close to being the all-purpose blues story, Eddie Taylor's explanation is reminiscent of John Lee Hooker's line in "Boogie Children": "You better let that boy boogie, cause it's in him and it's got to come out."[14]

Clyde "Judas" Maxwell likewise had a mind to play:

"Now I was a little boy and I'd be around players, guitar players, [in the] old times. And I would just lay around and listen and watch. And they wouldn't say nothin, just sit around. And sometimes they'd put a box down and I'd pick it up and I'd hit it. Finally I hit it, and it sounded pretty good. Some of em say, 'you know, it look like to me you goin to play—you goin to be a good deal.'

"Well, I was about nine years old when I started doing it, but I was just about thirteen, fourteen, before I got good. I got about fifteen, sixteen years old, none them other players couldn't do nothin with me. See, I was young and my fingers was good, and I just wanted to do that. It was in my mind. That was my mind.

"I'd go to town and I'd get a chance to sing. And a record could come out, I would play it the next week. That's the way I learned.

"Well, I always had it in my mind and wanted to do that. Wanted to be a musician and I had it in my mind. I could keep things. At that time I was young and had a good understanding and everything and could memorize, then. Especially on that piece—I could memorize it near about by note, and I'd hear it and feel around and it didn't take me long to get home and get it all to myself. I'd fool around on an old guitar till I found the notes."[15]

Watching, listening, Maxwell caught the sound, and when his chance came he could play it so it "sounded pretty good." Like Johnny Young and Archie Edwards, he impressed the older musicians who recognized his gift. He had a good ear, a good memory, and his fingers worked then, unlike later in life. Along with his mind for it, these factors allowed him to beat the local talent and then turn to the blues players' greatest teaching aid, the record player.

Musicians were quick to embrace this fantastic invention, which caught the sound and froze it for convenient repeated reference. While records standardized styles and eventually hurt the musicians' business, they allowed the artist the opportunity to study musicians from outside the local community.[16]

Blues players affectionately recall 78 rpm records and old wind-up victrolas. You can still sense their magical impact. In some cases they provided an introduction to the world of the blues. Bob Lowery begins his story with a record player rather than a guitar:

"Well, how I come up, at first I would say I'm from Arkansas. That's where I was born, and we used to live on the farm and people used to have these old record players, like, you know, you have to wind up. And all the kind of music you would hear would be blues: blues and hillbilly music. Like, we buy these blues records, my friends would buy them or they didn't buy them, then somebody else would—some of my people. Anybody. You always hear the blues down there. They was real popular, and I don't care who was playing it, it all sounded good, you know. Everybody had all these blues singers' records."[17]

Live or recorded, the blues sounded so good. But recordings also provided access to progressive musical ideas, and aspiring artists could now choose their musical influences from the recording stars. John Cephas, like Clyde Maxwell, initially learned from local performers, but his models for style were his recorded favorites: East Coast stars Blind Boy Fuller and Blind Gary Davis.

"I never saw them. We— See, we used to listen to them on these old wind-up type of record players, you know. We used to have these seventy-eights, you know. Yeah, we started off, like, we used to have one of these—well, we used to call them a victrola, you know, with the big horn, you know. You wind it up and sound would come out the horn."[18]

Alabama-born Wild Child Butler also referred to record players, but like other artists associated with the Chicago scene, he downplayed the influence of records on his style:

"I did some of Sonny Boy's things. I used to sit and listen to some of his things when I got old enough. And my people had an old wind-em-up, they call them graphanolas back then. And I used to sit and listen to some of his tunes, and I went to blowing them. But I always would change my style. I didn't never want to be exactly like anybody else. I just wanted to be me."[19]

It is interesting that Chicago artists, unlike the Virginia musicians, spoke of making records but made few references to learning from them. While this may reflect a greater reliance on oral tradition—more artists to listen to and learn from face-to-face, I feel they chose to bypass recordings as inconsistent with their image. Other factors—availability of records, economics, when they learned to play—are also undoubtedly involved, but it appears that Chicago artists do not consider learning off of records appropriate to their self-presentation.

Wild Child Butler's emphasis on personal style exemplifies a tradition that values a recognizable individual voice. However, voice is achieved through listening to and copying other artists—going to school, so to speak. But once again the facts of studying or copying the records or the style of another artist goes against the stereotype that the blues player is a self-taught, self-expressive, natural musician.

Virginia artists, on the other hand, readily stressed their dependence on recorded sources. John Jackson provided an extensive story:

"It was two furniture dealers came up in the country with a horse and wagon, peddling furniture and had these record players on there. This wagon drove into the house one day and they sold my mother one and they left a bunch of records. And then they would come around about once a month, every six weeks, and collect whatever we were able to pay them on it, and they would bring a bunch of records for sale as well.

"And my older sister would buy records from them, and then they would order some from some ordering firm, but I don't remember whether it was Montgomery Ward's, Sears and Roebuck or Spiegler's, or who it was. But I know that some come by mail order. And it was people like the Carter family, the old Jimmie Rodgers, Blind Blake, Lemon Jefferson, Frank Stokes, and a lot of— It was mostly black blues players from mostly in the South.

"And so that's how we come by so many of the records that were made then. Then we'd put on a record and I'd get the guitar and just play right behind the record, and that's how I mostly learned to play—by listening to records."[20]

Fellow Virginian Archie Edwards adds a parallel account:

"My oldest brother would go to parties at night, and he would pick up old recordings from anybody that he could get em from and bring em home, you know. And we'd put em on the old record player and we would listen to them. So my younger brother, Robert—who lives around the corner—we would listen to the records, and I would pick the guitar, and if I'd make a mistake he would stop me and tell me where I made the mistake. After that, he would play, and I'd listen and I'd correct him. So we both learned professionally at home before we was fourteen, fifteen years old."[21]

For Archie, the ability to learn from records distinguishes his generation from that of his father, who although a talented musician, did not learn in Archie's words "professionally"—that is, to play like the record sounds:

"I got into it a little deeper than my father because he was never gifted enough to listen to the records and get the chords from the record player, and get the chords like the professionals play. Now, I can listen to a record twice. I'll play it just like the record, like the artist played—like Blind Lemon, John Hurt. I can listen to those people a couple of times, tune my guitar, and play it. So I kind of learned professional because I grabbed the stuff from an old record player. Mississippi John Hurt, Blind Lemon, Frank Hutchinson—all those old-timey dudes, you know. And everytime we get ahold of a record, I'll play it around three times and whip it out on the guitar."[22]

Like Archie Edwards, Kentucky-born J. T. Adams differentiates between musical generations by the ability to use records to keep up-to-date:

"We learned mostly from records cause they [his father's friends] played an older style, you know, than we played. They was mostly banjo pickers, but they could play guitar. They played, you know, before we did, and we played more what was going on then, you know, when we were young and playing."[23]

Despite the advent of phonograph records and their importance in providing new techniques, musicians were still inspired by other musicians. The human actor—a man or woman of stature in the community, whether saint or sinner, traveler or hometown hero—provides the crucial link between generations of musicians. And although the subjects of this book derived much of their repertoires from records, the purely traditional and eminently human process of identification and empathy with another artist inspired their decisions to become musicians.

Blues players invariably point to one or two individuals as key inspirational figures. These can be relatives, friends of the family, teachers, or local musical stars. They may provide inspiration or instruction, or serve as a model for the younger artist to pattern himself after both musically and as an exemplar of the blues life.

Bukka White, on a Takoma recording, paid tribute to the legendary Delta artist Charley Patton. In this spoken narrative, the listener can sense the terrific impression Patton made on him:

"I tried to be the second behind old Charley Patton, uh, really did, and to tell the truth, the first drink of whiskey I ever drink Charley Patton give me a little in a spoon. He said, 'You too young to drink too much whiskey, but I'm gonna give you enough to know what it's about.' And I still think about it and wish I'd asked him to give me the spoon."[24]

The scene is reminiscent of an initiation, sealed with the spoonful of sacramental whiskey. The older musician struck the youngster as an attractive figure to emulate, and while the emulation included playing mu-

sic like old Charley Patton, it was a more expansive desire to *be* like old
Charley Patton. It is the visible or projected characteristics and personality traits as well as musical style that the younger musician imitates on
the road to becoming a musician.

Almost every musician can list some similar influence whose musical
ability or personality captured his imagination. John Cephas tells of his
aunt's boyfriend:

"The very first blues music I heard, my Aunt Lillian had a boyfriend
and his name was Haley Dorsey. And he used to go around from house to
house, and he was very good at playing the guitar. And he used to spend
a lot of time with my aunt, and every time he would come around he
would bring his guitar. And I was just a little tot, but I would love the
sound of what he was doing, and he later showed me a few chords on
the guitar."[25]

Bob Lowery points to an unrecorded local musician as the man who
inspired him to try to play:

"Then there's one fellow, I'd like to say, that they used to call— His
name was Ben Maxwell. He never did no recording. He used to come out
to the house with his guitar. He couldn't play too many songs, but man,
what he played, it sure was good. And I said if I ever get to be a man,
I'm gonna buy me a guitar and learn how to play it if it's the last thing I
do."[26]

Fred McDowell echoed this sentiment as he recalled listening to his
uncle play: "I said, 'If I ever get grown, I'm gonna learn to play a guitar.'
Boy, it sounded so good to me."[27] Johnny Young listened to his Uncle
Anthony: "So I used to sit and listen, and I said, 'God dog! That sure do
sound good.' "[28] And for Honeyboy Edwards inspiration came from the
great Tommy Johnson: "Every night I would listen at them play. Sounds
so good to me."[29]

The combination of the attractiveness of the older musician, the romance of their life-style, and the intoxicating sound of the guitar proved
too much to resist. On the one hand the artist wants to make the sound,
and on the other hand he wants to become the musician.

Beyond providing inspiration, the musician's hero may also be a
teacher, father figure, or guide into the world of the blues. Big Joe
Williams was all three to a young Honeyboy Edwards. Other musicians
likewise informally adopted their apprentices. James Cotton lived with
Sonny Boy Williamson, Hubert Sumlin with Howling Wolf, and Lee Crisp
with Sleepy John Estes. Lee Crisp claimed:

"Old John, he's practically like a near about father of mine. He just near about learned me. He used to call me Leander all the time and, uh— He really did. He just was a teacher of music for me and was like a daddy, cause he was old enough for my father and he just taught me the whole ropes—how to do it, travel. And I actually learned time. I played music in time. So that's the way I started off."[30]

These relationships are part of the blues legendry but once again reflect the reality of a small group of men and women teaching each other and living together.[31] Blues scholar Sam Charters has reviewed this pattern of influence from a competitive perspective: the younger musician learns from, and then displaces, the older.[32] This may be too severe an assessment of an admittedly competitive situation. Actually, the younger artist is simply taught enough to be able to make it on his own. As Honeyboy Edwards said: "I see how he was doing it. I said, 'Hell, I can do the same thing.' "

While there may be some tensions when the younger musician decides to strike out on his own and the older, in effect, loses a free sideman, within the context of interviews about life experiences, the positive aspects of the relationship are usually stressed.

The major point is that Honeyboy Edwards' father figure, his mentor, Big Joe Williams, "learned him the ropes" and taught him the necessary "way of living" to allow him to strike out on his own.

Byther Smith had wanted to be a musician down in Mississippi but did not really develop until he came to Chicago. His inspiration may have been his cousin, J. B. Lenoir, one of Chicago's biggest blues stars, but Smitty picked out Robert Junior Lockwood as his main influence:

"Lockwood, he helped me a lot and was a great friend of my cousin, J. B. Lenoir. And they was living next door, and he really taught me a lot, by how to play the blues the way I do. And I give him a lot of credit because the things that he told me, he helped me to turn on to the field like I am. Because he just told me that if I wanted to succeed with my guitar playing, I would have to develop a style of my own. I tried to pattern a lot behind my cousin. I tried to fake up Chuck Berry's style, and he just really sit me down and talked to me like I was his kid. That's really what give me a big turnover."[33]

Artists who learned from records also have heroes. Archie Edwards, who grew up surrounded by musicians, patterned his playing on the recordings of Blind Boy Fuller and John Hurt. In this sense, they were his teachers as well as heroes, although at a distance. But because he loved their music and learned their songs, they became part of his repertoire and himself. And he managed to meet them both: Blind Boy Fuller tenuously in retrospect; John Hurt, in the flesh as a friend and a musical partner.

"He [Blind Boy Fuller] was really big here on the East Coast—one of about the hottest thing that ever came up the highway with a guitar. And the funny thing— It's a long story about it—

"I was walking the highway one evening, me and my brothers and sisters, a couple of kids. We had to walk a couple of miles, on the old dirt road in the country, to go to school. So we passing along this highway one evening, coming from school, and this little old filling station on the highway—they called it Clayton Money's filling station. He sold liquor there.

"So I see these two white fellows with these two colored fellows in the car with them. So they pulled off the highway into this service station yard. And this colored fellow had this solid steel gray guitar, and he played a song or two and slung his guitar around his back, you know. And the white fellow would hand him a cup of liquor and he would take a drink out of it.

"And I said, Well, I'll remember that because I bet that guy is some-body famous. And then I came to find out about thirty-five years later it was Blind Boy Fuller and Sonny Terry."[34]

Despite the intervening time of thirty-five years plus, Archie has con-nected himself with his hero as well as the famous harp blower Sonny Terry. Now the event stands out in his life as a major episode and calls our attention to the elasticity of time in life story narratives. This excel-lent example further demonstrates how the narrator selects which epi-sodes from his past have the most significance and meaning and best represent his current role of blues musician, his current self-awareness.

Another revelation occurred later in Archie's life connecting him to his other major hero and prime stylistic influence, Mississippi John Hurt. In this narrative destiny is fulfilled:

"Mississippi John Hurt, I— Man there's a story about him you will never believe to save your life. I learned to play one of Mississippi John Hurt's pieces—well, two of them, 'Candy Man' and 'Stagolee'—the two pieces he had recorded in the twenties that made him famous, you know. I learned it in about '31 or '32. From '32 when I was a kid up to '64, I still played his songs and I always had a feeling that I would meet him some day.

"To go back further than that, during the war I was lucky enough to go to Mississippi. I was stationed in Mississippi for a while. And every-where I went, I asked people did they know Mississippi John Hurt. Some did and some didn't.

"I didn't find him in Mississippi, and went overseas and all that stuff. I came back and got settled down in Seat Pleasant, Maryland. And we got the Sunday paper one morning. And I didn't read the paper. Something happened—I think I went somewhere with a couple of guys. I told my wife, I said, 'Put the newspaper on my side of the bed on the chair and don't throw it away because I'll read it later.'

"So on Thursday, I believe it was, I picked it up and was reading it and I found the picture in the newspaper of this man sitting, playing the guitar. And I read it and it said, 'Mississippi John Hurt is now appearing in Washington, D.C., at the Ontario Place nightly.' I said, 'Well, I didn't find him in Mississippi, but I found him in Washington.'

"I told my wife, 'You see this? Now this is the man I began looking for all my life.' I said, 'Now he's here in Washington.' I said, 'I'm going down and meet him and play the guitar with him.'

"She said, 'Oh well, don't you think that's quite a big step for some-body like you?' Say, 'That man's a pro.'

"I said, 'I don't care. I'm going to go there and meet him and we going to have a nice time.' And sure enough I did.

"I called the man, called down to the club to check it out. I said, 'Is this true that Mississippi John Hurt is appearing down there?'

"Say, 'Yeah. Do you know John?'

"I say, 'I sure do.'

"He said, 'Are you from Mississippi?'

"I said, 'I'm not.'

" 'But how do you know John?'

"I said, 'Well, it's a kind of funny thing. We have a mutual under-standing, I guess, between the two of us, because I learned to play some of his music and I know we have something in common and that's how I know him.'

"He said, 'Well, come on down to the club and meet him and talk to him.'

"So I went down and met John and talked with him. Man, me and that cat got hung up on some damn guitar—you talk about a hell of a time—it was a beautiful thing between me and John Hurt cause for the last three years of his lifetime he'd come to my house when he wasn't out on the road at a gig. He'd come to my house and we'd sit and play all night."[35]

After years of anticipation the chance meeting inspired Archie Edwards to begin to play seriously again. In this way John Hurt helped him twice: as an inspiration off of records, and as a friend later in life. According to Archie Edwards, John Hurt told him, "After I'm gone I want you to carry on my music. Don't let it die."[36] And since John Hurt's death he has been faithful to the task of carrying on his onetime partner's musical legacy.

Learning from a hero involves imitation, or as it is sometimes called, seconding behind their style. This can be done either through personal contact or through recordings. There is also the element of keeping someone else's music alive as a formal tribute, or as Archie does for John Hurt, carrying on and passing along an individual's style.

While Archie and John Hurt are from different regions of the country, their musical styles are irrevocably linked. This is due to Archie's learning "just like the record" and from his later decision to carry on John Hurt's musical legacy. This is not an isolated or unusual occurrence within the blues tradition. Learning by imitating an accepted artist may include appropriating that style (at least as a stage in development) or exact imitation as a formal tribute. Most blues players, as they are learning, try to play like, and to be like, their hero.

While it is important to keep in mind the regional affiliations of this rather homogeneous group with regard to the entire spectrum of cultural traits and musical values, we must also consider a tradition of artistic patterning on an influential artist as a crucial element of the process of musical development.

The apparent connection between such artists as Son House, Robert Johnson, Muddy Waters, Elmore James, Boyd Gilmore, Homesick James, James Thomas, and Hound Dog Taylor certainly suggests the perpetuation of regional values over time. But even more we see schools of artists grouped around specific styles associated with people who put their highly individualistic stamp on tradition. There is a personal handing down, or over, of musical content, and a conscious patterning of one's style on that of specific artists. Though they lived and performed at the same time, Elmore James perpetuated and in a sense assumed the music of Robert Johnson after Robert's death. When Elmore died, his musical personality was carried on by Hound Dog Taylor, Homesick James, James Thomas, and J. B. Hutto, not to mention the several Elmore James Juniors in the Chicago area alone.

Without discounting the importance of isolated and idiosyncratic artists, it is useful to view blues musicians in a manner like that of the biblical "begat": T-Bone Walker begat B.B. King, and B.B. King begat Mr. Bo, and a literal host of others; Bukka White followed old Charley Patton, Muddy Waters followed Son House, Elmore James continued Robert Johnson; yet each artist had a distinct and recognizable personalized sound, an individual musical voice that set him apart and, in fact, allowed him to become the musical model for the next generation.

Observing and conceptualizing the whole sound of an accepted artist and then reproducing it is crucial to the development of a musician. Muddy Waters said, "I was really behind Son House all the way."[37] Johnny Shines followed Howling Wolf and one night earned the name Little Wolf:

"So Wolf got up and went to take a crap or shoot some craps and I picked up his guitar and started to play. All his pieces were falling into place. When he come back I had the joint jumping; he just stood there and looked. So then they went to calling me Little Wolf."[38]

Carrying on in the manner of an already accepted artist is part of the blues tradition and allows such seemingly contradictory statements as "I'm the original Muddy Waters Junior."[39] James Thomas plays in the styles of Elmore James, Arthur Crudup, and Little Son Jackson but has also developed his own style, which is at once an amalgamation and a transcendence of his chosen models.[40]

Keeping in mind that reference to a major influence is very much in accord with a standardized interview format, statements of major influences, heroes, and teachers do show us a real view of the world of the blues musician—a world linked with the chain of tradition. Jimmy Reed, when asked "Did any other particular musician make you decide that you wanted to be a musician?" answered, "All I could say would be Sonny Boy Williams because I was so stone in behind what he was playing till it just felt to me like I could do some of it too."[41] He, in turn, influenced many artists, including JoJo Williams, who told Jeff Titon, "When I first started, I picked up most of my part from Jimmy Reed. I adored his sound, and at the time I went for it I kind of fell in on his style of playing."[42]

Narratives descriptive of the relation to other musicians, whether relatives, teachers, local heroes, or stylistic models encountered face-to-face or on record discs, are stock matters of the bluesman's story. Not all artists mention specific individuals as influences on their own music, preferring to strike the posture "I taught myself" or "I learn a little from everybody." However, in the evaluation and selection of appropriate life experiences, contact with other musicians, especially the most famous ones, bear repeating. The musician's organization of life as musician would make this the predictable case. It is noteworthy that Eddie Taylor's mother went to school with Memphis Minnie and that Memphis Minnie nursed him as a child. It is important that John Lee Hooker's stepfather, a professional musician, used to be visited by Blind Blake, Blind Lemon, and Charley Patton. They were the most important blues musicians of their time, and any mention of these legendary figures adds to the aura of the speaker. While we find considerable blues name-dropping in the interview, this is because older musicians really do exert a terrific amount of influence over young people, and musicians do seek out and keep company with their peers. Furthermore, the interview places a high value on listing personal knowledge of, or contacts with, legendary predecessors. Literally, the interviewer asks a series of "Did you knows?" In most cases, the musicians did, and they run through a listing, resurrecting the memory of old partners, taking a census of the living and the dead.

7

The wages of sinful music

James Thomas of Leland, Mississippi, worked days as a gravedigger and
part-time furniture mover. Tall, slender, and sensitive, he has become a
recognized folk sculptor as well as blues musician. Back in February 1976
he appeared on "The Today Show" along with fellow bluesman Sam
Chatmon. Each man was allotted time for a brief spoken self-introduc-
tion to present himself to a large television audience. Mr. Thomas chose
this statement:

"I'm from Yazoo County, where I used to work for my uncle—play all
night long for one dollar a night."

The announcer's immediate response: "We're gonna pay you more
than that."[1]

The salary paid the purveyors of the devil's music reminds us that the
bluesman is a wage earner. People sing the blues to make money and
have been doing so for at least seventy years. This aspect of specialization
determines whether they are professionals and whether they can maintain themselves as musicians. On the bottom line, it is a matter of survival: if the artist makes money he can afford to play the blues.

No romantic, content to live on love or art, the bluesman recognizes
that art, working, money, and eating go together. This pragmatic and
sometimes frankly mercenary attitude toward the dollar is also a feature
of blues songs—what anthropologist Charles Keil wryly termed the
finance-romance equation. The bluesman as realist appreciates that
money makes things easier, or, as Chicago guitarist Jimmy Dawkins simply put it, "I don't think money is everything, but when I don't have any
money, hell, I don't like it."[2]

But money means more than groceries and, especially for the aspiring artist, reinforces his sense of his own value and the value of his art. In

a recollection of a working camp experience, Sunnyland Slim points out
the importance of money to the uncertain artist:

"So I had about a dollar or so and I didn't want to get broke, so I said
I believe I'll go out there and sing the blues, play the blues real good. So I
seen Brother Montgomery, he was playing out there. I didn't know him
then. That's where I got to know him. He played so good. I was broke
and wanted some of that food I see. Hit around for my dollar; I never did
want to spend my last dollar out there.

"So he was singing, said [slurred], 'Hey now, can you sing? Go
ahead and sing one.' I got started singing there, and all the hustling
women started coming down with boots on. It's so muddy down
there in 1923 and, boy, them old gals started giving me a quarter, you
know. She had made some money off them peoples, you know, and the
hustlers make some money they just give me some. Started to give me
a little money and so we just started to have a little fun, you know what
I mean.

"So finally Brother got drunk. He got up, played 'Rolling and Tum-
bling.' I left there, and I had about seven or eight dollars myself. That
puts you in the mood for doing something. Money puts you in the mood
for doing something. I was content better then, about playing by myself,
so I come to Memphis. That's where my career happened."[3]

In the musician's story, early paying jobs stand out as career milestones marking the transition from amateur time-waster to wage earner.
Just as accounts of the first guitar represent an initiation into the world
of playing music, the first real jobs serve as an initiation into the ranks of
the professional blues musicians.

In Sunnyland Slim's account, the combination of work camp setting,
receptive audience, hustling women, and the presence and implicit blessing of his hero, Little Brother Montgomery, make the event outstanding.
But it is the almighty dollar, that most tangible symbol of success, that
provides the spur to his career. That seven or eight dollars does put you
in a mood to keep on trying.

Blues players, like other workers, view financial success as a gauge of
achievement and openly admire those who have attained the financial
security so elusive in their business. Big Bill Hill and Muddy Waters demonstrate this respect in a conversational tribute to John Lee Hooker:

BILL HILL: John Lee Hooker got some money.
MUDDY WATERS: He don't play. No, he don't play. He don't beg.
BILL HILL: No, he don't beg, man! He take out a fifty-dollar bill and
lay it on his knee and a woman's eyes get as big as that damn cup. Ha,
ha. He lay it on her lap. He don't play. No, that cat make advances. He

got five or six hundred dollars in his pocket. He don't play. You got to cope with this cat's money.[4]

Impressing fellow musicians with one's financial success can take the form of extreme generosity, and compulsive, even competitive, bouts of extravagance are spoken of with a certain awe. In some stories the excess of spending and consumption takes on the appearance of a potlatch ceremony reinforcing stereotypes about the musician's inability to handle his money. But extreme generosity adds to the artist's prestige and he hopes he will be paid back in kind during leaner times.

Among fellow musicians, the bluesman speaks of his success and maintains a posture of doing all right even if he has been out of work for a while. Here the bluesman as businessman keeps up a front for his fellow workers. But backstage bragging to other musicians is very different from dealing with the general public, who feel somewhat uncomfortable with a well-to-do blues singer. Blues is supposed to be about being down and out, and singers are supposed to be singing of their own lives, so the public expects the profile of "Poor Lightning." And musicians, whether broke or flush—and historically the former is more common— are aware of this aspect of their stereotype. Most have gone through hard times and witnessed suffering, and any temporary success needs to be balanced against the cost of getting there. Musicians generally share the conviction that blues and dues are bound together and, considering the reality of the black experience in general and the blues profession in particular, the dues have been paid time and again.

The popular image of the blues player's Southern experience focuses on racism, economic oppression, and confrontations with rednecks. The artist in some cases literally escapes from the South to Chicago—although now the direction is reversed.[5] Mississippi especially meant hard work or (as Honeyboy Edwards noted) even being forced to work.

Despite the stereotype that a musician will not work, in reality musicians were often forced to work two jobs. Because music provided only a supplemental income, musicians found themselves forced to farm by day as well as play music at night. So even though some musicians like Honeyboy Edwards claim to have escaped day work, other musicians tell of playing music all night, then getting up to go to work the next day. As Johnny Shines noted in Chapter 5, you can't be a musician and a field hand at the same time. Yet many artists did just that. This practice explains why a musician would be tired, but contradicts his reputation for being lazy.[6]

Sam Chatmon, who had quite a successful career himself, referred back to his father's hard times:

"My father, he played in slavery times, and then you had to play if the boss told you to. Had to play all night, go on home, go out to the fields, and go to work."[7]

Fellow Mississippian Clyde "Judas" Maxwell also complained of working night after night and then trying to farm:

"I'd play so much I couldn't eat. I'd come in home at midnight—be playin maybe two or three nights, playin for different parties Thursday, play Friday night, Saturday night. Sunday's a holiday—I'd come in Sunday sit at the table—say, 'Come on in sit down and eat.' So I'd sit down, maybe bite off a piece of biscuit. That's all I could eat. Have to get up and work. Get up and catch a mule."[8]

Howling Wolf paid his dues scuffling for jobs during and after the Depression. Beginning his career relatively late in life, he worked hard to get to the top, earning even the sympathy of fellow bluesmen. Jimmy Dawkins paid him a rare tribute: "Howling Wolf, he had it hard. He struggled for thirty years walking those corn rows trying to get a break."[9]

According to Howling Wolf, early jobs down south meant hard work, low salaries, and long hours: "Back in the country, the people weren't able to pay you too much. Sometimes you'd work all night for a fish sandwich—glad to get it too."[10] In another interview he told Pete Welding, "Some of the jobs I had taken was fifty cents a night back in Hoover's days. Seven in the evening till seven the next morning, and I was glad to get it in those days."[11] While further detail is included, his basic tone emphasizes the difficulty of survival during the Depression. In a final statement, also from the Welding interview, Howling Wolf continues his complaint:

"When I'd go out on them plantations to play, the people played me so hard: they look for you to play from seven o'clock in the evening until seven o'clock the next morning. That's too rough! I was getting about a dollar and a half, and that was too much playing by myself."[12]

Notwithstanding the apparent inflation of these statements, Howling Wolf's consistent point is that he came up the hard way and so can legitimately sing the blues.

Whether at suppers down south or in taverns up north, the musician describes himself as playing "all night long." When paired with day jobs in the fields or in the factories, it is a real source of complaint. Musicians dream of working music full-time, although few ever make it. But music is what they wanted to do, and looking back to those early days, the artist is proud to have survived.[13] John Jackson recalled:

"I was completely and totally music crazy at one time. When I lived in southwestern Virginia, why I used to walk thirty miles with a guitar on my back playing house parties on the weekends and just get back in time to go to work on Monday morning."[14]

The environment of racial and economic oppression that gave black Americans the blues also provided the context in which the musicians matured. Despite the hard reality of black life in the Depression South, it was also a time of accomplishment, when the artist as a young man came of age as a musician. But, however proud of his accomplishments, the artist runs into problems of self-presentation. He may be misunderstood by an audience conditioned to hear protest. When Johnny Young told me, "All I got was two dollars a night and a hamburger," I immediately registered complaint consistent with my preconceived notion of life in Mississippi. But when I asked why he worked for so little, I hurt his feelings, and he impatiently explained that two dollars was in fact a lot of money to make in those days, especially for a youngster. Forced to qualify the amount in order not to play himself cheap, his posture shifts from dues-payer to successful wage earner, a position consistent with his image as child prodigy and musical star.

Like Johnny Young, Kansas City piano man Roy Searce played as a youngster and was managed by his mother:

"People would come by and ask my mother, 'I want this boy to play for my party.' She say 'Okay, but have him home at nine o'clock.' She wouldn't even ask me, and I would work for the party, get maybe fifty cents and a sandwich."[15]

While the pay was average, the hours were better, and his complaint is that he wasn't asked.

No matter what the amount, any contribution to the family income was an accomplishment then. The fact that the youngsters were paid at all proves that the community recognized their talent and accepted them as artists. The money—however low by today's inflated standards— along with the recognition, mark these scenes as successes.

Archie Edwards gives a glowing report of house parties where no money changed hands:

"Most of the time I used to play for house parties, but in those days people didn't have much to pay you. About the only thing I got out of playing when I was a kid was a soda and a couple of pieces of hot fried chicken. At these house parties I wasn't old enough to drink whiskey, so the proprietor or whoever was in charge of the house party would always give me cold sodas and hot fried chicken, biscuits—very good."[16]

Relaxing in my living room in Bloomington, Indiana, after a successful concert, James Thomas recalled a job:

"I remember one time it was froze up and my uncle had an old car at that time. So we had a drum and Poppa Neil, who was in that book, and me an him and my uncle got together, said, 'Let's go somewhere and try to play this evening, get us a little money.' So we went and played for a man. We made, I believe it was nine dollars apiece—nine dollars—and divided, three dollars apiece. And, oh man, we bought ourselves something to eat when we come back. Three dollars was, back in them times, would help you a whole lot, you know. Maybe get you some cigarettes or whatever you use."[17]

Here again an explanation of the comparative economics shows the event to be a great success. Three dollars at that time—albeit after the Depression—was a substantial payment, and the phrase "oh man" intimates the sense of the achievement. Contrast this to the dues-paying statement on "The Today Show," where working all night for a dollar meant hard times.

Bob Lowery tells of his first job as an even greater triumph:

"That was back in El Dorado, back in El Dorado playing with some band from Little Rock. Now they was pretty good back then, and they like the way I played. They liked it, and I guess somebody else might like it, so I just started in right then. I think I got three dollars and seventy-five cents that night. That was a lot of money! I didn't know what to do! I had a heck of a time."[18]

He made a fortune—the appropriate reward for a successful debut—and as with Sunnyland Slim's initial account, the episode stands out as an important transitional event. Here the artist becomes aware of his potential and receives confirmation as a musician. The acceptance by other musicians, their recognition of his ability, and the exceptional amount of money make the event a milestone in his life.

Sunnyland Slim recalls a full work week:

"That man hired me one night for the motion picture show. I was playing pretty good by then. They were going to give me a dollar and a half the first night. Most of the white people be down on this floor, colored people be up there where they had the piano, big old upright piano. You know, it really took so long to change reels in those days. That was in '22 or '23.

"He gave me a dollar and a half the next night, and the fellow that had been down to the joint around there, little fellow, we'd go out. I didn't know nothing about no price of no playing. But he said, 'Hey man.'

So this fellow asks me, says, 'You go out there play with me,' says, 'I can give you two and a half every Saturday night and I'll be there to come and carry you out to play out there.' And I says, 'Yeah.' Two and a half, that was a lot of money then. So I'd be around and play before I started playing for Mr. Tolliver round there.

"Stay up there and play all night for a dollar. That was a lot of money. You weren't getting but sixty-five cents a day for working, seventy-five cents from sun up to sun down. So he gave me a dollar and a half that first night at the motion picture show. Gave me two and a half, said, 'You stay with me Sunday. I'll bring you home Sunday evening.' I'll make another dollar and a half. That's what I got that week. There's a lot of people. If it rains, you didn't make that in two weeks, see."[19]

Whether two dollars and a fish sandwich can be considered bad pay for having a good time or good pay for hard times,[20] the storyteller, in conjuring up the event, has several options as to the best way to present this information. As an example of the economics of authenticity, stress can be laid on hard times, hard work, and low pay. The prerequisite of suffering and musical participation in Southern hard times is accomplished by stressing the position of coming up hard, as in Lee Crisp's statement: "I had a pretty rough way of starting. I just stand in the alley blowing my harmonica, well, for a quart of beer."[21]

When recreating a similar episode, other artists focus on the joy of participating in an event like a supper or a session in a juke. The sheer fun and self-esteem overshadow the need for a dues-paying reference. In still other cases we find an emphasis on youthful talent, which is accomplished by placing oneself in a musical context at an early age where, regardless of the amount of payment, the fact of professionalism is in itself outstanding. Pride in professionalism is also indicated by qualifying the amount earned and stressing the value the community placed on one's performance. Finally, there is the recreation of the wonder of being paid for, and perhaps even making a living at, what had previously been done simply for pleasure.[22]

The topics so far have generally dealt with the steps of becoming a musician and are separated from the present by intervening time and space. Instruments, family attitude, learning, and early jobs can be recalled nostalgically as highlights of the developing artist in the rural South, or they can be presented as obstacles overcome and dues paid. Often infused with a romance uncharacteristic of the bluesman, they remind us that regardless of later letdowns and rip-offs the young man must have been deeply impressed by the idea of actually becoming a bluesman.

Times may have been tough, but other things were better: the musicians were young, people took care of each other, the world was less violent and less hectic, and their style of music was more popular. As Clyde Maxwell put it, "I was first a little boy—then at that time they liked music more."[23]

The intrinsic reward of playing music, along with recognition, esteem, and being attractive to the opposite sex, was incentive enough for many amateur blues players. Making money for playing, whether it was substantial payment or merely a token, when conjured up in contrast to later years of hustling in the business, made it all the more worthwhile. Unlike today, the money was worth something then, and as Honeyboy Edwards noted, "A hundred dollars rattled and talked shit a long time, but it ain't worth nothing now." With nickel beer, sausage at seven cents a pound, and hustlers turning tricks for a quarter, the musician's two dollars had him doing as well and often better than other workers similarly trying to keep body and soul together.

Poverty and suffering existed as part of the musician's past, part of the milieu in which they worked. But the good times should be remembered as well, the accomplishments and the joy of making it as a musician. Let us not deny the artists their success or the respect they earned. Honeyboy Edwards' line provides a fine summary with typical blues ambivalence—"It was a rough time, but we made it good."

8

"Wasn't only my songs, they got my music too"

Up to this point the bluesman's story tells about his becoming a musician. The young man generally wishes to become a musician after being exposed to other musicians. He secs himself as having a God-given gift or talent for music. He acquires an instrument. Overcoming obstacles, and with the help of an inspirational figure or teacher, he eventually is initiated into the ranks of professional musicians by being paid for his work. Reaching maturity as a working musician, he loses his innocence and gains wisdom through experience.

Working the blues teaches its own lesson: survival. Coldhearted people and cold Chicago winters have taken their toll. The dangers of night work in tough clubs, the exhaustion of travel, and the killing effects of alcohol have done some artists in and driven others out of the business. Descriptions of the harsh reality of playing the blues in the present day sharply contrast with the idealized accounts of the bluesman's younger days. Now cynical, even bitter, the mature artist has traded his innocent ideals for the wisdom necessary to survive in a dog-eat-dog world. The friends, heroes, and admirers of the past are now replaced with dishonest employers, con artists, undependable, jealous sidemen, and an unpredictable audience. Yet despite the disillusionment, the dream of making it stays alive.

Accounts of present working life explore the contexts in which the musician works and warns of the dangers he faces. Explaining the conditions of his world, he passes on advice on how to deal with occupational hazards like alcohol, violence, and rip-offs. But while emphasizing his dues —often having learned his lesson the hard way—he also jokes or brags about the same topics as if to say, "See what I've gone through." Avoiding topics at odds with the bluesman's life, he presents a one-sided picture of music and musicians in nightclubs or on the road. Working the blues is a hard life, and he has made it through so far, but now he wants some of the rewards he is due.

We assume the bluesman is immune to the suffering inflicted on mortals who carouse beyond their capacity. One night following the show at Theresa's (in Chicago), everyone packed off to a club with a 4:00 A.M. license, The Peyton Place. I found the club thanks to the expert navigation of bass player Odell Campbell, from whom I recall the line "Are you sure that you aren't a policeman?"

The Peyton Place absorbed the Theresa's crowd, and the blues continued, featuring Hound Dog Taylor, Sammy Lawhorn, Odell Campbell, Lefty Diaz, and so on. There was, in fact, a great deal of audience overlap from event to event. If you were into the blues, you made the rounds. This night, taking care of business, I spoke to Hound Dog Taylor about an interview. "Sure, sure," he said, and invited me to lunch the next day. I agreed to drop by around noon. Business settled, we partied into the night.

The next day, after arriving home at eight o'clock in the morning, I found myself too weak to go calling. Chagrined by my lack of endurance, I called Hound Dog about eleven o'clock to cancel out on lunch. A woman answered. I asked, "Is Mr. Hound Dog Taylor there?" "Just a minute," she said. So I waited. It was quiet, then I heard some movement on the other end. Suddenly, I was startled to hear a strange, moaning sound. "Eeeh, eeeh." Over this strange and painful exhalation the woman's voice directed, "Talk, talk, it's a telephone."[1]

Blues musicians drink. They drink for many reasons: inspiration, anesthesia, strength, nourishment, to be sociable, as part of their act, and of course for recreation. Blues and booze are tied together in reality as well as in the public's mind. Just mention blues, and everyone wants a drink. Such a Pavlovian response requires conditioning, and liquor has been part of the scene wherever musicians worked at picnics, suppers, jukes, taverns, and after-hour joints.

The image of the bluesman working for drinks and tips has him half drunk all the time but never quite includes the crippling hangovers that afflict his audience.[2] In reality, working taverns six to eight hours a clip, the musician recognizes the dangers of alcohol; still, most artists drink— barring doctor's orders—or at one time did. As hero of consumption, competitive drinker, and unofficial nightclub host, he is pressured to take a drink. Mixing with the audience, recognizing regulars, greeting big spenders, the bluesman interacts with the audience, whose members show their friendship or approval by buying him a drink.

Furthermore, he needs to establish that he understands the people in the audience and shares their joys, sorrows, and habits. And turning down a drink, unless done with considerable grace, can make him appear as if he thinks he's better than they are. Saying no can be interpreted as a rejection of the patron as well as the drink; all told, the bluesman needs to rationalize abstinence instead of the opposite, as Byther Smith explains:

"They can't accept me like that because they say, 'Hey man, look, I'm going to have a drink.' 'Okay, go ahead,' you know, 'Hey man, come and have a drink with me.' 'No thanks, I don't even drink.' 'But what do you do?' 'I talk to you. I play my guitar. I go home. I go to work.' You know. I says, 'If you want to, I'll tell you some jokes.'

"You know, like that, run down some people to you. But I can find so much other things to do, you know. But don't get me wrong. I tried it all. I tried to drink. I tried to smoke. I tried to gamble. I tried to be a gang leader, and it just didn't pay off. It didn't show me nothin. It's nothin to it."[3]

The bottle is such a pillar of the bluesman stereotype that a drink amounts to a secondary stage prop. But the line between social drinker and victim of excess concerns reliability. From a business perspective, lines like "He likes to drink but you don't ever see him drunk" or "He could be drunk but he could still play" describe fellow musicians. Being too drunk to play, however, can cause serious problems by weakening the band's show, making it tougher to get a job the next time around, and in general driving still another nail into the bluesman's reputation.

So musicians accept drinking but not drunks. Eddie Taylor refers to his long-time partner Jimmy Reed:

"From '56 on it was pretty hard cause you got to watch him. He wouldn't do his shows—couldn't get him to lay off the bottle. You got to eat, you got to sleep, you got to take a bath, these things you got to do. You couldn't take your eyes off Jimmy, Jimmy's got a fifth of whiskey. He'll get somebody, give them a five-dollar bill, tell them to get him a fifth of whiskey. He don't care, you know, do that just to keep from doing his shows."[4]

The tragic combination of alcohol and epilepsy ended Jimmy Reed's career, though he was on the road to a comeback just before he died.

Because musicians are expected to drink, they need to rule alcohol and not have it rule them,[5] and as Otis Rush suggests, they are careful:

"I've gotten high, drunk, or what not, I don't fall out on the floor or anything. I respect liquor. I can get pretty soaked. Occasionally I do, but I don't do it often."[6]

Drinking for courage or to get a feeling, to help you put everything you have in a performance, is common in the blues tradition. Blues performance demands intensity and a willingness to give of yourself. Summoning maximum energy, with or without stimulants, is hard work, and the level of intensity the artist displays can verge on trance. Total commitment, however, must be balanced by self-protection and control or it can be destructive. The blues artist can become a bandstand kamikaze, driving himself deeper down into the blues in search of knowledge or a voice. For the stone bluesman, this act is no gentle game but a journey of the soul from which there may be no return.

Some artists lose themselves or embrace the bluesman stereotype, hell-bent on self-destruction. Big Joe Williams said of Elmore James, "He did it too hard in a way of speaking, you know, drinking pretty heavy, and like he sung, he lived, and everything he sung, he sung it real hard."[7]

But blues songs more often celebrate the joys of tonight's high times than bemoan the ravages of tomorrow's hangover. Likewise, the bluesman jokes about drinking, recognizing that the public enjoys this part of his profile. Piano player Roy Searce utilized an alcohol theme in his introduction to a song by Big Joe Turner. "Big Joe Turner could drink more whiskey and make up more words than any man. He'd say, 'Please give me another drink of whiskey,' and then he'd drink up half a pint."[8] As usual, this introduction drew a laugh from the audience. Whenever a blues player refers to drinking, people laugh with appreciation and recognition, secure that their beliefs are correct. And musicians, though they pay the price for the association with liquor, are quick to take advantage of this side of their stereotype.[9]

For better or for worse, alcohol is part of the blues life as a right and an obligation. From that first drop of whiskey in Charlie Patton's spoon, the young artists follow in their heroes' footsteps,[10] acting like they act and drinking what they drink, and as Johnny Shines notes, they become conditioned to alcohol:

"A lot of musicians believe it today: if you don't have a drink of liquor you can't make it. That's because he been taught that. I remember a time when me and Sunnyland both, we couldn't play if we didn't have a fifth of liquor sitting up there on the piano."[11]

While many artists believe alcohol helps their performance and the blues event as a whole, they have also lost friends to the bottle. Despite their reputation for excess, musicians warn of the need for moderation. J. T. Adams recalled his friend fellow Indianapolis bluesman Pete Franklin:

"He just drank himself to death. Well, it's mostly a habit. They just get to running with those types of people, you know, drinking, and they always drinking. Somebody buying them a drink and they don't know how to turn it down."[12]

Besides the bottle, the bluesman also copes with physical violence—although the two are often related. But here too, stereotype and reality merge. According to popular opinion, the blues artists' world includes nightly murders and fights, and in the real world artists have traditionally played tough clubs where audiences worked hard at blowing off steam. But tales of violence are somewhat exaggerated—or in any event represent unusual working conditions. Still, musicians tell of dangerous clubs, "buckets of blood," and of witnessing shootings, cuttings, and other mayhem. Although they avoid working such places—if they can—they know most people are interested in violence, that fights or murder make a good story. And since they have experienced or witnessed violence, they have a story to tell.[13]

The bluesman, stage center, is capable of being either hero or scapegoat. For an audience or an individual turned evil and ugly, there is no more convenient victim, and the musician knows this. It only takes one crazy drunk or jealous husband to end it all, and while a few bluesmen are fighters, most prefer to be thought of as lovers. Both can be dangerous.

The intentional violence directed toward the musician can be attributed to his visibility and attractiveness. Simply being in the spotlight can be dangerous, because others may envy your position. Byther Smith illustrates the problem and how the performer learns to cool down dangerous customers:

"He come up to me and says, 'You think you are really something because you up there playing that guitar,' he says, 'and you got every woman in here looking at you.' He says, 'You think you're something don't you?' I said, 'No. I'm not as much as you because you're more than I am because you had money to pay to come in and see me.' I says, 'I didn't have no money.' So I had to think of something to tell him to make him feel that he was as much as I was, you know. Because I told him, I said, 'I'm not as much as you are because you had the money to come in, to pay and to spend.' I said, 'I don't have no money to spend.' I said, 'That's why I'm working here, because I don't have anything!'[14]

The bluesman improvises on and off the bandstand.

No matter how well the bluesman learns to cope with tavern patrons or how fast he can jump out the window, he most fears being the unintentional victim because there's nothing he can do to prevent it. Unintentional violence is quite literally out of control. James Thomas points out the problem of random violence in a southern club:

"Well, it's dangerous now in these nightclubs. It's like you in a big nightclub and they get to shooting, you don't never know which way that bullet's going. Cause plenty people done got killed—wasn't shooting at this person, but kill somebody else. There was a man in the country killed a man, killed two men, but one of them he wasn't intending to kill."[15]

Otis Rush parallels this statement in the Chicago context:

"It's very, very, very hard. It's dangerous. Cause anybody can start a fight and get it. Hey, a bullet don't care who it hits, or a chair or a brick, or something, you know—

"Yeah, well, there's a lot of places I won't play because of, uh, peoples are so evil now today. There's a lot of confusion all over. I try to pick up a few places I won't be running into that, cause I'd rather play my guitar. I don't want to fight."[16]

How does the artist counteract so much "evil" and "confusion" without allowing it to consume him? Otis Rush tries to keep away from the dangerous clubs, in a sense taking the music out of the volatile atmosphere in which it developed.

For Byther Smith the fear of being shot by accident almost came true:

"I was playing with Ricky Allen. We was out of Joliet one night, playing out there, and they got to fighting in that place. They got to fighting in that place, and man, I have never been so scared in my life.

"And it didn't scare me at first, but when I got ready to take my equipment down and looked at my guitar—I had a red fender guitar like this one I have over at T's [Theresa's]. They had about three shots, and one guy or two guys had got shot. I heard em say that three of them had got shot, but I know they shot three or four times in that place and one bullet went in.

"A boy was playing organ—you know how they got that great big Hammond organ speaker—I'm standing up there and I was leaning up against that organ, just playing. I was just playing and a bullet hit up above my head up there. But I thought this was the man playing the organ, hit down on the organ. I never even opened my eyes. I was just standing up there. I heard the guns shoot, but I thought they was shooting just cause it's New Year's night, you know. And I thought there was some people in there shooting fireworks and things. And all of a sudden I heard them screaming and hollering, 'He shot him. He shot him. He shot him.' And I decided I better get down behind my amplifier.

I chose to duck, and when I pulled my guitar off—I don't know when the bullet hit the guitar, honest to God I don't. I jumped on behind this speaker cabinet for the organ, I laid down behind there. Peoples running all up on that bandstand going down to the basement and hid.

"When we got ready to take down that night and I was looking at my guitar and I saw this busted, you know, the wood busted. After looking at it, and the corner, right where the guitar come right down across this part of it, of your body, there's a bullet from about a twenty-five automatic was stuck in that guitar.

"And on my way home that night I got to thinking. Supposing that went on through there, and maybe he'd missed the guitar and got me. And I was driving around, I got so nervous like that. I pulled over to the side and stopped. And the highway patrolman pulled up behind me there and a state trooper asked me, 'What's wrong?' And I told him, I says, 'I didn't mean to park here.' He says, 'You'll have to go.' I said, 'I'll go, but you have to give me a minute to get myself together.' I says, 'I just got off of work and guy got to shooting and people got killed up there, got shot, and I got to thinking about it. I'd like to show you my guitar, how close I come to the bullet hitting me.' He said, 'Okay, sit there until you get yourself together.' I said, 'I'll be all right,' I says, 'but right now I just can't drive.'

"So he pulled out there in front of me, went on. But then I was just like that, and the more I got to thinking about it, you know, just pressed down on me like that. It was really bad."[17]

While tales of violence tend to be blown out of proportion, the working artist who must go on stage night after night cannot afford to forget about it. Otis Rush has paid his dues:

"Yeah, it is dangerous. Very, very much so. Cause there's been so many fights. Hey, you up there playing music, right? What the hell do you know about what's happening out there, somebody fixing to blow somebody's brains out, you know. I've seen it happen in so many places I've played. Somebody lay out dead in front of the bandstand. I've seen it several, several times. I say several, six or seven times saw people get killed."[18]

Sometimes the bluesman feels a premonition, as Byther Smith did, a sense of danger in the atmosphere of a place:

"There used to be a place over here on Lake Street. I went there and I worked couple of times and I refused to go back the next time. And I called the man up and told him to get somebody else to play because I couldn't stand the atmosphere of the place.

"It used to be a place out on Roosevelt Road they used to call 'the Bucket of Blood.'[19] I went there one night, hooked up my equipment, and I just got to looking around and I took down my equipment and walked out. Now, I had to pay a fine because I had signed a contract.

"Now, I had to pay a fine. I had to pay twenty-two dollars that night for leaving. I went there and hooked up my guitar and tuned up with everybody, and I got to looking around there and it just look like death was in that place. And I told the man, 'Man,' I says, 'look, I ain't playing.' I says, 'I'm not going to play here.' And I never did go back to that club. I never have been back in there no more. Never did."[20]

Archie Edwards, like Honeyboy Edwards, spoke of jealous husbands and boyfriends:

"Now something—it never happened to me, but I have known— other people tell me that they have been to parties where the husbands, boyfriends, of some women would get jealous, angry with the musi- cians—because he might play a song that some of the women might like and they might smile at him, say something to him, and there might be a fight over that. But I guess it never happened to me because I was too young to cut my eyes back at them."[21]

John Cephas laughed at the memory of blues events that turned into battles royal:

"Everybody get steamed up drinking that corn liquor, and some would start fighting. I've been to some free-for-alls back in the country where everybody would be fighting. Nobody knows who's fighting who. Breaking all the windows out, tearing the doors down. I've been to quite a few of those."[22]

John Jackson told of a more chilling encounter in which a man wear- ing "convict shoes" accused him of stealing his guitar. A fight broke out, and the man later returned with a shotgun. This episode, which made a great story years later, had the more immediate effect of convincing John to give up playing for ten years.[23]

While violence is part of the bluesman's life and enough artists have been killed to reinforce this aspect of the bluesman's stereotype, accounts of violence distort the picture of the bluesman's usual working experi- ence. All things considered, he is more likely to be ripped off than as- saulted.

The musician copes with a world eager to cheat him. Stories of rip-

offs, though slightly less dramatic than tales of violence, are all too common. Working two jobs, musicians have relied on others—usually fellow
musicians—to find them work. But they have also placed themselves in
the hands of agents, managers, producers, and club owners, generally to
the musician's disadvantage. Cast as villains, management figures are
portrayed as lining their pockets at the musician's expense. But musicians
continue to need help to get beyond the small tavern circuit. Having been
burned so often, however, they develop a healthy suspicion. Wild Child
Butler spoke of his caution:

"You run up on all kind of people in this business. That's why I'm
really funny about who I talk to, you know, or fool with, cause there
really some bad peoples out here in this business. I been got and I have
paid so many dues. I really did that. I don't know when they'll stop. I'm
still paying them. I don't know what's going to come out of it."[24]

Ripped off across the board—personally, collectively, culturally—the
complaint "I never saw a penny" describes the history of the blues. Rip-
offs occur at all levels of the bluesman's work: writing, recording, and
performing. Once again the stereotype of the down-and-out artist, his
work stolen, paid off with a bottle of booze, corresponds to real corrup-
tion. Sunnyland Slim expressed the cynical realism of the blues artist who
has learned his lesson the hard way:

"You can't write—you can't, man, can't write, can't claim nothin and
don't get no paper for it, you know what I mean. It's not yours, no
matter what anybody do— You can't claim nothin if you ain't got the
papers on it. You can't. That ain't your coat there if you ain't got nothing
to show for it."[25]

Sunnyland is still angry. It's hard to be ripped off, whether it's having
been beaten out of some money or having your life's work stolen. While
most artists complain about being cheated financially, others, like Sunnyland, are angry about being denied their place in history. When someone
has a song stolen, the bitterness is twofold: it hurts the businessman
financially, but it hurts the artist by cheating him out of his due credit.
Harmonica Frank Floyd also complained of being cheated:

"I try to be honest, fair and square, with everybody. That's my motto.
And can't none of them say I've crooked anyone and can't stand people
that crook me. However, these people have done it and ——— of Nashville Tennessee is another hasn't paid off for the record that he's got out.
He said he'd pay for it later, but he didn't pay a god derned penny—and I
didn't give no permission for none of them guys to record my records. So

I should have a little say over what belongs to me, it looks to me like. Wasn't only my songs—they got my music too. See what I mean."[26]

His indictment of the music business sounds discouragingly familiar. Yet I took the option of deleting—or as the bluesman says—"not calling no names." Generally careful about mentioning names in interviews, people get angry when they talk of being ripped off. But careless comments can wind up costing the musician in the future. Wild Child Butler was still so angry he wanted me to talk about his nemesis:

"Well, all my songs now, I never got a dime for no writing and they copyright it, ———Enterprises. Mercury sent me some things that said they gave me a piece of money, but they said they're lying, that Mercury never gave them no money, but I never even got nothin for a line I wrote. Yeah, it really is. I never got nothin for nothin I wrote. On the L.P. I ain't never got a dime out of nothing I wrote. I ain't never got nothing.

"And by the way, I didn't have no special pay. I had my file lying there in the cabinet. They wouldn't even give me my copyrights when I got my release from them. The guy tell me, 'I'm gonna send them, I'll mail them.' Every time I call them they lie to me. The great ———, I hope you talk about him— He's a big— I didn't think he would lie to me like that. They tell me, 'All right, we gonna send em, we gonna send em,' and I know she had them down at the office, but they don't even send me the copyrights."[27]

Even in this case, however, Eddie Taylor's admonition—"Don't talk too much yap, yap, yap. You know, say the wrong thing at the wrong time at the wrong place. You know, that can ruin you."[28]—may be applicable.

Although blues artists talk about their records with pride in their story, they complain that the record industry rips them off as well. Generally treated like a replaceable part in a badly run machine, the blues artist sees his sessions as poorly planned, cheap, slipshod affairs. But to be honest, blues records get little distribution and almost no air play. So while thousands of records are produced, few people actually get rich, least of all the artist.[29]

Artists know that their records, "Money Taking Woman" or "Build Myself a Cave," provide a frame of reference for their fans, and so they can supply names, dates, and labels. Speaking of records is akin to listing publications, and even if the artist "never saw a penny," if the record was released it would show up in the hands of a collector and the artist would be asked about it. So he keeps his recording history in order as with Wild Child Butler ("My first record was 'Aching All Over,' and the flip 'Dying Chill' on a small label, Sharpshot"[30]) or Byther Smith ("My first recording was 'Thank You, Mr. Kennedy' and 'Champion Girl' "[31]).

First recordings, like first guitars, first paychecks, or even first interviews, tend to stand out in memory at least as a convenient beginning. Recordings that do not sell present different problems. Painfully aware that record sales determine fame and fortune and are an artistic judgment as well, musicians rationalize a record's failure or even cite conspiracy—the figures were juggled or it was held back in favor of another artist's lesser record.

They reasonably believe that if they make a good record the public should want it, and they tell unusual tales about how their record hit the top ten in Puerto Rico or Canada. They know this because they heard it from a friend who heard it on the radio.

Paranoia—"My record would have been a hit if not for so and so" or "I could have had a big break if not for so and so"—has been justified in the blues business. This was especially true in the early 1960s, where a combination of recording monopolies and a diminishing market placed the artist's future in the hands of a few powerful people. Eddie Taylor claimed:

"Course I could call names of important people. Before ——— died, he had ABC, and Columbia were asking for me and [he] told them they couldn't get me cause I was his man, I had a contract with him. And I never had a contract with him, you know."[32]

Traditionally in a weak bargaining position, the bluesman copes with the situation as best he can and stoically takes work where he can find it. This often means giving up artistic control, but as Eddie Taylor rationalizes, it's up to the man with the money:

"If I'm recording for you, you paying for the studio, you paying the fellows, you paying me. I can't get in the studio and quit just because I feel bad about that. I just go ahead and do the best I can."[33]

But the inequities of the system drive some artists out of the business. Fed up with the hassles of being cheated and tired of being angry, Big Chief Ellis quit:

"The reason I had to give it up cause I was getting ripped off. Practically every record company I recorded for owes me money right now. In fact, I had to threaten a couple of them to even get money from them. I went down to wreck this company. He knew I meant business. He made me out a check right then. He knew I was out to wreck this company. I had got tired of getting ripped off, and that's the reason I had to give it up, cause they'll record you, pay you for the recording, then you don't hear no more. This mostly happens to blues and religious."[34]

He returned to music later on but retained his suspicious nature.

Even in day-to-day performance the bluesman gets ripped off. On one end of the spectrum James Thomas spoke of working small rural cafes:

"Oh, they tough and you can charge fifty cents at the door. Well, cause who you have at the door, they gonna cheat you out of some of that. So it's tough everywhere you go. Somebody gonna slip in, some stay until they get tired, go out, and give the ticket to some of his friends. They there till they get ready to go. It's always ways to slip in."[35]

On the other end of the spectrum, Wild Child Butler spoke of a blues superstar being taken by his own manager who booked him in a major Chicago club:

"She books him, she gonna get him thirty-five hundred dollars a week and he gets—his manager—they say he went down there and booked him for twenty-six hundred dollars and took the whole gig over. She booked him for thirty-five hundred dollars, and his own man went down and booked him for twenty-six hundred dollars and took the whole gig over."[36]

Byther Smith passes on another lesson:

"Don't have em charge anything, because there are so many peoples behind that counter at different clubs and different places I've known. People do it—they get the band fellows to drinking and they gonna charge. You come in here, you buy one drink, and they buy, say, 'This is on me, here.' But they gonna put it on the band's tab. That's in order— Because you're a customer, that's gonna make you come back, say, 'Gee, I went to the club over at such and such a place and I bought one drink and then they give me a set, see."[37]

But losing can also make a good story if a clever con is involved and the difficulties are now settled. Blues musicians appreciate the ability to be able to "take it" and may even con each other. And as Byther Smith points out, even the victim should appreciate a truly bold or clever move:

"So I get dressed and go on out there. I get there about five minutes before work time. Sammy Lawhorn was sitting up there. When I walked in, Sammy says, 'Hot dog. Here comes my baby. Everybody gotta bring it in for my baby.' I was bringing my guitar and amplifier in. Sammy says, 'Queen Bee, gives me Smitty's money now. I'm gonna drink it up.' And that woman paid Sammy. See, he's sitting at the bar, he's not working, he's just sitting at the bar. So she goes and pays him. [Laughter.]

"Now, when I get off work I'm standing there. I say, 'Okay, Queen Bee, come on and give Smitty his money so I can go.' Just like that, you know. She says, 'Uh, Smitty, I done paid you. I gave your money to Sammy Lawhorn.' Honest to God, and I thought she was kidding. So I go and put my stuff in the car and come back in there and said, 'Woman, you better pay me.' 'You ain't getting nothing. I done paid Sammy Lawhorn, and Sammy done drink that money up.' Sammy done got drunk and went home."[38]

Squeezing ironic humor out of misfortune and being able to handle life's unexpected setbacks are values implicit in blues songs. Here, however, we should note the equally traditional game of beating a fellow musician out of his money.

Because of the nature of the business, distrust is a healthy state of mind. Whether beaten out of his short change or clipped for $900, rip-offs have taught the artist caution: don't sign anything, get the money up front, and keep your eye on everyone, including fellow musicians.

Such tales, ranging from straightforward complaints to entertaining anecdotes, show the musician confronting his real-life problems. A night person, out on the streets at four in the morning or hitting an after-hours club to wind down after a show, the bluesman knows his work can be dangerous. But he also knows that the danger enhances the romance of his story.

If these trials above summed up the bluesman's life, working as a bluesman would be enough to give anyone the blues. There must be more to life, and there is, but as Johnny Shines argues, the public doesn't want to accept it:

"See, one thing about it, people think because you're a blues musician, and especially black, you don't know anything to talk about but sex, murder, gambling, you understand, and getting drunk and so on like that. But that's not all there is. It's more to life than that. If that's the only life you lived, you haven't lived. You just haven't lived at all."[39]

The bluesman can have a house in the country like John Cephas or live in the suburbs like Byther Smith. He lets his dog run on his well-kept lawn. He has a wife and two daughters and worries about credit card bills. Even his work-related problems are more realistically represented by doing free favors for other musicians, keeping a band together, and keeping out of trouble while on the road. But the public prefers the bluesman as nocturnal adventurer, the creature of the songs, and feels more comfortable tying the artist to whiskey and women rather than paying off the equipment or insuring the bus.

Since the musician's story shows professional life and how the artist became a blues musician, certain subjects like home life or nonmusical work, while very much a part of the individual's world, do not fit with the bluesman image. Because they do reveal the man behind the mask, they are avoided, and the musician sticks with a consistent if lopsided picture of his life.[40] Family life does not fit with the bluesman image, nor is it really the subject of blues songs, which leave that subject to the church. Traditionally family has been portrayed at odds with the musician, pulling him away from the road and the company of other musicians. Seemingly incompatible with family and hearth, the bluesman's hours and habits—at least as portrayed in blues songs—show him a long way from home or perhaps about to break up somebody's happy home, going home, or leaving home, but almost never at home.[41]

Where musicians did touch on family, they often still referred to music. Byther Smith, whose family was home when we spoke, mentioned his daughter's music lessons and how his wife had bought him some new equipment after he got angry and sold his. Johnny Young mentioned how much his wife loves his music in comparison to his ex-wife, who tried to make him quit. Honeyboy Edwards mentioned his former wife, Bassie, then spoke of his current setup, which included fellow bluesman Walter Horton.

While musicians may assume a lack of interest in their family, I felt they held family separate—a private retreat for the private person away from the blues life and the blues interview.

Blues musicians also circumvented or rushed over nonmusical work, although many have spent years at another job and take pride in their nonmusical work. But nonmusical work is also inconsistent with the bluesman image, and from the perspective of musician's lore, the day job has traditionally been a "slave," whether picking cotton or plowing mules in the South or working in the mills in Chicago. Honeyboy Edwards' account of Floyd Jones leaving the mills to play music exemplifies the bluesman's attitude. Floyd the millworker, portrayed as a suffering working stiff, is contrasted with Floyd the bluesman—successful street-corner hustler. In contrast to the image of the bluesman as down and out, musicians themselves pity the poor working stiff.

Artists casually referred to other jobs in the context of comparison to (or of leaving them to concentrate on) music. For example, Johnny Young spoke of shoveling coal, washing dishes, and cutting logs as dues-paying, but then he came back to music. Even with an exceptional job like grave-digging, which would interest the audience, James Thomas' emphasis was on putting it aside for the blues:

"When I go to the funeral home and work I gets, uh, twenty-five dollars a grave, that's opening and closing. So I make more money playing than I would doing either one of those jobs. But it's right around home, and when I'm there I just do that work, you know, pick up extra money. Cause they wouldn't pay me a hundred and fifty dollars for that little while last night. Plus my ticket back home! They wouldn't pay that."[42]

Above all, James Thomas is a professional musician first and foremost who picks up extra money doing convenient day work.

That day work suffers by comparison shows the musician's priorities: you do day work until you decide to go professional, or fall back on it when times are tight. In one final example, Archie Edwards contrasts playing music to his job as a policeman at the welfare office:

"Working with something you love—that's not really work cause you don't worry about it. And I love to play the guitar. I'll play for hours and hours. That's something that I want to do. Enjoyment takes the stress and strain out of whatever you're doing. If you like to do it, no problem. But anything that you do, if you don't like to do it, it will drive you crazy.

"Like I quit that job as a police officer. I made up my mind to get that burden off of me because it was worrying me to death cause, see, I was doing my job, but the other people wasn't doing their job. When the clients come in to the building, instead of the workers coming down stairs to see them, to help the clients so the clients can go about his business feeling good, why they'll wait to the last minute. They wait till the client starts raising hell, then they want me to get the client out of the building.

"Why, you got to be crazy. I'm not gonna use no physical stress and strain on this client. You got to see him. Throwing him out of the building is not gonna solve the problem. Give him a chance to go get a gun, come back and shoot everybody, see what I'm saying?"[43]

Sensibly avoiding subjects he wishes to keep private or sees as detracting from his image, the bluesman talks instead of other musicians. On the bandstand or on the road, blues players still form a close-knit, self-conscious mutually supportive group. But tales of work often show the musicians in a negative light, in contrast to the "good old days." But even though jealousy, distrust, and competitiveness may cloud their relationship, musicians still need each other. Through an informal network, they continue to help each other find work, and if they have no job of their own they may perform anyway to help another musician's show. Trading what they call favors, they work for little or no money, hoping the favor will be returned. As Eddie Taylor explains, it's part of the business:

"Everybody ain't greedy about money, everybody ain't greedy. If I know you and you giving an affair or giving something and say, 'Come and play for me. I can't pay but such and such a thing.'

"Well, if I got a good heart I'll say okay. It may not be but ten dollars, it may not be but five dollars. You know. Especially, you buy your wife or girlfriend a drink. Even if it's ten dollars, it's gonna go anyway on a pack of cigarettes. So you have a party. Anyway, in this deal, you can't be stuck up. You got to try to do right, do well, you know, do people favors that want favors."[44]

Wild Child Butler also accepted the system:

"Now I get calls. Guys call me all the time—'I got a group. Hey man, you want to come up? I'll get you the side men, and tonight you my special guest. Okay?' I say, 'What is it, a favor?' I know it's a favor. 'Yeah, it ain't much money.' I gets there and I see my name in the headliner.

"And I think I done had jobs and I didn't know it. Because someone else did it with the group that I be with. Well, reckon I done got there and saw my name in the headline. Well, so what? I there then. I go on hopin some day I go back."[45]

Favors can work both ways. As a guest artist the bluesman keeps in the public eye even if he's not working. If he has a big name he helps the other band by appearing on their show. But if he does not have a following, he needs the exposure and depends on the goodwill of working bands. Wild Child Butler shows this other side of the coin:

"Last year I was on with Wolf. Last Christmas Eve I did a number on Wolf's show, then Wolf gave me his whole show. I did the whole show for him. He was working at Big Duke's on Madison. I was there that night around the last show. I got up to do a few numbers, and Wolf say, 'By the way you like the young man, Wild Child, I'm gonna let him close the show, finish it.' And Wolf turned his whole show and the band over to me and let me work it. Now, if I'm in a house with Wolf I really know he will call me up on stage with him."[46]

But musicians can also be coldhearted, freezing out the guest who needs a break. I recall one night a man (I won't call no names) striding confidently to the bandstand, guitar in hand and a smile on his face. He stood there half a set waiting to be noticed, but the band chose to ignore him. Unsure whether to leave or wait for the band to break, he just kept standing there. But the band did not break until after he finally left. Head down, confidence shaken, he went next door and got drunk.[47]

Ego destruction of this sort is also part of the blues business. It is a method of keeping aggressive, untalented, unreliable, or even blackballed musicians off stage. With regard to amateur artists, it involves nipping potential competition in the bud. After all, the same person given a good break may get stronger and steal your job.

In the good old days there were enough jobs to go around, but in the 1960s and early 1970s, times had changed and, according to Byther Smith, became "dog-eat-dog":

"They used to be— Musicians used to be playing door to door to each other. But each man is making— Along then scales weren't where it's at now. I think then the scales weren't no more than about fifteen, sixteen, seventeen dollars. The highest that was paid was eighteen then. But they really respected each other so much until this group would be playing right here in this door and across the street in the next tavern is another group. You didn't find all that dog-eat-dog for musicians. Now the musicians have wrecked the jobs. You can't hardly get a job, a decent-paying job, just on account of this

"Musicians used to respect one another better than they do now. Now they don't have the respect for a musician. I'm speaking of musicians in general of each other. They, along then, the musicians, didn't go around and try to undermine for jobs like they do now. See, today in town the musicians have wrecked all the jobs by undermining each other.

"If you playing in a club and you making, say, one hundred and fifty dollars a night with three pieces—if you got four pieces you making about one hundred and seventy-five—here I come with my band and I sit in on your show. You was kind enough to say, 'We have Smitty here. Let's give him a wonderful round of applause.' Then I say, 'Hey, I have my own band here. Can they come up?' And you say, 'Yeah. Let em come up.' And you, you and your band walk down and you be courteous enough to give me a play on your show.

"Then I come down and go behind your back. Now this is the way it is today in town now. Say, 'Hey, look, what's this man working for? I'll work cheaper.' I didn't even give the proprietor a chance to tell me what you working for. But right away I say, 'I'm gonna work for you cheaper.' Then you gonna say, 'Well, how cheap?' 'I'll do it, man, I'll do it for you for fifteen dollars a man.' 'Well, how many pieces you got?' 'I got four.' Well, maybe you got four.

"Well, quite natural the club owner's gonna go for that, cause they heard me play and I'm sounding pretty good, but I was on your equipment. Now the club owner doesn't know what kind of equipment I have. I may not have anything. You understand? So, I may not have nothing to play on, but yet I come in and undermine you for the job. And this is what it is with the musicians nowadays in time."[48]

Once again the contrast between past and present is vividly portrayed. While it may be human nature to idealize the past, for the blues artists the difference is very real. At the time of this interview, competition for jobs among blues bands was bitter. In the past the pay may have been less, but the blues were more popular among blacks, more clubs hired blues bands, and more musicians could work. You could afford to be friendly. Back then you could promote fellow musicians. Now they are the competition. Eddie Taylor spoke of deceitful musicians:

"And I know a lot of more people, big musicians living right now, because he didn't do anything, he wouldn't say that, but I won't call nobody's name. But people asked him about me and he say, 'No. No. I don't know his phone number.' Well, this— What can I do about it? I don't hate anybody, but I know about it."[49]

Jealousy has been singled out as a major cause of current problems. "You find the average musicians," Byther Smith claimed, "they are jealous. They really are jealous, and this is what really have hurt musicians." Wild Child Butler also saw individual conceit as a destructive factor:

"And I found a lot of jealous-hearted musicians, you know, in Chicago. I imagine that's the reason some of them hasn't got no further. I really saw this and I play— Like there is some gigs I go on I see the guy, 'Well, I want to be last. I'm the biggest star.' You know, I watch this. It's not many blues musician—why they like this?"[50]

Johnny Young also displayed concern with ranking and privilege when he corrected me after I mentioned that I saw him working with the Aces: "They was working with me. I was the star."[51]

The drive to become a musician, positive and attractive traits in the aspiring artist, may after years of frustration turn into negative egotism. Self-promotion can verge on megalomania, and self-confidence can turn to bitterness as other artists appear to get all the breaks.

Keeping a band together demands patience. James Thomas tried to keep a band in Mississippi but got fed up trying to keep everybody happy:

"We—I slacked up in clubs. Mostly peoples, they cut these clubs out in most places like little small places we used to play. Well, they didn't want to pay nothin. When we was playin they didn't want to pay but twenty-five dollars—that's twenty-five dollars have to be divided out between three, maybe four, sometimes. Cause you most have, if you get a good group, you have an extra man to come in and help and if you don't let him play, he goin to be mad with you. Maybe the next time the other man can't go and he be vacant, but he won't go, so you have to go ahead and join with them all. You know, let all of them play some and divide that twenty-five dollars up."[52]

Now a solo act, James Thomas does quite well.

But in Chicago, where a band format is necessary, dissension causes

greater harm. Band leaders steal musicians from other bands, and sidemen look to usurp the leader's position. In the constant scramble, the
leader walks a thin line between maintaining discipline and not offend-
ing his musicians. Otis Rush provides insight into the problems of leadership:

"Like, matter of fact, there's some trouble right now. A bit—nothing
serious. Changing around. But, like, I say anything can happen, and if
you can't get along I get rid of them. I can say, 'Go your way, I'll go
mine.'

"See, you get tired, and then we get back to this award for musicians.
When you say something like that, if you look back over the big, big
bands and all this on down to blues, you might say up to the blues,
there's always a group start out together and they wind up splitting up.
Yeah, music is sort of like divorce.

"You got four or five guys, and you hit off well and start going around
doing a little business, you know, looking pretty good and up—hey, he
want to take the band over! Hey, 'Going to get my own group,' where
everybody want to be a leader, you know? So everybody can't be a leader.
So if you don't pay him what he asks and somebody else say, 'Here's two
dollars more,' he's gone. It's something like Joe Williams, Count Basie, all
on back."

"Everybody wants to be a star," I responded.

"Right," he laughed. "Everybody wants to go to heaven, but nobody
wants to die."

"After so long there's just something happening in the air. And that's
it. So there that particular person, that leader that's [started] all those
guys together. Now this guy, he's got to try to build this thing over again.
Well, there's a lot of musicians out here, but, hey, you know—you try to
pick out the one that you won't have any trouble with. By the time you
got em all together, got right, there he is.

"So you constantly goin backwards and forwards in this kind of thing.
I guess I had ten thousand men play with me, all at different times I
imagine, believe it or not. Earl Hooker was playin guitar for me once—
stayed with me too for six months, that's longer than with anybody in
the world I heard of him playing with."[53]

Despite the consolation of philosophy, the constant turnover detracts
from artistic consistency and leads to ulcers. These personnel problems,
whether rooted in ego or economics, pose the greatest threat to the musician's livelihood and peace of mind.

But through it all—the fights, the accusations, the breakups—musicians continue to rely on each other for local work and spend even more

time together on the road. Travel is part of the bluesman's image and a necessity of working life, and blues artists traveled together, whether walking that lonesome road or riding the band's bus. Today the grind of overseas tours, often as part of festivals or other package deals, continues to throw the musicians back into their own company.

Surrounded by foreign language, foreign food, and unfamiliar customs, musicians stick together, and once back home, they laugh at their overseas scrapes and boast of their ability to handle any situation.

Language, a problem at least offstage, is a source of amusement at home. The competitive blues player loves to show off how he copes with unfamiliar situations and strange tongues. Big Joe Williams, holding court at a festival, rapped with Big Bill Hill and Bob Koester, the owner of Delmark Records:

> X: Man, how do they do? Do they speak English?
> JOE: I talk to them.
> BILL: Do you speak French?
> JOE: Pretty well. Enough to get what I want. They say something. I say, "Oui, oui, oui, oui." [Laughter.]
> BOB KOESTER: You are the biggest liar in Bluesland.[54]

Big Joe spoke with Howling Wolf:

> JOE: I was just coming back from Mexico this time.
> WOLF: That where they talk all that blah, blah, blah?
> JOE: Yeah, man. I met a girl talk like that. I tell her—no sabe. [Laughter.][55]

Hound Dog Taylor told Jim O'Neal of his adventures in Sweden involving foreign language and foreign food:

> "When me and Koko Taylor was in Sweden, she said, 'Don't be surprised, Hound Dog.' I thought she meant something else, you know, but when we walked into the restaurant, man, I'm telling you, all those people stopped. This one old boy had his head bent down and his spoon about halfway between his soup and his head. I told him to go on and eat it, I wasn't going to take it away from you. Pretty soon the waitress came over and I said I wanted eggs and bacon. She didn't know what the hell I was talkin about, and Koko said she didn't think these folks ate eggs and bacon. So I pinched that old waitress on the butt and said, 'Give me some of that!' And that got us thrown out of the restaurant."[56]

Tales of the road also pit the musician against his road manager. In partial reaction to the grueling work schedule encountered overseas, musicians enjoy accounts of rule-breaking and escape. Big Joe Williams entertained Muddy Waters and Howling Wolf:

"On the tour we riding on that bus. I tried to get away, slip away. Lord, I asked this woman, said, 'Gee,' I whispered. I said, 'Come on, honey, let's go way back to [the hotel].' I said, 'Come on, honey. It's a regular party, a party night.' She said, 'What the hell you trying to do?' Said, 'I'm trying to get away from this bus.' So I got away. I done cut out through the rear and we both got lost. So we get a cab and we still got lost. But we got to the party and John Lee Hooker, he came out there too."[57]

Because they travel so often and are forced in effect to spend so much time together, musicians value a good storyteller to liven up the boredom of the road.[58] Their occupational legends provide a behind-the-scenes look at the blues life. But once again stereotype and reality merge as musicians favor topics that closely parallel the bluesman stereotype. For example, Arthur Crudup tells a story about his old partner Sonny Boy Williamson, with whom he and Elmore James formed a blues super-group:

"Sonny Boy would get too advanced. This white woman in Little Rock, she like him, and he was in her house taking it easy. He has his shoes off, and a white man came by. Sonny Boy, he left there running. Me and Elmo was going back home in my old car and we ain't seen Sonny Boy. Elmo was saying, 'Where's Sonny Boy?' And I was saying, 'I don't know.' My radiator was leaking and stopped by a ditch to get a little water. Sonny Boy calls, 'Motherfucker, open the trunk and let me get in!' He was hiding in the ditch there."[59]

Musicians enjoy the scrapes of other bluesmen. The worse, the better. They tell these stories about their peers as a type of irreverent gossip, but such tales also embody their values. Quick wit and the ability to keep your cool in a bad situation are stressed from story to story. Musicians admire those who break conventional taboos and get away with it because of their wit. They may laugh at their colleagues' discomfort, but they respect the improvised escape. Another example of telling stories "on" somebody, more a recollection of in-group gossip than a retelling of a hero legend, was told by Joe Willie Wilkins about Roosevelt Sykes. Here he was speaking to Big Joe Williams as well as to me.

"So we were working this job outside and they got this stage with stone steps up to it and then it drops off. Roosevelt Sykes was there. We were all high. He was dressed in this real nice suit, so he had to go to the bathroom, you know, and he goes to step off the back of the stage, but he don't know how far the ground is on that side, so he's like this and down he falls, over the edge there, and we run over and he laying there in the mud on his back. We say, 'Roosevelt, what you doing down there?' So he's just laying on his back and looks up and says, 'Just relaxing,' but he was hot."[60]

Stories of the road suggest a real musician's life-style that includes liquor, jealous husbands, travel, and keeping cool when things get hot.

Storytelling as a leisure-time activity can also have competitive over-tones as musicians try to outdo one another with accounts of their outrageous behavior. This competitive spirit also carries over into their conversational games, as demonstrated by Howling Wolf, Big Joe Williams, and Muddy Waters at Ann Arbor:

WOLF: Hey, how come you don't make me acquainted with your newcomer?

X: Paul Oscher, this is Wolf.

WOLF: What he do?

JOE: This is a harmonica player.

WOLF: Don't like no harp blowers. Don't like no harp blowers. Who is he? What he do, the other guy?

X: Who's this? Hey listen, this is the [racketeer?] of the whole group. This is the hardworker.

WOLF: I don't like no drummer neither. All I like is a Jew's-harp picker. I don't like no drummer or no harp blower. I likes a Jew's-harp picker.

JOE: I know. I get mad when I play because I know that they can't even hear the guitar.

MUDDY *(to Howling Wolf):* Didn't I tell you about playing my goddamn tunes? Everything was mine out there. Everything but that "Back Door Man."

WOLF: I'm sorry, Brother Mud. Hear what I'm speaking. You have it made. I have a hard time getting my shit.

MUDDY: You don't know where to go.

WOLF: Oh.[61]

JOE: I just missed you. I came to Austin the next night after you left—over at the gas company, out with Lightning. I left out with Lightning and went to Oakland. I got through and flew back.

WOLF: I didn't see you. Now when the Wolf leave a place, he lifts both foots like a rabbit. Nobody can see where he go.[62]

Competition carries into the interview as well. If several musicians are talking about themselves in the same interview, watch out. Blues musicians, like members of other occupational groups, practice the great American pastime of duping the outsider or putting one over on the greenhorn. Keeping in mind that the interview itself is part of the music business, it provides the artist a chance to have fun while he's working.

The musician as jive artist can entertain himself and his friends by bullshitting the interviewer. Jim O'Neal told me how one Chicago artist and his fellow bluesmen played this musician's game in Europe:

"He tells a lot of good information too, but he just likes to have fun. One time he told me he was over in Europe and he was on tour with some other bluesmen, and they all got to lying—all the other people were lying in these interviews—and he thought that was great fun, so he started it too, telling all these tales."[63]

Telling lies for amusement is one way of taking advantage of the interview as a chance to have a good time. Bogus information may be passed off at face value or, in other cases, shown to be a lie and performed as such. In these latter cases, anyone dense enough to accept the information at face value deserves the inconvenience.

Dealing with the critic, the bluesman can draw on the romantic stereotype derived from the content of blues songs and based on the ideal that the bluesman's life mirrors his onstage performance role. But contrast this with the way he acts with fellow blues artists. In a sense, poor Lightning becomes bad Lightning, intent now on impressing his peers with his successful tours, recordings, and trips to Europe.

But the two sides of the bluesman's role can become entangled. The artist may be caught out of character or shifting character, as happened to Bobby Bland in an interview with *DownBeat*'s Ray Townley:

TOWNLEY: Do you consciously program your stage shows to get a certain response?

BLAND: No, it just happens. If the audience makes it happen, then it happens. I don't plan anything, because I don't think this is a good policy. Because it may not work out that way. If the spirit hits you, then let go.

TOWNLEY: I read something about you in a book, *The World of Soul*, by Arnold Shaw. I think you probably read it.

BLAND: Yeah, I read it. There's another book too. What is it? *Urban Blues.*

TOWNLEY: Shaw contends that you have a routine where you'll come on to the audience with certain songs to demonstrate a weakness toward lovers. Do you remember that? Then you'll come on strong with a certain tune that asserts your masculinity.

BLAND: Ha, ha, ha. Okay, all right, all right.

TOWNLEY: Know what I'm talking about?

BLAND: Yeah. Exactly. That's all right. You caught me this time.[64]

The clichés of "it just happens" and "the audience makes it happen" are consistent with the natural musician playing spontaneously from the heart. Note also Bland's awareness of the scholarly literature in which he participated. This is an ideal example of the two dominant roles projected by the working bluesman: the natural musician playing his own soul and the skilled professional manipulating audience response to commercial advantage.

All musicians and other show business personalities, including the bluesman, need to maintain an image not too far at odds with what their fans and supporters expect. But sometimes the artist just gets fed up with the hype and dismisses the stereotype to reveal a union card. Byther Smith prefers the worker image:

"I'm just only playing my music, that I know. I'm just like— It's just like if you would say, well, 'Smitty look, uh, I understand that you are a body and fender man, I'd like to get you to fix my car.' I'm not trying to outfix someone else over there. I'm not trying to outdo no one else over there. I'm only just giving you what I know.

"It's not the idea I'm trying to impress nobody, like a lot of guys will say, 'Man, I'm gonna get up there and play and I'm gonna make that lady over there go for me. I'm gonna make that lady over there see me, you know. I'm gonna make such and such a person hear me, I'm gonna let em know that I'm the best here. I'm gonna let em know that I'm the band leader here.' None of this crosses my mind, it never crosses my mind.

"I feel, like, when I go to work I'm just only going to a job. I'm just going to a job. There's nothing there that I'm going there to impress anyone. It's nothing. I'm just— This is just a job to me. You can come every night of the week if you want to, it's still just only a job."[65]

Unfortunately audiences prefer the competitive display Byther Smith rejects and for that matter do not want him to be just another worker. They want him to live out a life they dream of: romantic, self-indulgent, and adventurous. After all, what's the use of being a star if you have to work just like everybody else?

Despite occasional complaints, most musicians capitalize on their image and work to keep their romantic stock rising. They do not want to be considered average workers, because they're not. They are artists, poets, philosophers, blues doctors, who have worked hard to achieve that role and who won out over other would-be musicians.

Behind the glamour lie the years of hard work and dues-paying, and at times the musician wonders if it was worth it. Still, as the blues go global, new opportunities present themselves: better-paying jobs, more recording options, even more credit where credit is due. And the artists appreciate the opportunities—but, as Jimmy Dawkins testifies, they also remember where the sound came from:

"I appreciate it, especially from the colleges and universities, cause most of the time I go to eight-dollar-a-night taverns. You know—but I'm proud of it. You know, I think the greatest thing that ever happened to me was not being able to hire a band. Myself and Magic Sam, Luther Allison, and Freddy King, we learned how to play because we didn't have the money and couldn't get the money to pay a band. We had to use a bass, drums, and we play the guitar and sing. And this is the greatest thing that could have happened to us. That's where you have to work."[66]

Having graduated from such a tough school, the survivor wears his scars proudly but wants to put the dues behind. Now he feels he's earned something better and hopes that's what the future will bring.

Where, oh, where is Bessie Smith,
With her heart as big as the blues of truth?
Where, oh, where is Mister Jelly Roll,
With his Cadillac and diamond tooth?
Where, oh, where is Papa Handy,
With his blue notes a-dragging from bar to bar?
Where, oh, where is bulletproof Leadbelly,
With his tall tales and 12-string guitar?

—Melvin B. Tolson[1]

9

"Well, that's it, that's my life story"

The public knows the bluesman as a two-dimensional, larger-than-life character. The name bluesman conjures up a shadowy composite image: trickster, hoodoo man,[2] lone wolf, the devil's son-in-law, too lazy and too proud to work for a living. Whiskey and women are the bluesman's stock-in-trade, and he is low down, down home, and down and out.

According to Johnny Shines, the average person associates the bluesman with sex, murder, gambling, and getting drunk. While he overstates the case slightly, his words ring true. But he gives too much credit to the white man as the source of the bluesman stereotype. Black folk culture provides the primary source of the bluesman's reputation, as it does the subjects of his story. Furthermore, the musicians themselves reinforce the stereotype through their song lyrics,[3] their stage act, and in some cases their offstage behavior.

Blues musicians are not passive victims of stereotyping. They also consciously manipulate their own image. From childhood on they have confronted a set of beliefs about their character and work which, as we have seen, affected their lives. For better or for worse, they learned the advantages as well as the disadvantages of their ambivalent role. While musicians may chafe at being typecast, they often share their public's beliefs concerning who they are and what they do. Johnny Shines argues that they have been brainwashed.

But earning the right to play the blues and be recognized as a bluesman demands an ideological commitment and the creation of a public persona. Ralph Ellison described the Kansas City blues shouter Jimmy Rushing as a bluesman who "had to make a choice, had dedicated himself to a mode of expression and a way of life no less righteously than others dedicated themselves to the church."[4]

Taking a blues name like Sunnyland Slim signifies a remaking of the self. The artist experiences an internal transformation represented in his story by acquiring a guitar, running away, or hearing another musician.[5] He also adopts the external trappings of the musician because he admires other musicians and wants to be accepted as a musician himself. Although society pressures the artist to conform, musicians act the way they do because they wish to be recognized as musicians.

Younger artists learn by observing older musicians and imitating their heroes and teachers. Blues critic Albert Murray noted: "Most of the slouching about, the jive talk, the joking and even the nonchalance is as deliberately stylized as is most of the stage business on the bandstand during a performance for a regular audience. Nor are any of the blues musician's role-defining mannerisms, whether on or offstage, likely to be lost on the apprentices."[6]

When Lee Crisp claims that Sleepy John Estes taught him the whole ropes, or Honeyboy Edwards states that Big Joe Williams "learned him the ropes," they allude to a working knowledge of the full range of musicians' traditions, including how to play the part as well as play the music.[7] Once the artist gets the part down, he can become the model for the next generation, not only perpetuating musicians' traditions but reinforcing the public stereotype as well.

Image projection, approached with enthusiasm by younger artists, becomes ingrained and even resented in later life, but it is nevertheless a necessary condition of the blues musician's life. Musicians perpetuate the glamour of their profession even after the joy of music becomes the job of music. They also go beyond patterning their own highly visible act on that of their fellow musicians. They become the ideal. This realization can take the form of a dangerous self-fulfilling prophecy, as noted in the obituary of Chicago bluesman Lee Jackson: "A horrible pattern exists and a stereotype has developed . . . a formula blues life."[8] Here the author, Justin O'Brien, reasonably mourns the loss of a fine musician. But the traditional merging of individual personality and the bluesman character need not be tragic. Other musicians glory in their blues name and embrace a blues life-style because it suits them and they too believe "You have to live the blues to play the blues." Proudly declaring themselves a breed apart—not only from nonmusicians but also from other types of musicians—they capitalize on their reputation and enjoy their notoriety.

Of course, not every artist accepts the notion of a blues life any more than he accepts a blues name or, for that matter, tells his life story. Instead he may try to restrict the blues to a mode of expression, or even a job, from which he can return after the last set is over. But reluctance to play the part makes the job even harder, as Byther Smith attests:

"I've had a couple of clubs that I was playing in that the owner, proprietor of the house, they have gotten rid of me because of my way of performing on the bandstand. You know, I don't have a whole lot of mouth to blah, blah, blah to people, and I'm not cursing over the mike. And when I come down, I don't go to the bar and buy ten or fifteen dollars worth of whiskey or something on credit."[9]

The public expects blues artists to act like bluesmen should, not only in the club but also on the street and even at home.[10] Because of the stylistic features of their art form, blues artists have been singled out for their ability to fuse daily experience and artistic expression. Their off-stage life supposedly supports their onstage act, and their onstage act supposedly carries over to offstage life.

As part of the blues business, the artist's story extends, and to a degree justifies, his onstage act. Public expectation and the competitive nature of trying to make a living playing the blues pressure the artist to validate or authenticate his claim to his overly romanticized role.

Restricted by the interview context and his oral format, unsure of what his audience knows, he seeks points of mutual understanding. Working to a live audience, he limits his account to what he can effectively narrate as well as what his audience can comprehend.[11] In a nonstop, one-shot situation, which generally characterizes the way he tells his story, he selects topics consistent with his role. These may include his favorite episodes—milestones of achievement or stones in his pathway—which, as his most polished beads, are often entertaining as well as informative. Finally, by adding emphasis and drama, he effectively highlights subjects associated with the ideal bluesman character, both as he sees it and as he understands his audience to see it. He creates a version of his life shaped into an effective narrative.[12]

Black folk tradition, popular stereotype, and the lore of the musician's subculture guide him as he selects meaningful details for his story. The recurring questions of the interview, which reflect popular beliefs and make up a frame of reference, also help him shape his account. Awareness of a blues hero, an ideal figure whose life is portrayed in blues songs, provides still another guide. And finally, the blues itself—his artistic system—contributes characteristic content and gives his story its special flavor.

Inverting the conventional view that the artist turns his experience into a song, the artist applies his artistic idiom to the subject of his own life. The language of the blues resonates throughout the musician's story.

When Johnny Shines preaches, "The blues come from right here in America. That is your American music, and if you don't appreciate it, it's just like a child being born don't appreciate his mother,"[13] when Yank Rachel boasts, "I learned it the hard way, out in the country, all by myself—so far back in the woods my breath smelled like cord wood,"[14] or when Wild Child Butler simply complains, "I have paid so many dues,"[15] their words echo blues songs. Drinking white whiskey, running back in the alley, or dancing until the house breaks down—these images from their stories also have parallels in blues songs. Proverbs, such as Otis Rush's statement "Everybody wants to go to heaven, but nobody wants to die,"[16] express values found in the blues, which in turn articulate the values of black folk culture.

But in using the resources of his art form, the bluesman draws on a conservative system with its own appropriate content and characteristic attitudes toward life. Since each artist shares this same general system, and since each is associated with the subjects of their songs, they are tied together through their repertoire.

Because blues songs are sung in the first person, as in "I woke up this morning . . . ," they have often been described as autobiographical. Ralph Ellison's often quoted definition describes the blues as "an autobiographical chronicle of personal catastrophe expressed lyrically."[17] The comparison is misleading because blues is not sung autobiography. Nevertheless, the public generally believes the artist sings about his life and lives the life of his songs, and the artist makes use of this assumption.

Furthermore, he can apply the stylistic techniques of blues performance to his storytelling. Because storyteller and subjects are one and the same, the artist can act out his adventures in his story, as he does in his songs, bringing it to life through the power of his own personality. Combining the musician's feel for rhythm with the bluesman's gift for communicating emotion, he can add an emotional intensity to his narrative which lends it the stylized feeling of the blues.

In a circular fashion the bluesman uses his life to authenticate his art and then turns around and uses his art form to talk about his life as apparently autobiographical songs merge into blues-tinged autobiography. But no matter how stylized the musician's story becomes, it retains its historical dimension.[18]

Blues artists are the oral historians of their own lives as well as of their art form. In fact, they often switch back and forth between themselves in particular and the blues in general. Their story merges into the story of the blues, obscuring distinctions between the individual and the art form. Although a personal or interpretive view of history, their narrative remains an ordered and memorized account of past events.[19] As

Johnny Shines indicates, musicians take their historian role seriously:

"You know, in paying your dues there's many incidents in life you go through, so many changes. And they're all to be recollected because they're all history, and in order to be reckoned with, you don't forget them."[20]

Like their academic counterparts, blues artists are jealous of their knowledge and eager to list their credentials and stress their eyewitness vantage point. Sunnyland Slim, a walking encyclopedia of blues history, compared the veteran's historical perspective to that of a younger "expert":

"And in Chicago I'll say this much, ———— tells a lot, but he wasn't in the class with me and Brother, and Roosevelt. See, he couldn't tell what a man who goes back sixty years could. What Brother or Roosevelt could tell, or Big Bill could tell. You know, that's for sure, what happened in them days."[21]

Sought out as experts, bluesmen defend their own reputation, and at times savage the credibility of their competitors. As noted in the preceding chapter, bluesmen have been known to "put on" the interviewer on occasion. Yet artists like Sunnyland Slim or Johnny Shines or Honeyboy Edwards are serious about setting the record straight. Sunnyland Slim tells the truth about early Chicago blues, shifting from his own story to the general history of the blues:

"Chicago was not the blues. When I come there, I didn't stay because my kind of music wasn't appreciated. Brother could [stay], but most of the musicians wasn't there. They just record and go back to Memphis, like Memphis Minnie. Roosevelt go back to St. Louis or Memphis. Go back to Helena once in a while. Lonnie Johnson go to St. Louis. Bill [Broonzy], he would go to Rosedale.

"But after Mississippi, Alabama, Georgia, Arkansas, Missouri, the colored people wanted to come up there where they be recognized. They could say what they want to people and some of them—a lot of them— had houses. And when they did pull out, the people running them joints, they had a little money. They got in beers and started having more joints [and] blues. And Chicago really got the blues in '38, '39 on up. That's when Chicago really got the blues.

"But before, well, you find Jelly Roll and some of them big bands, big shots, but not nobody like me. We got around here now. But the South was full of it. It's always been blues down there—always will be until the end of time."[22]

Musicians involve themselves personally in the past by concentrating on events they witnessed, using examples drawn from personal experience or, on rare occasion, personalizing something they heard about. Of course, everyone, bluesman included, values a firsthand account. But the bluesman's tendency to place himself on the scene shows a strong correlation to the primary characteristic of his art form, which is to involve himself personally in the subjects of his song through subjective presentation and emotional intensity.[23] Jim O'Neal noted this tendency in regard to deathbed scenes:

"There are all kinds of stories about the death of Little Walter, or Johnny Ace, Sonny Boy, or Elmore, you know, but not many of them were there that actually know. Then you hear stories about so-and-so died in my arms. This happened so many times that there must have been a whole crew of people holding him up."[24]

More often a question of storytelling style than deceitfulness, such deathbed scenes demonstrate the artist's concern for dramatic effect as he adds the emotional intensity of his personal feelings.

Blues singers personalize history perhaps to a fault. Yet they also show a control of the facts that often amazes the interviewer. But just as the blues must be understood primarily as an art form, with its own rules and values, and only secondly used as a historical source, so too the bluesman is a poet first and foremost, whatever the historical value of his words.

The truth in the blues concerns the human condition in the context of the black American experience. The artist's vision of the past often reflects more interest in truth than in facts.

Yet as we have seen in Honeyboy Edwards' story, the facts and the truth, like reality and stereotype, need not be mutually exclusive. Edwards' account of Robert Johnson's death skillfully blends the facts, invested with the authority of his firsthand participation, with the artist's need to find meaning in the past. As artist and observer, he is an adept analyst of human motives, especially those described in blues songs, and adds the blues-like warning to beware of people who smile in your face. While the facts are there for the historian, the artist's concern is with the truth—not only in relation to the event itself, but as a universally applicable lesson.

Musicians do not necessarily personalize all their historical information. They may also use traditional tales or perhaps occupational legends to illustrate the past. Both Bukka White and Wade Walton slip into traditional John tales in order to explain the sharecropping system.[25] Though both were talking about their own lives, no confusion resulted, and they certainly were not intending to deceive their listener. Quite the opposite. They use these standard vehicles to explain history through example to make sure their audience understands what they mean.

As witness and truth-teller, the bluesman blends history and poetry, using tradition to provide examples to illustrate his point and infuse meaning into the cold facts of past events. Similar philosophical and aesthetic values temper his vision of his own past and color the narrative he creates to portray his life.

As author, narrator, subject, and actor, he is free to alter his account as he sees fit. Looking back over his life, he selectively reveals what he now sees as the noteworthy events of a musician's life. Both consciously and unconsciously, the traditions of his art form influence what he includes.

As he translates his experience to narrative, his story becomes more and more a collective enterprise.[26] The shared traditions of the blues ties one musician's story to another's. Blues musicians lead similar lives to the extent that they face similar beliefs growing up, especially in the rural South. Patterning themselves after such blues heroes as Charley Patton or Blind Boy Fuller, they perform in much the same contexts and work and travel with each other. They share common experiences, a common role, and a common artistic system that shape the way they perceive and describe the world around them.

Blues artists share an awareness of what makes an ideal blues life. Through his experience as a storyteller, he learns his audience's preferences by observing their reaction to his tale. His story now fits a blues "mold." His account of his life is determined by himself, blues musicians in general, and the public at large.

Tradition dictates suitable subjects for blues composition and determines suitable subjects for the musician's story. These subjects all describe the reality of the musician's life: homemade guitars, church opposition, the gift of music, a famous teacher, playing suppers or jukes, coping with alcohol, and working in clubs where the atmosphere often turns violent. At one time they may have defined the musician to his community and perhaps to other musicians as well. Now, however, with some variation and distortion, they define the musician to us.

10

"I've had hard luck, but it will change some day"

Champion songwriter Willie Dixon, once the most powerful figure on the Chicago blues scene, spoke at a conference concerned with the poetry of the blues. He stood out even among the notable scholars and musicians assembled for the conference. Having put in more than forty years as a composer, musician, and record producer, he knew the blues business inside out. A major spokesman for the blues in the tradition of W. C. Handy, he now intended to lead a campaign to preserve and promote the blues. With this on his mind, he took the podium, the final speaker of the long day. He began to preach, but he did not speak about the poetry of the blues; he spoke in the poetry of the blues:

"Blues are the facts of life, good and bad, right and wrong. Blues always tell the truth—the blues tell you of the past, the present, and what you hope for the future."[1]

Dixon's statement typifies the way the bluesman approaches defining what he does. Because bluesmen are artists, their definitions tend to be artistic, sharing the language, images, and techniques of blues songs. And because they know the blues as a system they have worked with most of their lives, their definitions are expansive: the blues are about life. Musicians use the blues to define the blues, but they also use it to describe and rationalize their lives. Where the blues—in Dixon's terms—tell of past, present, and future in general, the musician's story tells of his own past, present, and future. This translates coming of age in the rural South working the blues and hoping for some future success. But to understand the bluesman's view of the future, one has to understand his view of the blues, because the two are linked. As the blues go, so goes the blues musician.

For over half a century the bluesman has been asked to explain the blues. Tiresome as the question becomes, it also signals to the artist that he has arrived, that he is recognized as capable of providing a meaningful definition. One could even consider the bluesman's life in relation to a sequence: learning the blues, playing the blues, and explaining the blues. Depending on the artist, time, place, or intentions, definitions vary from straightforward statements to powerful provocative analysis to a list of examples to a prose blues song. Because these definitions may be prepackaged and feel like the same song without the music, they have made scholars uncomfortable.[2] But being artistic statements does not invalidate their meaning; in fact, it does just the opposite. Their definitions reveal more and are even more consistent than those supplied by critics. And because of their artistry they also have more impact.

The critic can only talk in formal terms about twelve-bar, three-chord protest songs, but the blues player generally bypasses formal definitions, perhaps because he knows that the blues takes many different forms. He prefers to focus on what he does or what the blues does. While definitions fall beyond the sequence "I was born—I picked up a guitar, so-and-so taught me," they are still apt to be included in the bluesman's story, if for no other reason than they are answers to predictable questions.

Actually, musicians talk about blues throughout their story: a sound, then a need, a type of work, an artistic system, a feeling, a way to talk about life and a way of life. As the motivating force in their lives, blues provides the meaning to their story; it is what they do, and in this sense it is their life or their life's work.

Musicians talk about the blues and their own lives as if they were one and the same, using their experience to illustrate a point about the blues or using an example from the blues to make a point about their lives. California bluesman J. C. Burris provides an eloquent explanation of the blues, comparing them to himself:

"Blues are more than music. They are a way of telling about life—not everybody's life, just the lives of some people. You make em and sing em from life. They have a history, for sure. They come from the cotton fields and tobacco patches and went somewhere else. Like I did. I wrote a blues called 'The Cost of Living' the other day after a trip to the store. It's my way of saying something to Mr. Reagan. He has got the evening news to tell his side of the story. And I've got the blues."[3]

This onstage rap introduced one of his compositions, and it is as much a part of the performance as the song itself.

The bluesman claims that the blues rises out of true things pulled out of real life, perhaps the composer's own life, perhaps some stranger's life. The personal-experience component, which looms so large in the popular imagination, is outweighed by the inherent truth, common applicability, and effective phrasing of the subject matter. The late Big Chief Ellis claimed:

"You see, blues is a thing that'll never go out of style. See, blues is a living thing. Every blues you hear a person singing, somebody has lived that life, it happened to somebody. That's the reason blues is a living thing. Blues makes you happy sometimes, make you sad sometimes, cause it's a living thing."[4]

Blues is about being broke and hungry and misunderstood because that is life for many in the blueman's audience. The trials he sings about may have also been part of his life, but not necessarily. What is important is that he understands them and empathizes.[5]

Chief Ellis stated that, while he had never really suffered, he understood the blues because he had been misused:

"Some of the best times in my life I spent playing the blues. Actually, I never really suffered in my life. We wasn't rich, but my father always had enough money for food and things, you understand. I never really knew the Depression was on. I've known people who didn't have what I had, but for me to say that I've actually had to suffer, I've never had to suffer one day in my life. I've suffered in that I couldn't get things that I wanted, but I never missed a meal in my life.

"But I know about the blues. I've been misused by many people. This gives you the blues, you know what I mean? Being misused without a cause—you see, if there was a cause it'd be different—but being misused without a cause is the roughest."[6]

The bluesman doesn't need to suffer to sing the blues, but he needs to convince the audience that he knows what he is singing about. The blues artist as truth-teller draws on his awareness of those things most likely encountered by his audience, using personalization as a performance technique.

The statement of shared experience in the stylized language of the blues utilizes intensity of expression for authority. The bluesman must sing and play with deep feeling—or soul—to be successful. On stage, in performance, he enacts the tension and the joy shared by his audience and communicates feeling in sound. Artists are proud of this skill which is derivative of an oral tradition and are quick to criticize people who play without feeling or, as Byther Smith told me, who "don't measure up to the foundation of the blues."

For the beginner, sound was enough, and blues was simply a type of music to be assimilated and performed—something to play and sing so people can have a good time. But the real musicians learn to play with feeling, with soul. And while the sound always remained central, emphasis later shifts to feeling—what the artist feels, but most important, what the audience feels. Johnny Shines explains what the bluesman needs to do:

"You see, you got two different people here—you got a musician and a technician. You have a man here that plays ten or fifteen different instruments. He's not a musician, because you didn't feel a damn thing he did. He didn't tell you anything. All the songs he played, you already knew. You could sing them with him. You knew them all by heart. He didn't tell you anything out of his soul. Nothin, cause he don't have no soul for music.

"I can teach you everything I know as far as the fundamentals of music, but I can't teach you how to feel it. That have to come from God, and if God don't give it to you, baby, I can't give it to you."[7]

The artist as truth-teller expresses the audience's vision of reality through his personality and conviction, much as individuals in church corroborate the validity of a general belief in the Holy Spirit through testimonies of their own experience. Blues concerns are secular, but the bluesman provides testimony in agreement with the audience's beliefs.[8]

A blues singer asks, "Have you ever been mistreated? Then you know just how I feel." And the audience responds affirmatively, sharing a bond of sympathy. He may even interject phrases to bring the audience closer, to engage them in the dialogue: "You know what I mean?" or "Can I get a witness?" The audience responds, "That's right," and encourages him to "tell the truth," "tell it like it is."

The personalization of experience in the blues validates and intensifies the message. Through its reliance on subjective, personalized presentation, the blues presents common experience as idiosyncratic—which means not that songs are never based on personal experience but that they do not *need* to be.

The artist can draw on his own experiences for inspiration, but he is as likely to rely on his observation of community life. Chicago harp blower Wild Child Butler described his method of composition to me one evening over a glass of Pernod in a late-model automobile:

"See, the blues is your best—I found to me, in my life. I've found that the blues is a man's very best friend, anyone's best friend, cause it don't never ask you where you're going, it don't care where you been. And it don't care who you are, and that's the way blues is. That's what I love about it. I just love to sing em. I'll sing em, I love to sing the blues, you know.

"Sometimes I get— I don't have to be just sad and down and out all the time to sing the blues. I just will sing them anyway. It just comes to me to sing em.

"I can look at you too, you know, like that, and I can make a song about that person, but I put myself to it. But I can make a song about it, I can look at it, I can make a song about it. That's the way it is. It's a lot of people, you know. Sometimes I have songs I have wrote, definitely I write the song, maybe an idea. But in a way, to me, sometimes it ain't my idea, cause I look at that person and I see his shape or what he going through with. In a way I done got it from him—if it weren't for him doing it.

"But I can put this together, I feel with it. I can sing about it. But I ain't never been able to figure did he write it, or I'm writing it, cause this didn't come to me till I saw him, you know, like this. So I think both of us do it sometimes. But I don't never know the people's names. But I have watched them on the streets, you know. I've lived in the ghetto. I live in the ghetto now. You know, I come, I watch, I see this."[9]

The bluesman's world of feelings begins with his sensitivity to what is happening to the people in the world around him. He watches people and "feels their considerations." As Fred McDowell claimed, "I don't care who they are, I don't care who they is, I got a feeling for you. I don't like to see anybody misuse nobody."[10]

Although blues present the way it is, there is ample room for the poetic imagination. Archie Edwards provides a thoughtful example of the composition process:

"Well, it is to a certain extent the way life is actually, or the way you might visualize it. Just like when I wrote when the little girl walked down the street, you know, and I wrote that song about, 'Baby, Please Give Me a Break.' Well, it really wasn't, I wasn't worried about anything, but you know older men—I mean I'm not an old man yet—but older men might say about a young girl, might say, 'Baby, please! Give me a break,' because she's looking just the way he would expect a young woman to look.

"Furry Lewis, back in the twenties, he wrote a song called 'Every-body's Blues,' so this is something like an everybody's thing. You might see a good-looking woman coming down the street—you're afraid to say anything to her, but you're gonna say, 'My God, baby, would you please give me a break?' Right? My age and her age, if anything happened between us, she'd have to give me a break, see what I mean?"[11]

The bluesman's skill is keyed to his ability to turn an insight and a phrase into "something like an everybody's thing." Edwards also notes that his song had nothing to do with being worried, but rather derived from coming up with the right phrase that encapsulated his own feeling but was applicable to older men in general. His feeling was true and his phrase was true, and the subject matter was right for the blues. From his perspective, blues combines reality and imagination:

"Some of it is actually everyday living, some of it is the hard times, hardship that people go through, and then again sometimes you just sit down and start imagining things. You might not have ever seen it. That's like when I wrote that song about 'Call my baby long distance cause I want to talk to her so bad, when the operator asked me for my money took every cent I had.'

"Man, I didn't ever do nothing like that, but I was just imagining if I was in that predicament. Like an artist paints a picture, an artist sits down and starts to thinking about certain things, and I might start writing a song about it but I don't experience it.

"Artist will put his on a piece of paper, you put yours through your fingers on the guitar. An artist might draw a picture. Everything they put on the paper is not real, but they can imagine it. And some person comes and looks at it, says, 'My God, that person is—look at that expression!' "[12]

The artist forges his songs from his experience, from the reality he witnesses, and from other blues songs that provide a model of acceptable content and style, but his song should be about appropriate blues subject matter, so the artist must be selective, looking for blues-like situations. And the most agreed-on subject is of course the opposite sex. Eddie Taylor, asked to define the blues, pronounced:

"What's the blues? Blues is a woman. That's the man's side out of me. Now she done did you wrong in some kind of way or you done did her wrong in some kind of way. You know it don't have to be the woman all the time. It could be that you wrong. In other words, you know what I'm trying to say. I mean it's love and a woman."[13]

Chicago disc jockey and TV personality Big Bill Hill has promoted the blues in Chicago for decades. When he spoke of the blues, it was as if he was on stage rather than just lecturing me. As in many blues songs, Bill Hill shifts his attitude from aggressive to sympathetic. What begins as preaching ends in humor created through overstatement:

"Now there's thousands of American people born with no hurt, go to college, big cars, money, a certain allowance. You have no right to dig the blues—unless your woman quit you. A woman make a man sing the blues, especially when you been rich and got broke because your woman left with your friend." (Laughter.)[14]

I have heard similar raps from blues artists who, even when trying to restrict blues to the down and out, eventually allow that anyone can get the blues over a woman. Being hurt in love is the common denominator.[15] Blues is about misunderstanding and being misunderstood, being put down and put out by your lover or partner. John Cephas adds, "Blues is about your feelings, feelings about your girl done you wrong, your job, your hardships."[16] As John Cephas implies through his order, there are simply more blues about "your girl done you wrong or you done her wrong" than subjects like jobs or hardships, though public opinion usually inverts the order. Blues is the truth about real things that happen to people. It is a way of talking about life, but it takes talent and hard work to control the idiom.

Roosevelt Sykes, a true blues veteran with fifty years of seniority stood in the warm sunshine at Ann Arbor. Decked out in rakish straw hat and a light summer suit, he lived up to his name "The Honeydripper." Patiently he explained the blues:

"Well, in the first place, the blues is a talent. Blues is a talent, you can't learn that. Nobody teaches it, there's no schools for it. Nobody can teach it to you. You see, God gives every man a talent—it don't come in schools. It's just something you born with—can't nobody give it. You have it, you can't buy it, you can't give it away. You got it, so it's something you born with. Blues is a part of a man. It's the way he feels.

"Now, some people don't understand. They think a blues player have to be worried, troubled, to sing the blues. That's wrong. It's a talent. If every man with a worry could play the blues, why—another guy worried to death and he can't sing a tune. You ask him to sing the blues, he says he can't sing it.

"You have to work hard. It will come to you. It's there for you. Lots of folks got talent; they don't even use it, but do it better sleeping than another fellow could do it woke.

"So blues is a sort of thing on people like the doctor. I'll put it this way. There's a doctor, he has medicine, he's never sick, he ain't sick, but he make the stuff for the sick people. See, you wouldn't say, 'Call the doctor.' 'I'm the doctor.' 'Oh, you're a sick man?' 'No. I just work on the sick people.'

"So the blues player, he ain't worried and bothered, but he got something for the worried people. Doctor, you can see his medicine, he can see his patient. Blues, you can't see the music, you can't see the patient cause it's soul. So I works on the soul and the doctor works on the body. Both are important, they all mixed to one. Two makes one."[17]

What rings so true in his exposition? Is it the authority of his fifty years of experience? His clarifying analogy? Or in retrospect was it the sound of conviction in his voice? Rejecting the simplistic notion that all one needs to sing the blues is a worried mind, he locates the blues where it should be· as an art form and a professional skill that involve reaching out to touch the people. His blues provides invisible medicine for the soul. It is a healing force that the good blues doctor uses to cure the disease. Blues is a talent, an art form; it is what Roosevelt Sykes does, it is his life.

After so many years of working with the blues system, the musician finds the blues to be a way of observing, organizing, and understanding the world, as well as describing it. The artist takes in the world around so that it makes sense in relation to the blues—he filters the world through a blues aesthetic. Turning his poetic vision inward, he looks at events in his life, he remembers homemade guitars, he feels a musical gift, he sees violence around him, and he teases the boundary where the real and the ideal overlap, recreating the past and shaping the present. But looking to the future, the musician turns philosophical—as he does in explaining the blues. Facing what is ahead, he speaks of his hopes and fears, using the blues as a sustaining artistic and philosophical reference. In looking ahead, we see the bluesman doing for himself what he gets paid to do for others. To extend Roosevelt Sykes' analogy, he enacts the proverb "Physician, heal thyself."

The bluesman faces the future ambivalently. It is a source of anxiety and a space for dreams. The future remains a mystery, but the traditional perspective of the blues provides a heritage of facing the future with strength, determination, and an ability to make do. The artists see themselves getting older and note the passing of their peers and partners. But younger artists carry on and keep the blues going. In Chicago, sons of blues players play blues. Tradition is maintained.

There are other good signs too, such as an apparent resurgence of interest in the blues. Of course, a few top acts will reap most of the benefits, but something may trickle through to help the working musician. However, there can be little appreciable financial gain in the face of accelerating economic troubles, and there is no security. But this factor is not new to the blues musician, whose art makes few references to security.

Confronting the future, the blues musician blends his survivor's self-confidence with honest self-appraisal and a cynicism born of experience. The blues complain as fact. Wild Child Butler claimed:

"I been got and I have paid so many dues. I really did that. I don't know when they'll stop. I'm still paying them. I don't know what's gonna come of it. I want to do it before I get too old. You know, I'm getting older, I'm not getting any younger."[18]

Wild Child echoed the blues message to keep holding on: "So that's the way it is. But I still keep on singing the blues. I'll be singing the blues anyway. I have had hard luck, but it will change some day."[19] This phrase has countless parallels in blues songs. If you don't let the bad luck crush you, your luck will change some day. The sun's gonna shine in my back-door some day, the wind gonna rise and blow my blues away.

The blues is less a complaint than a contract with honesty. Otis Rush knows he cannot change the world, he cannot make everybody love him and he cannot stop them from talking about him:

"There's a spotlight on you up there on the stage. People goin to talk about it. They're gonna talk about you anyway, whether you up there or down here. But, being a musician, I'm in the spotlight all the time—like, the spotlight is on me. Like I say, a lot of people like us, a lot of people don't. So that's what makes the world go round. I got friends, I got some that doesn't like me."[20]

Lee Crisp also accepted the fact that people are going to talk. To him the most important thing is what you make of yourself. It is your responsibility to hold yourself up:

"A man can make what he wants out of himself. That's the way I was taught. It's not the musician that makes a man bad. But if he's bad, he's just bad, and there's no more harm in playing music than in cutting a tree down.

"You see, it's just like drinking. You can drink too much and do anything, and just run it out. You don't have to throw yourself away because people say you ain't nothin, you just, you suppose to be something, yourself. You hold yourself up regardless of what the people say. And I always did feel that way.

"My grandmother, when I was coming up said, 'Lee, always hold yourself up no matter what anybody say. Hold your head high, you die hard.' So that's the way I do. I don't care what nobody say. I know what I am. And anybody should be the same way. You be here, you're acting human, you act civilized. They talked about Christ as they gonna talk about you."[21]

Lee Crisp expressed the values of self-definition and self-evaluation which he inherited from his grandmother: accept yourself and hold your head high. In a statement of hard times totally devoid of self-pity, John Jackson also preaches self-acceptance:

"I'll tell you, there was no one was raised up that had no rougher time than I've had. But I really don't like to talk about it. Cause whole lots of times if you talk—I've always had a feeling I'm talking to make people feel sorry for you, or sad, or trying to say that somebody's mistreated you. I really appreciate the way I was raised, cause if I wasn't, I wouldn't have the chance I have today, or the kind of understanding that I have. I really appreciate the way I was being raised by my family and by my self-experience. There's no way in the world I would have learned what I know, if I hadn't had this real hard drag-out time."[22]

Though the musician has pride in his art form and in himself, he is aware that there are many who scorn his life's work. Black ethnic rejection almost overwhelmed the artist in the 1960s. But in the same militant rejection of the blues were sown the seeds of a new and lasting relation between the artist and the community.[23]

The musicians appreciate the renewed respect for their work. But the blues player knows he kept the faith when others mocked him for it. For a time it seemed as if he were crying in the wilderness sustained by his belief in himself alone. Archie Edwards would not put the blues aside because he realized their value:

"The greatest feeling that I have had in my life is to be able to sit and tell people that I did it myself. And it's looking so good now, so if I don't make a dime I still think I've got a lot out of it. Cause it's good to be able to say that all down through life the things that I believed in and what I did is beginning to come back to the front again, you know. It brings you up. I feel mighty good about being able to play the guitar.

"Many people used to say, 'Why don't you play jazz guitar? Why don't you do this? Why don't you go to school to study, you know, get into the deep stuff?' I say, 'Oh no. This is deep enough. This is actually deeper than you think.'

"See, most people don't know actually how deep blues is, and once you know how to do it yourself, you'll know how deep it is, because it's the next thing to a spiritual. A good spiritual, it puts you right in the deepest part of religion. One day it's gonna be a big boom, and who's gonna be there? Me."[24]

Archie's work has been worth it. His own sense of accomplishment, of pride in himself, is adequate reward for the effort. But he also senses a swing that will bring him even greater rewards and will vindicate his belief in the blues. His statement is a testimonial to the blues as well as a reaffirmation of his own dedication. He knew all along how valuable the blues were, and maybe now others will come to understand. Archie's statement keys on self-determination, holding fast to values, and, in a sense, waiting out the opposition. Roosevelt Sykes:

"Blues players feel as though only a few people like the blues. More people likes the blues than they thought. Lot of people wouldn't admit it. But we kept pluggin away. Like myself, I just kept pluggin away."[25]

Sykes' collective "we" connects the blues players who endured the tough times. Now, as a respected patriarch, his confidence and industry inspire others. Joe Willie Wilkins, in a prose blues, echoes Sykes' philosophy. Determination and hope transcend the agonizing moments of self-doubt and despair:

"So I'm gonna keep on trying to play, and maybe one day something liable to happen to me. Thing about it, I work hard in my life on the guitar, you know. I'm not gonna stop playing the guitar. Sometimes I get in a place that you think you done worked all your life hard. And then sometimes you feel as you're throwed away in a corner alone, by yourself or something, you know. But as Sykes once said, 'Well, things gonna clear up. Work hard.' "[26]

Roosevelt Sykes' advice is the basis of the blues: "Keep on keeping on, and your luck is bound to change some day." Eddie Taylor said, "You got to just keep doing right and if you gonna get it, you gonna get, and if you ain't, you ain't. That's all I can say on that. You know, that's the way I feel. Keep doing right and somebody will get you."[27] His fatalism is couched in his belief in the necessity to keep on doing right.

Honeyboy Edwards keeps on:

"There's lots of guys around ain't never recorded, never done nothin. They holler and go on. See, I lay dead long time after I got them breaks like I did. I never give up guitar-playing, I never have give it up because I know somethin sometimes will come by, I believe."[28]

Byther Smith assessed his career as a musician without bitterness but looks to the future for the lucky break that will bring recognition and reward:

"I really got into it at that particular time, and up until now I haven't found no faults about it. I love it. So I feel like I would like to keep going a little further, I just haven't got that lucky. I really haven't got the lucky breaks like a lot of guys. So I will, I'm just waiting on, just— I wish I— Inside of me, I do feel that I'm going to get one lucky break."[29]

The bluesman has reason to complain. With the burden of negative stereotypes, constant rip-offs, racism, and almost no media exposure, the dues-paying never stops. If ever a group could blame others for failure— inept record producers, crooked agents, fellow musicians who forget their phone numbers—the bluesmen could.

The potential for paranoia is great, yet most artists accept the responsibility for their lives. It may be a question of being in the wrong place at the wrong time, being with the wrong people, or, like Honeyboy Edwards, moving too fast. As Eddie Taylor put it, "Well, I had some good breaks, I messed them up myself. Used to have a temper, you know. You want the truth, you don't want no lying."[30] Individuals may have helped him or held him back during his life, but in the final analysis his life is his own and he accepts the blame and the credit.

Determination, hard work, and talent have carried the musician up to now. It is, however, not enough in itself. One needs a break, a lucky break, to reach that elusive goal of being a star. He waits for a break that may never come, working and hoping the work will pay off. He will not give up although bad luck follows him or, as Wild Child Butler said, "Or I'm following it. I don't know which one it is. So I guess one day things will change, but I ain't giving up. I'm not about to give it up."[31]

Without tangible reward, without recognition, the artist wrestles with self-doubt, and because he is going nowhere or getting robbed, he may quit. But as in Johnny Young's case, the talent is still there nagging him, pushing him back to the blues.

Chief Ellis quit because of disgust with the rip-offs, but then came back. He could do this because he kept "the feeling":

"You never lose the feeling. Once you've ever loved the blues and played them, you'll never lose the feeling. You may lose the touch, but you'll never lose the feeling. If it wasn't for the feeling, I would never have been able to come back playing. I'm like the Dixie hummingbird, I'll never leave the blues."[32]

The artist renews his pledge. Wild Child Butler contributed his oath: "You know the blues is all I know. I'm gonna always play them anyway. I don't care. Till the day I die. I always love the blues. I just love em."[33]

J. T. Adams can no longer play with the command that he demands of himself. His complaint verges on the pathetic, but stops short:

"I got to the place where I don't know what's happening to me. My fingers are numb. Hear those joints pop? I know I got arthritis. I don't know what other thing I got though. I imagine it's mostly arthritis. I quit playing with Ray and them last year. I got to the place where I couldn't execute, you know. I just give it up—but I keep on messin with it.

". . . My hands are just plumb numb. I used to play the shit out of Blind Lemon, but it looks like I won't play any more. I'm just hitting at it. But I'm better at times than others. I picked it up the other day and I said, 'I believe it's coming back to me.' "[34]

The mix of honest, even brutal, self-appraisal offset by guarded optimism tunes J. T. Adams' comments into the blues worldview. The unwillingness to concede to self-pity, to despair, is a blues value he applies to his own life.

The blues says, "You might be beautiful, but you got to die some day." Recently James Thomas, who was a gravedigger and who sculpts skulls from clay, became incensed when a religious zealot lectured him that he was getting older and had to die some day. James Thomas was indignant. "Tell me something I don't know,"[35] he said.

But the blues artist can pass his music along and in this way keep his memory alive. Archie Edwards referred to this practice in relation to his role as blues teacher:

"I'm trying to keep the blues—what you call black heritage—I'm trying to keep it rolling. Yeah, and it doesn't matter who I teach it to, cause Mississippi John Hurt asked me, he said, 'Brother Arch,' he said, 'Whatever you do, teach my music to other people.' He said, 'Don't make no difference what color they are, teach it to them.' He said, 'Because I don't want to die and you don't want to die. Teach them your music and teach them my music.' "[36]

The artists keep the blues alive, and because they have put so much of themselves into it, a little bit of them keeps on living. John Cephas adds:

"And you know they're so good to hear. So this is our effort to keep the blues alive. I can play some upbeat stuff, I can sing it, but I would rather do this to let the people know what the black man's culture is, what his heritage is. This is what the old folks was all about as far as the music was concerned."[37]

Yet John Cephas' music, which he performs with a talented young harmonica player, Phil Wiggens, is not revivalist. He combines songs he learned as a young man from 78 rpm records with more progressive rhythm and blues standards, and he sings in a sophisticated soulful style.

His music reflects the future as much as the past, a future that draws its strength from tradition.

Accepting the past, acknowledging his debt to the artists he learned from, the bluesman pays tribute to his predecessors by calling their names in performance or playing their songs. Yet the blues is today's music and the future's music because, as John Cephas says, they are so good to hear, and as his mentor Chief Ellis claimed, because they are "a living thing."

Since the turn of the century the blues have helped people make it and have given the community something of their own at house parties or in taverns. And if some people do not appreciate what the musician does, at least the artist should:

"A lot of people don't know what musicians have to go through with, you know. A lot of folks, when they say, a musician, 'Aw, he ain't no good.' Musicians don't know why they do it, cause I wonder what the world would be like if they didn't have no sounds of music. No sounds at all. Hey, what would happen? Go crazy, wouldn't it?"[38]

Most blues artists would agree with Otis Rush that what they do has value, and even if it does not keep the world from going crazy, perhaps they keep it a little saner, a little more human. The blues help fight despair by providing hope, but not through a Hollywood happy ending. This would destroy their credibility. The blues presents an honest view of life and, although poetic, avoids the sentimental. The blues is realistic and cynical, and the blues artist is likewise. In blues songs there is a guarded hope that some things can get better. The balance between honest appraisal and hope for a positive change partially determines the ambivalence of the form.

The blues artist, in assessing his life, also has recourse to falling back on this central feature of the blues worldview. He too must maintain a delicate balance between self-appraisal and self-assurance. The determination to succeed, and even the deep inner awareness of one's artistic gifts, are so often removed from the reality of current circumstances. But the blues has always worked as a vehicle to initiate self-confrontation.

Wild Child Butler considered his chances of future success in Chicago in a blues-inflected narrative:

"I moved here, working round here, and I come to know the people. And I found it out then didn't nobody— It was tough when nobody work together. They tell me this, you know, I still would use them on my session, but every time they do a session I found out, well, the man say he wanted *his* artists on this session, you know. I wasn't good enough. So

I realized, it come to me then, I just wasn't good enough to play on Chicago musician's session. That's why I don't call myself a Chicago blues musician.

"I'm from the lowland, the swamp. I'm from where the blues came from, and that's where I'm going before it ends up and something happens to me. I'm going back to the lowlands—that's where the blues came from right off, that old country farm.

"But I'm going to—when I get back—I'm anxious to build me a house back, way back out, you know, on them plantation farms, cause we buying down there now, on them plantations. They selling, you know, parcels. That's where I always want to live. I'm not too crazy about the city. I like to come to the city and have fun and do around and head back, you know, head back to the lowlands.

"But one thing about the lowlands, you don't have to have a lot of money. You can always stay, stick. But you have to have money in the city. But in the lowlands, you can make it. That's what I like about it. You can always stay back in there and make it. You know, in a way, I guess I knows how to live in there because I was born in there."[39]

Going back down home is a goal of many blues players. For Wild Child, the rural South, the lowlands, the swamp, offers the security lacking in Chicago. His image extends from himself to the blues, returning to where it was born.

Self-determination, inner conviction, and the support of other musicians keep the artist going. But after all these years in the blues business and nothing to show for it, the despair sometimes shows. Johnny Young's passionate plea for a home falls like a collective weight on his country, which did not notice him until he was gone. But meanwhile the bluesman uses the blues to fight despair and hopes the future will bring some reassurance that their lives were not in vain. And all this before the funeral. But folk wisdom admonishes us to do our crying for the living.

There is a sense of resignation inherent in the blues—not a giving up, but rather an acceptance of human nature steeped in wisdom derived from observation. The blues artist is a realist with little faith in the perfectibility of man, or woman. He has observed the ways of the world, the way people will do you. However, he is not immune to being deceived and is capable of being hurt by the betrayal of friends and loved ones. Back in the 1940s John Work wrote: "The blues singer has no interest in heaven and not much hope on earth; a thoroughly disillusioned individual."[40]

As usual, the singer is linked with the protagonist in the blues songs. But even if disillusioned, the bluesman keeps on keeping on, scarred but undefeated by life's setbacks. The blues teaches the artist—and us—that we can never get beyond our capacity for being hurt because it is in the nature of living.

In the blues, emphasis is on surviving, living within conditions, making the best of situations as they occur. Less concerned with shaping events than with being able to respond to them, to improvise, and make do, the blues deals with knowing the world more than with changing it. The world it portrays is to be survived, not remade. But the blues focuses down into the community, into the daily lives of the audience, and touches on human concerns of immediate interest.

The blues serve to remind us that the fracas tearing us apart is only the most current in a sequence of continual changes. Live through it, it will happen again. The life portrayed in blues really describes no ending, happy or otherwise, but speaks rather of change, generation, and flux. Even death is generally balanced by the active movements of the living. The blues celebrates life-affirming sexual love in a direct or playful manner and leaves the celebration of death to the church or to the ballad tradition.

Within the system of blues poetry, "I woke up this morning" introduces a blues song and "So long baby, sorry I got to go" takes it out. But another image, "Moon going down, sun begins to rise," better represents the form. In the old folktale, Brother Rabbit stated, "This is life. Some go up and some go down." The blues inherited this traditional wisdom and complained, "I been down so long," but then affirms, "But I won't be down always." The values enunciated in the blues are supportive and life-affirming. Though the world presented in the blues is unstable and security is transitory, the blues teaches a resiliency and toughness of spirit very much applicable to the present. Contrary to the interpretations of scholars early in this century, the blues are not expressions of self-pity; rather, they teach us how to transcend despair and how to enjoy our existential victories. It's important that we learn from the blues—from those courageous men and women who perform them—the lessons we are able to grasp.

The ranks of the bluesman are being depleted. The deaths of so many members of the blues community do not mean the death of the blues. The blues continues as an art form regardless of its status as a philosophical system or a survival ritual, and the blues will continue to change even as it is perpetuated. Blues may move to the suburbs, beyond the critical influence of its co-ethnic audience, but the blues artists will continue to enforce their own standards of excellence. Young, white imitators, as notable for their sincerity as their inability to achieve deep expression, make us more aware of the talent of these important folk artists—the true bluesman. Those artists whose statements you have read in this work and who are now dead include Howling Wolf, Joe Willie Wilkins, Big Chief Ellis, Fred McDowell, Hound Dog Taylor, Big Bill Hill, Big Joe Williams, Jimmy Reed, Arthur Crudup, Johnny Young, Roosevelt Sykes, and Sam Chatmon. J. B. Lenoir's memorable admonition "You're gonna miss me when I'm gone" applies to each.

The passing of so many of the older musicians adds a sense of poignancy to the narratives inconsistent with the tough, unsentimental image of the bluesman, a sense of wistfulness coupled with the realism and fatalism inherent in the blues. The bluesman's art demands a frank confrontation with the real world and a transformation of sorrow into new determination through the use of irony and humor. Sam Chatmon, who had seen several generations of blues artists come and go, exemplified this talent:

"A lady from California told me about Bob Jefferies was dead. A man who plays with me every time that I go out there. I know when I go I'll sure miss him. But I told him, everybody got to go now. But I ain't going to draft myself. The Lord got to do the drafting. I ain't gonna volunteer."[41]

The blues as an art form has been declared dead so many times that its artists no longer bother to deny the rumor. The coffin lid has never been nailed down, nor does it appear likely in the immediate future that it will be. Blues artists have realistically accepted the changes in the popularity of their music, but they do not accept its death. Like Sam Chatmon, the blues will wait for the Lord to do the drafting. It's not gonna volunteer.

Notes

Chapter 1: Johnny Young's story

1. See Pete Welding, "Johnny Young" (1965), in *Nothing But the Blues*, ed. Mike Leadbitter (New York: Oak Publications, 1971), pp. 76–77, and the obituary notice, "Johnny Young," in *Living Blues*, no. 17 (Summer 1974), by Jim O'Neal with Bob Reidy and Barry Pearson, pp. 6–7.

2. He recorded for Bernard Abrahams, Ora-Nelle label, Ora-Nelle 712.

3. Mike Leadbitter and Neil Slaven, *Blues Records: 1943–1966* (New York: Oak Publications, 1968), pp. 367–68.

4. Sam Lay had previously worked with the Paul Butterfield Blues Band as a drummer. Following his stint with this extremely popular group—their record sales were phenomenal for a blues band —Sam Lay put together a band that played around the Chicago area.

5. Actually, Eddie Taylor claims credit for the so-called Jimmy Reed sound: "It's my sound. I learned it on the guitar down in Leland, Mississippi. That's my sound."

6. The common broom served many functions in black folk culture. It provided materials for homemade guitars and could be used as a rhythm instrument. Playing techniques included pounding it against the floor, using a sweeping motion, as Johnny Young describes, scraping the wooden handle against the floor, drawing the handle over or between one's fingers, and whatever other methods a creative individual could improvise. See W. C. Handy, *W. C. Handy: Father of the Blues* (New York: Collier Books, 1941), p. 16; and William Broonzy and Yannick Bruynoghe, *Big Bill Blues* (New York: Oak Publications, 1964), p. 34.

7. "Sonny Boy" John Lee Williamson, born in Tennessee around 1912, was a popular performer and recording artist in Chicago until he was murdered in 1948. Another artist, Rice Miller, also used the name Sonny Boy Williamson, creating some confusion and at times even a little heat.

8. "Johnny Young," obituary notice in *Living Blues*.

Chapter 2: David "Honeyboy" Edwards' story

1. Pete Welding, "David Honeyboy Edwards," in *Nothing But the Blues*, ed. Mike Leadbitter (New York: Oak Publications, 1971), pp. 132–40.

2. See also "David Honeyboy Edwards," *Living Blues* 1, no. 4 (Winter 1970–71): 19–24.

3. Seeburg refers to a brand of jukebox (the word "juke," probably of African origin, deriving from "juke" or "jook" as in "jook house" or "jook joint"). Another traveling bluesman who contributes to this book, Joe Willie Wilkins, was at one time referred to as "the walking Seeburg."

4. A version of this legend can be found in the above-mentioned Welding interview. While the information is essentially the same, the account, narrated roughly ten years earlier, is much more tentative and far less dramatic. As far as I can determine from the printed text, it's as if he hadn't told the story very often at that point and so is less sure of himself.

5. Patton recorded for Paramount. For more information, see John Fahey, *Charley Patton* (London: Studio Vista, 1970).

6. For more on Tommy Johnson and his music, see David Evans, *Tommy Johnson* (London: Studio Vista, 1971).

7. Big Joe Williams, a Delta artist who also contributed to this book, should not be confused with the blues and jazz vocalist of the same name.

8. Rice Miller, also called Sonny Boy number 2.

9. "Jewtown" refers to the Maxwell Street Market recently portrayed in the film "The Blues Brothers."

Chapter 3: "You know what you're going to get now? Interviews!"

1. W. C. Handy was the first black ethnic blues spokesman and for a while could be considered the single most important source of information on the blues. Scholars and critics alike sought out his expertise. In 1923, for example, folksong collector Dorothy Scarborough wrote, "Negroes and white people in the South referred me to W. C. Handy." Handy's reputation continued unabated, and in 1925 Carl Van Vechten could reassure his readers, "Nevertheless, Mr. Handy himself has informed me categorically that the blues are folksongs." See Dorothy Scarborough, "The Blues as Folksong," in *Coffee in the Gourd* (Austin: Texas Folklore Society, 1923), pp. 52–66; Carl Van Vechten, "The Black Blues: Negro Songs of Disappointment in Love—Their Pathos Hardened with Laughter," *Vanity Fair*, August 1925, p. 57; and Handy's own work, *W. C. Handy: Father of the Blues*, ed. Arna Bontemps (New York: Macmillan Co., 1941).

2. Leadbelly told his tale to John and Alan Lomax, Jelly Roll Morton to Alan Lomax, and Big Bill Broonzy wrote his to Yannick Bruynoghe. Other musicians from Mezz Mezzerow to Ray Charles have published autobiographies in collaboration with professional writers. On the other hand, blues recording pioneer Perry Bradford wrote his own autobiography, as did Johnny Shines, who has yet to find a publisher. See John and Alan Lomax, *Negro Folksongs as Sung by Leadbelly* (New York: Macmillan Co., 1936); Alan Lomax, *Mister Jelly Roll* (Berkeley: University of California Press, 1973; reprint of 1950 ed.); William Broonzy and Yannick Bruynoghe, *Big Bill Blues* (New York: Oak Publications, 1964); and Perry Bradford, *Born with the Blues* (New York: Oak Publications, 1965).

3. Several of the better books are Paul Oliver, *Conversations with the Blues* (London: Cassell & Co., 1965); Mike Leadbitter, ed., *Nothing But the Blues*, (New York: Oak Publications, 1971); George Mitchell, *Blow My Blues Away* (Baton Rouge: Louisiana State University Press, 1971); Robert Neff and Anthony Connor, *Blues* (Boston: David Godine, 1975); Mike Rowe, *Chicago Breakdown* (London: Eddison Press, 1973); Arnold Shaw, *Honkers and Shouters* (New York: Macmillan Co., 1978); Peter Guralnick, *Feel Like Going Home* (New York: Fusion Books, 1971); and Peter Guralnick, *Lost Highway* (Boston: David Godine, 1979); *From Blues to Pop: The Autobiography of Leonard "Baby Doo" Caston*, ed. Jeff Titon, John Edwards Memorial Foundation Special Series, no. 4 (Los Angeles: JEMF, 1974); James Rooney, *Bossmen: Bill Monroe and Muddy Waters* (New York: Dial Press, 1971); Robert Palmer, *Deep Blues* (New York: Viking Press, 1981); David Evans, *Big Road Blues: Tradition and Creativity in the Folk Blues* (Berkeley: University of California Press, 1982); and William Ferris, *Blues from the Delta* (Garden City, N.Y.: Anchor Press, 1978). Various magazines publish interviews, including *Rolling Stone*, *Coda*, *Cadence*, and *DownBeat*. The best of these are the British *Blues Unlimited* and the Chicago-based periodical *Living Blues*.

4. Noted storytellers include Lightning Hopkins, Jimmy Rushing, Fred McDowell, Sonny Boy Williamson, and Big Joe Williams. Several folktales have been collected from Mississippi John Hurt, John Jackson, and James Thomas. See Bruce Jackson, "Stagolee Stories: A Bad Man Goes Gentle," *Southern Folklore Quarterly* 29, no. 2 (June 1965): 188–94; Chuck Perdue, "I Swear to God It's the Truth If I Ever Told It," *Keystone Folklore Quarterly* 14, no. 1 (Spring 1969): 1–56; William Ferris, *Blues from the Delta* (London: Studio Vista, 1970). For songs collected from a tale-teller, see Richard M. Dorson, "Negro Folksongs in Michigan from the Repertoire of J. D. Suggs," *Folklore and Folk Music Archives* 9, no. 1 (Fall 1966): 5.

5. I use the term "bluesman" not to imply any sexist prejudice but because it accurately describes the contributors, with the exception of Big Mama Thornton. "Bluesman" as used by such scholars as Sterling Brown and by the musicians themselves is the accepted term for a special group of black American musicians. Despite the impact of the classic blueswoman—Ida Cox, Sippie Wallace, Alberta Hunter, Ma Rainey, and Bessie Smith—specializing in blues has generally been a male activity both before and after the classic period. Talented female vocalists usually transcended the form to work more lucrative jobs as pop singers or jazz vocalists. Those who continued with the blues—Memphis Minnie, Koko Taylor, or Big Mama Thornton—closely parallel the male artists in terms of performance style and to some degree life-style.

6. The blues revival, like the folk revival, refers to the presentation of ethnic or traditional song and music to a nontraditional, often urban audience. For the blues, it means simply presenting the blues to a large white audience. According to Bob Groom, "The blues revival was essentially the discovery of blues by a large and appreciative white audience." See Bob Groom, *The Blues Revival* (London: Studio Vista, 1971), p. 6.

7. Initially I chose to use the term "life story" not as a rigid folkloric genre (if such a beast actually exists) but because it is common coin familiar to the public and the media. Furthermore, most artists could relate to it and used it themselves as in "my story" or "that's my life story." But today, folklorists and social scientists who use the term "life story" generally refer to an extensive document garnered over the course of numerous interviews and then pieced

together in a printed version. However, the subjects of this book work from a different perspective—which is not to say that they could not produce such lengthy documents (Byther Smith's story runs roughly seventy pages). What they tell is something that is focused and practiced, a consciously limited story that sticks with their bluesman role. They have not been asked about all their lives, nor are they expected to go into detail about nonmusical experiences they consider irrelevant to the reason they are being interviewed. For this reason I have decided to deemphasize "life" story and simply refer to the accounts as the bluesman's story. Other terms such as oral autobiography, oral self-portrait, or autobiographical account work as well.

8. Parallels to blues composition by subject matter, or where verses are linked together by subject as opposed to chronology, immediately come to mind.

9. Otis Rush, Wise Fools, Chicago, Illinois, December 1973.

10. Although Rush did an extensive interview (actually several interviews) for *Living Blues*, editor Jim O'Neal noted: "In his guarded conversation there is apparently little room for fond reminiscence, details of his career, anecdotes of himself or fellow musicians, or even explanations of his music." How unlike Johnny Young or Honeyboy Edwards. Jim O'Neal, Amy O'Neal, Dick Shurman, "Otis Rush," *Living Blues*, no. 28 (July–August 1976): 10.

11. Jimmy Dawkins, Ann Arbor Blues Festival, Ann Arbor, Michigan, August 1969.

12. Harmonica Frank Floyd, Bicentennial Smithsonian Folklife Festival, The Mall, Washington, D.C., September 1976. He refers to Greil Marcus, *Mystery Train: Images of America in Rock and Roll* (New York: E. P. Dutton, 1976).

13. John Cephas, The Cellar Door, Washington, D.C., November 1981

14. Jim O'Neal, at his home, Chicago, Illinois, August 8, 1974.

15. Cephas, 1981.

16. O'Neal, 1974.

17. Fred McDowell, Ann Arbor Blues Festival, Ann Arbor, Michigan, August 1, 1969.

18. Hoyle Osborne, "I Been Headed Up Ever Since," *Sing Out* 19, no. 2 (July–August 1969): 19.

19. Archie Edwards, at his barbershop, Washington, D.C., June 1978.

20. Edwards, University of Maryland, College Park, Maryland, December 1980.

21. Edwards, Martin Luther King Library, Washington, D.C., February 1981.

22. Edwards, University of Maryland, February 1981.

23. Harriet Ottenheimer addresses the issue of variation in her analysis of several versions of the life story of the New Orleans bluesman Cousin Joe, concluding: "Tellers of life stories probably vary their narratives as much as tellers of folktales—different audiences, different times, different dreams and even different selves. Perhaps we should be surprised not by variants in personal narratives but by consistency." While she overstates the case somewhat, musicians can present different versions of their lives or of a single experience— as bluesman or as gospel singer for instance. However, most bluesmen stick with relatively set narratives once they have developed them. Harriet Ottenheimer, "The Second Time Around: Versions and Variants in the Life Story Narrative of Cousin Joe, a New Orleans Blues Singer," *Louisiana Folklore Miscellany* 5, no. 2 (1982): 10.

24. Eddie Taylor, Northeastern University, Skokie, Illinois, December 1974.

25. John Dollard, *Criteria for the Life History with Analysis of Six Notable Documents* (New York: Peter Smith, 1949), p. 7.

Chapter 4: "I'm gonna get me a guitar if it's the last thing I do"

1. The large number of juniors shows an interesting aspect of the blues tradition where an artist will work in the style of another known performer and take his name. He may even be promoted by the known artist as his protégé or junior band and work the known artist's club when he goes on the road. Junior Wells is not of this tradition, but like other artists he began to perform at a very early age.

2. Byther Smith, at home, Chicago, Illinois, May 1974.

3. Ibid.

4. Johnny Shines, Childe Harold, Washington, D.C., February 1978.

5. Jim O'Neal, at home, Chicago, Illinois, August 1974.

6. For the best field study of this phenomenon, see David Evans, "Afro-American One-stringed Instruments," *Western Folklore* 29 (October 1970): 229–45.

7. For example, Edna Smith noted: "The children made play instruments. They improvised drums by stretching pig or goat bladders across the open ends of tins or bottles. The boys made zithers and musical pots. Then they formed bands to imitate the music of adult musicians." Edna Smith, "Musical Training in Tribal West Africa," *African Music: Journal of the African Music Society* 3, no. 1 (1962): 6–10.

8. Harnett Kane described improvised instruments in New Orleans: "Throughout enslavement, the Negroes had been fashioning rude horns, flutes and drums—anything that could produce sounds; actually, these were pebble-filled gourds, long whistles, pipes punched with holes, violins made from cigar boxes." Harnett T. Kane, *Queen New Orleans* (New York: William Morrow, 1949), p. 279.

9. W. C. Handy, *W. C. Handy: Father of the Blues* (New York: Collier Books, 1941), p. 16.

10. William Broonzy and Yannick Bruynoghe, *Big Bill Blues* (New York: Oak Publications, 1964), p. 34.

11. Anonymous, Indianapolis, Indiana, March 1975.

12. John Cephas, Library of Congress, Washington, D.C., June 1981.

13. Clyde Judas Maxwell, Georgetown University, Washington, D.C., July 1976.

14. "Even before I was ten years old, I was with my grandmother back out in the country; they had a spring over the hill, and I couldn't carry a water bucket but a small four-pound water bucket, and I used to have to go down there and get water, and I used to take that bucket and turn the bottom up under my arm, and I used to beat on it until my fingers bled trying to make it sound like a guitar. So that's how I say I guess I must have come to the world wanting to do that. That was just a talent for me." Tom Mazzolini, "K. C. Douglas," *Living Blues*, no. 15 (Winter 1973–74): 15.

15. Jerry DeMuth, "At Home with Sleepy John Estes," *DownBeat*, November 11, 1971, p. 10.

16. Ibid.

17. The various musical usages of the broom along with the wealth of

traditional beliefs associated with this common household item is uncanny. Surely a major study of the broom in Afro-American folklore is to be desired.

18. Eddie Taylor, "I Feel So Bad: The Blues of Eddie Taylor," Advent 2802.

19. Despite their importance, handmade instruments served only until a real instrument came along, as Chicago guitarist John Littlejohn indicates: "I never played guitar or seen one until my father won it in a crap game for fifty cents and brought it home. And before that I had a lil ole wire on the wall, trying to play that with a bottle on each end to hold it. That's where I first started to play the guitar" (in Dick Shurman, "Never Seen a Slide," *Blues Unlimited*, no. 72 (June 1972), p. 12.

20. Wild Child Butler, Chicago, Illinois, July 1974.

21. Mickey Martin, Indiana University, Purdue University at Indianapolis, Indiana, February 1976.

22. Paul Oliver claims, "The homemade instrument is almost a cliché of blues history" (Paul Oliver, *Savannah Syncopaters* [New York: Stein & Day, 1970], p. 84). See also Paul Oliver, *The Story of the Blues* (New York: Chilton Book Co., 1969), p. 51. Several other artists who made guitars are Big Joe Williams, Elmore James, Bunk Pippins, JoJo Williams, Sonny Boy Williams, Scott Dunbar, and Muddy Waters. Although generally for children, some adults play homemade guitars as novelty instruments. Lonnie Pitchford of Lexington, Mississippi, also plays a one-string guitar, but in his case construction proceeded in reverse. He took a six-string guitar and deleted five of the strings. Other excellent one-string players include One-String Sam, Napoleon Strickland, and Mose Williams.

23. James Thomas, Georgetown University, Washington, D.C., July 1976.

24. John Cephas.

25. Bob Koester, "Hoodoo Man Blues: Junior Wells' Chicago Blues Band," Delmark DC-612. See also Robert Neff and Anthony Connor, *Blues* (Boston: David Godine, 1975), p. 28.

26. In Joe Willie Wilkins' case, giving the child his own instrument was intended to prevent him from playing his father's: "My daddy played guitar, blues, all he knowed how to play. So I'd mess with his guitar, and he didn't want nobody messin with his guitar so much so he bought me a guitar of my own. So, 'Well, you got one, leave mine alone.' He wasn't jokin when he told me that." Jim O'Neal, "Joe Willie Wilkins," *Living Blues*, no. 11 (Winter 1972–73): 13.

27. Archie Edwards, at his barbershop, Washington, D.C., July 1972.

28. Bob Lowery, Smithsonian Folklife Festival, The Mall, Washington, D.C., August 1976.

29. John Jackson to Cheryl Brauner, at home, Fairfax, Virginia.

30. Babe Stovall to Rob Riley, New Orleans, Louisiana, February 1974.

31. Lee Crisp, Smithsonian Folklife Festival, The Mall, Washington, D.C., June 1976.

32. Sam Chatmon, Smithsonian Folklife Festival, The Mall, Washington, D.C., September 1976.

33. Harry Oster, "Angola Prisoners' Blues," Folk Lyric Recording Company, Folk Lyric LFS-A3.

34. Sheldon Annis, "I Was Born in Alabama: Bobo Jenkins," *Blues Unlimited*, no. 74 (July 1974): 18.

35. James Thomas, at my home, Bloomington, Indiana, March 1973.

36. Hubert Sumlin, Desperadoes, Washington, D.C., December 1980.

37. James Thomas, 1973.

Chapter 5: "They used to say it was the devil's music"

1. Mike Leadbitter and Neil Slaven, *Blues Records: 1943–1966* (New York: Oak Publications, 1968), p. 308.

2. "Corn songs" probably refers to corn-shucking songs, one among many terms used for preblues secular songs. While the most common term for dance music is "reels," other obscure terms such as "railroad songs," "ditties," and "levee camp songs" also show up in musicians' reminiscences. The implication is that before "blues" became a fixed term there was no single generic term for blues-like songs.

3. Sunnyland Slim, Childe Harold, Washington, D.C., February 1978.

4. Until recently, blues players often took special names, which became their musical identities An intriguing aspect of the blues tradition, these names derived from many different sources, including childhood nicknames, names given by other artists or by record producers, names associated with musical style, like Howling Wolf and Fast Fingers Dawkins. Names also come from instruments (Guitar Junior, Guitar Gable) or from techniques associated with instruments, as with harp blowers Shakey Horton or Shakey Jake. Names can be tied to geography (Memphis Minnie or Detroit Junior) or appearance (Big Bill Broonzy or Little Walter) or countless combinations (Piano Red, Harmonica Fats, Guitar Slim, or Memphis Slim). Nicknames, monickers, or more precisely professional names can be used to tie an artist to an established veteran or even to record for more than one label at the same time, but despite their practical purposes, names are magical and a declaration of who and what you are.

5. See the sermon of the Rev. C. C. Lovelace in Zora Neale Hurston, *Jonah's Gourd Vine* (Philadelphia: J. B. Lippincott Co., 1934).

6. An anonymous Maryland woman told University of Maryland student Lydia Murdoch: "But if you heard the same type of music on the outside, oh . . . you know, at a place of amusement or dance house, hop, or whatever, then it was a sin. The devil wanted you to dance and have these feelings. So if you heard these—somebody playing some string music, banjo, guitar, or combination of these—it made you feel kinda good. Your feet wanted to move, look like your whole body wanted to get into this rhythm, you know, then that was the devil's work. But if the same thing happened to you on Sunday night, that was the Holy Spirit moving you." John Cephas likewise points toward the musical similarities between blues and gospel music, claiming that only the words are different.

7. The blues encourages enjoyment of the physical world, which from a church point of view could be seen as promoting sin. But by a communal sharing of individual problems and despair, blues also restrains people from evil. The evil, confusion, and potential chaos that confront the blues artist and his audience can be defused by the mediating influence of the blues performance. It is, then, a method of survival, a collective effort to disperse loneliness, hopelessness, and despair. Blues cools rage, whether it is directed toward self or community, but through collective sympathy for individual problems it also works to prevent the death of feeling.

8. Johnny Young referred to this belief when he mentioned how his wife would go out Saturday night and still want to go to church. See p. 11.

9. William Broonzy and Yannick Bruynoghe, *Big Bill Blues* (New York: Oak Publications, 1964), p. 35.

10. A film version of Handy's life entitled *St. Louis Blues* starring Nat King

Cole also focused on the dramatic confrontation between the uncompromising preacher-father and the talented determined son, a theme popularized in *The Jazz Singer*. Handy also recounted his schoolteacher's opinion of musicians: "Musicians were idlers, dissipated characters, whiskey drinkers and rounders. They were social pariahs. Southern white gentlemen, he said, looked upon music as a parlor accomplishment not as a means of questionable support." W. C. Handy, *W. C. Handy: Father of the Blues* (New York: Collier Books, 1941), p. 13.

11. Chief Ellis to Susan Day, at home, Washington, D.C., April 1977.

12. Jim O'Neal and Bill Greensmith, "Jimmy Rogers," *Living Blues*, no. 14 (Autumn 1973): 11.

13. "I taught myself. I used to hear guys play, you know, and then the funny part about it, my father was a minister—my father wouldn't allow us to play what he called 'blues' in the house, you know, in the South. Well, I buys me a cheap harmonica, I started to play it there, and he told me I had to get out of there with that kind of carrying on." Amy O'Neal, "Snooky Pryor," *Living Blues*, no. 6 (Autumn 1971): 4.

14. E. T. Mensah, The American Cultural Center, Accra, Ghana, December 17, 1982.

15. Ellis.

16. Bob Lowery, Smithsonian Folklife Festival, The Mall, Washington, D.C., August 1976.

17. John Cephas, Library of Congress, Washington, D.C., June 1981.

18. Hoyle Osborne, "I Been Headed Up Ever Since: An Interview with Fred McDowell," *Sing Out* 19, no. 2 (July–August 1969), p. 17.

19. Church/blues tension is a definite motif of the interview and as such needs to be approached with caution. It does, however, represent real past conditions, and it influences the way the artists present their lives. There has been a tendency to discount the church/blues dichotomy lately. However, this also should be done with caution, because the tension still exists. It is also apparent that interviewers have consistently inquired of blues players about church attitudes toward their music, usually eliciting some statement of confirmation of church enmity followed by some rationalization or defense of blues or blues-playing. For example, St. Louis bluesman Henry Townsend told me: "When you use the term 'blues' [a lot of people] say that's the devil's music. Well, it's just as good as gospel. The only difference is the gospel people singing about biblical days and what they done, but I'm not at biblical times. I'm of this age as of now. They can certainly discard the idea that blues will send you anyplace different from gospel, because as long as it's the truth, one truth is no greater than the other. So I just stick to the truth, and if you can condemn the truth, then I haven't got a chance, because that's all I'm telling. And the 'devil's music'—I don't think the devil cares much for the truth."

20. There are similarities between the role of the blues musician and the role of various African musicians and the stereotyped beliefs about the character of musicians. See Alan Merriam, *The Anthropology of Music* (Evanston: Northwestern University Press, 1964); Paul Oliver, *Savannah Syncopaters* (New York: Stein & Day, 1970); S. A. Babalola, *The Content and Form of Yoruba Ijala* (Oxford: Clarendon Press, 1966); Samuel Charters, *The Roots of the Blues: An African Search* (Lawrence, Mass.: Merrimack Book Service, 1980); H. Olufela Davies, *The Victor Olaiya Story: A Biography of Nigeria's "Evil Genius of Highlife"* (Nigeria, n.d.).

21. Byther Smith, at home, Chicago, Illinois, May 1974.

22. Johnny Shines, Childe Harold, Washington, D.C., February 1978.

23. Mike Leadbitter, "Big Boy Crudup," *Blues Unlimited*, no. 75 (September 1970): 18.

24. Byther Smith, 1974.

25. J. T. Adams, at home, Indianapolis, Indiana, March 1976.

26. Wild Child Butler, Chicago, Illinois, July 1974.

27. Archie Edwards, at his barbershop, Washington, D.C., July 1977.

28. Wild Child Butler, 1974.

29. James Thomas, at my home, Bloomington, Indiana, March 1973.

30. Ralph Ellison, "Remembering Jimmy," *Shadow and Act* (New York: Vintage Books, 1953), p. 243.

31. John Cephas, 1981.

Chapter 6: "Sounds so good to me"

1. Recently he has worked with two younger musicians, billing the group as "Sam Chatmon and His Barbecue Boys."

2. Sam Chatmon, Smithsonian Folklife Festival, The Mall, Washington, D.C., September 1976.

3. Both tales play with apparent paradoxical ideas, Chatmon with telling the truth about lying, and Edwards with doing wrong but doing it right. Blues songs employ similar wordplay, and Paul Oliver has worked with this aspect of blues composition.

4. The idea of a gift provides a convenient explanation for musical skills consistent with so-called folk attitudes that down-play individual initiative or responsibility in favor of a supernatural cause.

5. Peter Guralnick, *Feel Like Going Home* (New York: Fusion Books, 1971), p. 46.

6. Mike Rowe and Mike Leadbitter, "I Was the Baby Boy," *Blues Unlimited*, no. 96 (November 1972): 4.

7. Pete Welding, "Johnny Young," in *Nothing But the Blues*, ed. Mike Leadbitter (New York: Oak Publications, 1971), p. 76.

8. Eddie Taylor, Northeastern University, Skokie, Illinois. December 1974.

9. Byther Smith, at his home, Chicago, Illinois, May 1974.

10. This simple sequence does not represent all musicians, and even within it there is ample room for diversity. For example, Johnny Young's emphasis was on gift; Honeyboy Edwards, on the other hand, spoke of his teachers and his own work. Nevertheless, both referred to sound, being inspired by local musical events and being taught by professional musicians.

11. Big Chief Ellis to Susan Day, at his home, Washington, D.C., April 1977.

12. Sunnyland Slim, Childe Harold, Washington, D.C., February 1978.

13. Eddie Taylor.

14. John Lee Hooker, "Boogie Chillun," Detroit 1948, issued on Modern, Kent, Crown, and United labels, among others, and a true blues classic.

15. Clyde "Judas" Maxwell, Georgetown University, Washington, D.C., August 1976.

16. For an excellent discussion of the positive value of phonograph records, see Norm Cohen, *Long Steel Rail: The Railroad in American Folksong* (Urbana: University of Illinois Press, 1981), pp. 21–38.

17. Bob Lowery, Smithsonian Folklife Festival, The Mall, Washington, D.C., August 1976.

18. John Cephas, Library of Congress, Washington, D.C., June 1981.

19. Wild Child Butler, in a car, Chicago, Illinois, July 1974.

20. John Jackson to Cheryl Brauner, at his home, Fairfax, Virginia, June 1979.

21. Archie Edwards, at his barbershop, Washington, D.C., July 1977.

22. Ibid.

23. J. T. Adams, at his home, Indianapolis, Indiana, March 1976.

24. Bukka White, "Remembrance of Charley Patton," *Mississippi Blues*, vol. 1, Takoma Records B1001.

25. John Cephas, June 1981.

26. Bob Lowery, 1976.

27. Fred McDowell, Ann Arbor Blues Festival, Ann Arbor, Michigan, August 1969.

28. See p. 8.

29. See p. 18.

30. Lee Crisp, Smithsonian Folklife Festival, The Mall, Washington, D.C., June 1976.

31. Frederick Ramsey, Jr., refers to this relationship when he wrote, "Blind Lemon was to Leadbelly what Ma Rainey was to Bessie Smith; he took the young boy and taught him his repertoire and way of living." Frederick Ramsey, Jr., "Leadbelly's Last Session," Folway Album, 241, Vol. 1, reprinted from *High Fidelity* (November–December 1953).

32. Sam Charters, *Robert Johnson* (New York: Oak Publications, 1973), p. 8.

33. Byther Smith, 1974.

34. Archie Edwards, 1977.

35. Ibid.

36. Ibid.

37. Peter Guralnick, *Feel Like Going Home* (New York: Fusion Books, 1971), p. 46.

38. Robert Neff and Anthony Connor, *Blues* (Boston: David Godine, 1975), p. 35.

39. Mojo Buford in Neff and Connor, *Blues*, p. 76.

40. See Bill Ferris, "Records and the Delta Blues Tradition," *Keystone Folklore Quarterly*, Winter 1969, p. 162.

41. Jim O'Neal, "Jimmy Reed," *Living Blues*, no. 21 (May–June 1975): 17.

42. Jeff Titon, "All Pretty Wimmens: Jojo Williams," *Blues Unlimited*, no. 64 (July 1969): 14.

Chapter 7: The wages of sinful music

1. James Thomas on "The Today Show," February 6, 1976; Bicentennial Tribute to the state of Mississippi.

2. Jimmy Dawkins, Ann Arbor Blues Festival, Ann Arbor, Michigan, August 1969.

3. Sunnyland Slim, Childe Harold, Washington, D.C., February 1978.

4. Big Bill Hill and Muddy Waters, Ann Arbor, Michigan, August 1969.

5. Many of the bluesmen, as transplanted Southerners, stated their intent to return to the South, which they now perceive as less racist than Chicago.

6. For further discussion, see Chapters 5 and 8. I am also reminded of words

attributed to Excello bluesman Lazy Lester: "They call me lazy, but God knows I'm only tired."

7. Sam Chatmon, The Mall, Washington, D.C., August 1976.

8. Clyde "Judas" Maxwell, Georgetown University, Washington, D.C., July 1976.

9. Jimmy Dawkins, 1969.

10. Peter Guralnick, *Feel Like Going Home: Portraits in Blues and Rock and Roll* (New York: Fusion Books, 1971), p. 124.

11. Peter Welding, "I Sing for the People: An Interview with Bluesman Howling Wolf," *Downbeat*, December 14, 1967, pp. 20–21.

12. Ibid., p. 22.

13. In a statement similar to Howling Wolf's, Muddy Waters tells of his early jobs. Moving away from complaint, his account is positive, because even though he had to work all night the people really liked the blues: "Played for those Saturday night fish fries. I used to sell fish too, then go to playing. Everybody used to fry up fish and have one hell of a time. Find me workin all night, playin, workin till sunrise for fifty cents and a sandwich and be glad of it, and they really liked the low-down blues." Paul Oliver, *Conversations with the Blues* (London: Cassell & Co., 1965), p. 45.

14. John Jackson to Elizabeth Wiles Dean, Fairfax, Virginia, n.d.

15. Roy Searce, Smithsonian Folklife Festival, The Mall, Washington, D.C., July 1976.

16. Archie Edwards, at his barbershop, Washington, D.C., July 1977. On another occasion he added, "So, man, I got a chance to get a grape soda, hunk of chicken on a biscuit. I was satisfied. A really good time—I really enjoyed it."

17. James Thomas, at my home, Bloomington, Indiana, March 1973.

18. Bob Lowery, Smithsonian Folklife Festival, The Mall, Washington, D.C., August 1976.

19. Sunnyland Slim, Childe Harold, Washington, D.C., February 1978.

20. Texas bluesman Black Ace also compared what he made to what other workers brought in, and like Sunnyland Slim he earned as much as the common laborers, but his work was play, and he got paid for having a good time. "So I would go around, play at house parties with this boy—make a dollar and a half whilst other folks was gettin that for one day's work on relief. Dollar and a half for that one day. I get three or four parties, man. I made a lot of money. I was making somethin playing at lil old house parties. Dollar and a half for fun!" Oliver, *Conversations with the Blues*, p. 50.

21. Lee Crisp, Smithsonian Folklife Festival, The Mall, Washington, D.C., June 1976.

22. The manner in which early jobs are described involves not only the nature of the experience but also the artist's current attitude toward the experience, as well as his goals for the interview in general. The difference between a youthful Honeyboy Edwards earning those nickels and dimes like his teacher Big Joe Williams, and Howling Wolf walking those corn rows in a sequence of low-paying jobs, is that one portrays a noteworthy beginning and the other an apparent dead end. Furthermore, Honeyboy Edwards never really made it to the big time. Howling Wolf, however, went on to become a superstar and uses his prolonged stint in the trenches to justify his later success.

23. Clyde Maxwell, 1976. Other musicians share his sentiment. For example, Baby Doo Caston told Jeff Titon: "In those days there wasn't too much like that

then; and whenever somebody could play and could play well, he was considered as somebody; he could go anywhere and had it made, you know." *From Blues to Pop: The Autobiography of Leonard Baby Doo Caston.* Edited by Jeff Titon, *John Edwards Memorial Foundation* Special Series, no. 4 (Los Angeles: The John Edwards Memorial Foundation, Inc., 1974), p. 25. See Honeyboy Edwards' comments on how people felt about musicians when he was young.

Chapter 8: "Wasn't only my songs, they got my music too"

1. Hound Dog Taylor, Chicago, Illinois, June 1974.

2. Actually, within the stereotype musicians may joke about their mornings after. A friend who works for the Smithsonian Folklife Festival told me about piano player Jimmy Walker, who when told he had to play at 11:00 A.M. said, "Don't you know a blues musician doesn't finish throwing up till noon?" We don't expect the musician to know what the morning looks like—a point that is driven home for a laugh whenever a blues player does a morning gig—yet over the years musicians have been getting up to go to work despite what the public wants to believe.

3. Byther Smith, at his home, Chicago, Illinois, May 1974.

4. Eddie Taylor, Northeastern Illinois University, Chicago, Illinois, December 1974.

5. Muddy Waters told Peter Guralnik: "Liquor's the thing that will get you—Well, I imagine, I guess if you get too much of anything I don't think you can make it all the way." Peter Guralnick, *Feel Like Going Home* (New York: Fusion Books, 1971), p. 53.

6. Otis Rush, Wise Fools, Chicago, Illinois, December 1973.

7. Big Joe Williams, Ann Arbor Blues Festival, Ann Arbor, Michigan, August 1969.

8. Roy Searce, Smithsonian Folklife Festival, The Mall, Washington, D.C., August 1976.

9. Big Bill Broonzy, who once recorded the sound of drinking on a record album cut, recommended his own autobiography: "I wouldn't care if it's just a story about how I live or how drunk I was the last time that they saw Bill. I would enjoy reading it because it's true." Broonzy ends the book with a final self-assessment: "Some blues singers can and do sing and don't drink but not Big Bill—he loves his whiskey, he's just a whiskey head man." William Broonzy and Yannick Bruynoghe, *Big Bill Blues* (New York: Oak Publications, 1964), p. 151.

10. James Cotton followed in Sonny Boy Williamson's footsteps: "When Sonny Boy stepped down he gave the chicks a better chance to get a look at me. I never had that before, and it really screwed up my mind. I started getting drunk, half showing up. Everything I thought a star was supposed to do." Robert Neff and Anthony Connor, *Blues* (Boston: David Godine, 1975), p. 38.

11. Johnny Shines, Childe Harold, Washington, D.C., February 1978.

12. J. T. Adams, at his home, Indianapolis, Indiana, March 1976.

13. Actually, fights in blues clubs are quite infrequent. In Chicago some clubs are in tough neighborhoods, but generally once inside a blues club you won't get into trouble if you behave yourself.

14. Byther Smith, 1974.

15. James Thomas, at my home, Bloomington, Indiana, March 1973.

16. Otis Rush, 1973.

17. Byther Smith, 1974.

18. Otis Rush, 1973.

19. The traditional name "The Bucket of Blood" has been applied to a number of rough taverns, but it is tied especially to Chicago. James Thomas spoke of a friend who he said got killed in Chicago: "He was up there about three or four months, and he got killed, place called 'The Bucket of Blood' in Chicago. You heard of it, 'The Bucket of Blood'?"

20. Byther Smith.

21. Archie Edwards, at his barbershop, Washington, D.C., June 1978.

22. John Cephas.

23. John Jackson, at his home, Fairfax, Virginia, August 1976.

24. Wild Child Butler, in my car, Chicago, Illinois, July 1974.

25. Sunnyland Slim, Childe Harold, Washington, D.C., February 1978.

26. Harmonica Frank Floyd, Smithsonian Folklife Festival, The Mall, Washington, D.C., August 1976.

27. Wild Child Butler, 1974.

28. Eddie Taylor, 1974.

29. There are exceptions: high-quality records, bad records redeemed by great performances, and even successful recording stars. Yet it is interesting to note that the artists who bragged most about their records generally referred to past successes or to a record yet to come out. For example, Roosevelt Sykes bragged: "The first records I put out was in '36, and I got royalty on them. Five cents on the dollar I reckon. Do you know I was drawing seventy or eighty dollars a month? Well, you know they were sellin some of those records?" (Ann Arbor Blues Festival, Ann Arbor, Michigan, August 1969). And Sam Chatmon stated: "Well, I started making records in 1929, fourteenth of June, 1929. So I was playing four, five, eight years or so before I started recording. After I made the record, the first number I made was a hit, 'Forty-Four Blues,' and every record I made was a star ever since" (Smithsonian Folklife Festival, The Mall, Washington, D.C., September 1976).

30. Wild Child Butler, 1974.

31. Byther Smith, 1974.

32. Eddie Taylor, 1974.

33. Ibid.

34. Big Chief Ellis to Susan Day, at his home, Washington, D.C., April 1977.

35. James Thomas, 1973.

36. Wild Child Butler, 1974.

37. Byther Smith, 1974.

38. Ibid.

39. Johnny Shines, 1978.

40. Albert Stone noted, "Furthermore, since our social selves, especially for women and blacks, are partly masks or imposed identities, both the autobiographer and her audience may feel further justified in playing around with historic identity. To stress the self as the creator of history—even at times as the fabricator of fantasies—maximizes ones freedom from circumstances and social stereotype. In this way an ideal self always coexists with an actual—that is, a determined historical identity." Albert Stone, *Autobiographical Occasions and Original Acts* (Philadelphia: University of Pennsylvania Press, 1982), p. 13.

41. See Richard Wright: "The locale of these songs shifts continuously and very seldom is the home sight hymned or celebrated" (in Paul Oliver, *The Meaning of the Blues* [New York: Collier Books, 1963], p. 9).

42. James Thomas, 1973. John Jackson is also a gravedigger—in fact, he is sometimes referred to as the "singing gravedigger"—but it is his hope to put that work aside and concentrate on music.

43. Archie Edwards, at my home, Hyattsville, Maryland, February 1981.

44. Eddie Taylor, 1974.

45. Wild Child Butler, 1974.

46. Ibid.

47. At Big John's, Chicago, Illinois, Summer 1965.

48. Byther Smith, 1974.

49. Eddie Taylor, 1974.

50. Wild Child Butler, 1974.

51. See Johnny Young, p. 11.

52. James Thomas, 1973.

53. Otis Rush, 1973.

54. Big Joe Williams, Big Bill Hill, Bob Koester, Ann Arbor Blues Festival, Ann Arbor, Michigan, August 1969.

55. Big Joe Williams, Howling Wolf, Ann Arbor, 1969.

56. Jim O'Neal and R. T. Cuniff, "Hound Dog Taylor," *Living Blues* 1, no. 4 (Winter 1970–71). 8.

57. Big Joe Williams, Ann Arbor, 1969.

58. Jazzman Dicky Wells recalls blues singer Jimmy Rushing's and pianist Count Basie's storytelling sessions: "Anyone lucky enough to sit in on a Basie-Rushing tall-tale jam should bring medals, because they would sure be in order. That Greyhound Bus Hotel was the place for them too. The wonderful things about people like that is that they can give out a tremendous amount of relief, the kind no money can buy. I remember how they changed many dull times into laughter in a second" (Dicky Wells, as told to Stanley Dance in *The Night People* [Boston: Crescendo Publishing Co., 1971], p. 78).

59. Mike Leadbitter, "Big Boy Crudup," *Blues Unlimited*, no. 75 (September 1970): 18. He told the same story at Ann Arbor, 1969.

60. Joe Willie Wilkins, Georgetown University, Washington, D.C., June 1976.

61. Muddy Waters and Howling Wolf were great rivals for the title of King of Chicago Blues. Over the years they had a tendency to steal each other's musicians and material, both of which are alluded to here.

62. Big Joe Williams, Howling Wolf, Big Mama Thornton, Roosevelt Sykes, and Muddy Waters, Ann Arbor, August 1969.

63. Jim O'Neal, at his home, Chicago, Illinois, August 1974.

64. Ray Townley, "Bobby Bland: Blue in Name Only," *DownBeat*, September 12, 1974, p. 18.

65. Byther Smith, 1974.

66. Jimmy Dawkins, Ann Arbor Blues Festival, Ann Arbor, Michigan, August 1969.

Chapter 9: "Well, that's it, that's my life story"

1. Melvin B. Tolson, "Lambda from Harlem Gallery," in *Black American Literature*, ed. Ruth Miller (Beverly Hills, Calif.: Glencoe Press, 1971), p. 584.

2. For a discussion of hoodoo in blues, see Paul Oliver, *The Meaning of the Blues* (New York: Collier Books, 1963), chap. 5; and J. L. Dillard, *Lexicon of Black English* (New York: Seabury Press, 1977).

3. For a discussion of the bluesman as character and narrative persona, see

Dennis Jarrett, "The Singer and the Bluesman: Formulations of the Personality in the Lyrics of the Blues," *Southern Folklore Quarterly* 42, no. 1 (1978): 31–37.

4. Ralph Ellison, "Remembering Jimmy," in *Shadow and Act* (New York: Vintage Books, 1953), p. 243.

5. Jean Starobinski considers such transformations as a condition for autobigraphy: "It is in the internal transformation of the individual—and the exemplary character of this transformation—that furnishes a subject for a narrative discourse in which I is both subject and object." Jean Starobinski, "The Style of Autobiography," in *Autobiography: Essays Theoretical and Critical*, ed. James Olney (Princeton: Princeton University Press, 1980), p. 78.

6. Albert Murray, *Stompin the Blues* (New York: McGraw-Hill, 1976), p. 230.

7. Big Bill Broonzy noted that younger musicians take up the vices of their heroes as well. "Some of the younger musicians use it because he or she is playing the same type of music or sing the same songs as some famous artist. They hear and they read about that artist using dope or drinking whiskey, and they can play and sing good, so they copy after them and they start drinking and using dope, and they get in a habit of every time they play or sing to get one or the other." William Broonzy and Yannick Bruynoghe, *Big Bill Blues* (New York: Oak Publications, 1964), p. 44.

8. Justin O'Brien, "Lee Jackson Obituary," *Living Blues*, no. 43 (Summer 1979), p. 48.

9. Byther Smith, at his home, Chicago, Illinois, May 1974.

10. Clifford James chides us for what he perceives to be a cultural predilection to accept coherent personalities in biography. Our view of the blues musician's life as consistent with his artistic presentation of himself illustrates James' point. Clifford James, "Hanging Up Looking Glasses at Odd Corners: Ethnobiographical Prospects," in *Studies in Biography*, ed. Daniel Aaron (Cambridge: Harvard University Press, 1978), pp. 41–56.

11. In their analysis of written autobiography, William Spengemann and L. R. Lundquist argue that the autobiographer is guided by his perception of society's beliefs about his character: "The writer explains his life by depicting himself according to culturally evaluated images of character. As he turns his private experiences into language, he assumes one of the many identities outlined in myth and so assumes his connection with his culture." William C. Spengemann and L. R. Lundquist, "Autobiography and the American Myth," *American Quarterly* 17 (Fall 1965): 504.

12. The bluesman's tale shares characteristics with written autobiography, although they are obviously different documents. Both are recreated versions of the past which rely on the manipulative power of their author for their artistic quality. As Albert Stone asserts, "A narrating self reinvents the historical actor." Dean Ebner describes autobiography as a "shaping of the past, as it were, into a coherent pattern with stages and self-consistency of character. It superimposes upon the welter of remembered facts in other words, the unity and order of a present mental outlook." Albert Stone, *Autobiographical Occasions and Original Acts* (Philadelphia: University of Pennsylvania Press, 1982), p. 13; Dean Ebner, *Autobiography in Seventeenth Century England: Theology and the Self* (The Hague: Mouton, 1971), p. 19. See also Stephen Butterfield, *Black Autobiography in America* (Amherst: University of Massachusetts Press, 1974).

13. Johnny Shines, Childe Harold, Washington, D.C., February 1978.

14. Yank Rachel, in my classroom, Indiana University-Purdue, University at Indianapolis, Indianapolis, Indiana, March 1976.

15. Wild Child Butler, in my car, Chicago, Illinois, July 1974.

16. Otis Rush, Wise Fools, Chicago, Illinois, December 1973.

17. Ralph Ellison, "Richard Wright's Blues," in *Shadow and Act*, p. 78.

18. Big Bill Broonzy begins his story, "The reason I'm writing this book is because I think that everyone would like to know the real truth about Negroes singing and playing in Mississippi." William Broonzy, *Big Bill Blues*, p. 29.

19. The bluesman's story shares creative principles associated with fiction, but to deny its claim to historicity does a great injustice to those speakers who view themselves as historians. These individuals have expended a fair amount of effort ordering, analyzing, and memorizing the history of their art form as well as their own participation in history. Blues life stories are historical because they are an account of past events, albeit viewed from a specialized but relatively consistent perspective. They are a special form of history selected and refracted through the individual speaker's sense of meaning, artistically recreated and even dramatically performed, but nevertheless illustrative of a true and meaningful version of history.

Albert Stone noted the dual status of written autobiography as he described an autobiographical act: "An autobiographical act, therefore, makes a writer at once creator and recreator of his or her personal identity. Individual experience and the consciousness through which it has been remembered are simultaneously presented in a distinctive narrative structure and through a pattern of verbal images and metaphors. The result is both deliberate artistry and a more or less trustworthy account of the past, a history." While noting the traditional nature of the bluesman's "verbal images and metaphors," we must also acknowledge the historical dimension of the account. Their story employs creative techniques that reflect its status as a mediation between the real and the ideal; it presents past events but is an interpretive or an artistic version of history. Stone, *Autobiographical Occasions*, p. 4. See also Jeff Todd Titon, "The Life Story," *Journal of American Folklore* 93, no. 369 (July–September 1980), pp. 276–92.

20. Johnny Shines, Childe Harold, Washington, D.C., February 1978.

21. Sunnyland Slim, Childe Harold, Washington, D.C., February 1978.

22. Ibid.

23. When asked to rationalize song performance as truly personal, the artist may have to rely on a secondary narrative to tell something about the song by relating it to his life or to his composition of it. Here lies an area of fabrication in which an unusual demand is made on the artist: he must legitimize his art to the interviewer through improvised narratives and rationalizations about songs which generally are more dependent on tradition than on personal experience. However, since the artist is aware of the content of the genre, which deals with life in general, and since he is an expert in the techniques demanded by his art form, he can usually respond as to the meaning of the song—its innate truth personalizing the explanation as he personalizes the song itself.

24. Jim O'Neal, at his home, Chicago, Illinois, August 1974.

25. Paul Oliver, *Conversations with the Blues* (London: Cassell & Co., 1965), p. 31; and Julius Lester, "Mr. White, Take a Break," *Sing Out* 18, no. 4 (October-November 1968): 61.

26. Janet Gunn shifts emphasis from the private act of life-story writing to the "cultural act of self-reading" with the author the first reader of his life experience. For the bluesman, the process of self-reading involves the eventual selection of details that portray him in his role. But as storyteller he also participates in later readings—which corresponds with Gunn's second moment

of the autobiographical situation, the reading of the autobiographical text. Thus the bluesman continues to witness his reader-audience's response to his tale and can further amend his account. Janet Varner Gunn, *Autobiography: Toward a Poetics of Experience* (Philadelphia: University of Pennsylvania Press, 1982).

Chapter 10: "I've had hard luck, but it will change some day"

1. Willie Dixon, speaking at "Black American Blues Song: A Study in Poetic Literature," Baird Auditorium, National Museum of Natural History, Washington, D.C., February 6, 1982.

2. See Harold Courlander, *Negro Folk Music U.S.A.* (New York: Columbia University Press, 1963), p. 123, for a discussion of Leadbelly's and Big Bill Broonzy's blues definitions.

3. J. C. Burris, Forty-third National Folk Festival, Wolftrap Farm Park, Vienna, Virginia, July 1981.

4. Big Chief Ellis to Susan Day, at his home, Washington, D.C., April 1977.

5. John Lee Hooker echoed Ellis' statement: "Every song I sing is something that happened to my life or somebody else's life in the world. If it ain't hitting me, it's hitting somebody out there." Blues compositions by certain artists may reflect their actual experiences, and the singer, like the novelist, may be at his best when working with the familiar. But a one-to-one correlation of experience and art is absurd. While some songs are partially autobiographical, most are composed of traditional content and are more reflective of other blues songs than of the singer's life. In blues, an ideal character confronts a typical blues situation, but the message is brought to life by the artist's personality. If authenticity of expression convinces the audience that the song is based on the inspiration of personal experience, then the blues artist is successful at his act. He has convinced the audience that his understanding and feelings are authentic, and they believe in him. Rube Lacey told David Evans, "Sometimes I'd propose it happened to me in order to hit somebody else, cause everything that happened to one person has at some time or other happened to another. If not, it will."

Still, a high value is placed on self-expression, and a song should be presented in a way that is recognizably the singer's. But this is accomplished through a repertoire of performance techniques, instrumental and vocal, as well as in composition. Personalizing a song, even one's own composition, is, as Albert Murray suggests, more a question of style than a direct unfolding of an actual life experience. See Robert Neff and Anthony Connor, *Blues* (Boston: David Godine, 1975), p. 1; and David Evans, "Rubin Lacey," in *Nothing But the Blues*, ed. Mike Leadbitter (New York: Oak Publications, 1971), p. 268; and Albert Murray, *Stompin the Blues* (New York: McGraw-Hill, 1976), pp. 98–99.

6. Ellis.

7. Johnny Shines, Childe Harold, Washington, D.C., February 1978.

8. For a discussion of the concept of witnessing and the blues, see Larry Neal, "The Ethos of the Blues," *Black Scholar* 3, no. 10 (Summer 1972): 42. For a similar application of witnessing regarding memorates, see Linda Degh and Andrew Vazsonyi, "The Memorate and the Proto-memorate," *Journal of American Folklore* 87, no. 345 (July–September 1974): 231.

9. Wild Child Butler, in a car, Chicago, Illinois, July 1974.

10. Fred McDowell, Ann Arbor Blues Festival, Ann Arbor, Michigan, August 1969.

11. Archie Edwards, at his barbershop, Washington, D.C., July 1977.

12. Archie Edwards, at my home, Hyattsville, Maryland, February 1981.

13. Eddie Taylor, Northeastern University, Skokie, Illinois, December 1974. Delta legend Son House, a star in the generation preceding Eddie Taylor's, explained, "You know, it ain't but one way the blues exist, and that comes between a male and female being in love, uh huh, and when one has been deceived by the other" (Son House, spoken in performance at the Ann Arbor Blues Festival, August 1969; also in Jeff Titon, *Early Down Home Blues* [Urbana: University of Illinois Press, 1977], p. 182).

14. Big Bill Hill, Ann Arbor Blues Festival, Ann Arbor, Michigan, August 1969.

15. These statements coincide with the remarks of the blues poet and critic Langston Hughes: "I'm not a Southerner, I never worked on a levee, I hardly ever saw a cotton field except from the highway. But women behave the same way on Park Avenue as they do on a levee: when you got hold of one part of them the other part escapes you. That's the blues." Langston Hughes, "Jazz as Communication," *The Langston Hughes Reader* (New York: George Braziller, 1958), p. 492.

16. John Cephas, Library of Congress, Washington, D.C., June 1981.

17. Roosevelt Sykes, Ann Arbor Blues Festival, Ann Arbor, Michigan, August 1969.

18. Wild Child Butler.

19. Ibid.

20. Otis Rush, Wise Fools, Chicago, Illinois, December 1973.

21. Lee Crisp, Smithsonian Folklife Festival, The Mall, Washington, D.C., June 1976.

22. John Jackson to Elizabeth Wiles Dean, Fairfax, Virginia, n.d.

23. Back in the 1950s, Ralph Ellison predicted this reconciliation: "Nor do I believe that as we win our struggle for full participation in American life we will abandon our group expression. Too much living and aspiration have gone into it so that drained of its elements of defensiveness and alienation it will become even more precious to us for we will see it ever clearer as a transcendent value." Ralph Ellison, "Some Questions and Some Answers," in *Shadow and Act*, 3d ed. (New York: Vintage Books, 1972), p. 269.

24. Archie Edwards, 1977.

25. Roosevelt Sykes, 1969.

26. Jim O'Neal, "Joe Willie Wilkins," *Living Blues*, no. 11 (Winter 1972–73): 17.

27. Eddie Taylor, 1974.

28. David "Honeyboy" Edwards, "Living Blues Interview," *Living Blues*, no. 4 (Winter 1970–71): 24.

29. Byther Smith, at his home, Chicago, Illinois, May 1974.

30. Eddie Taylor, 1974.

31. Wild Child Butler, 1974.

32. Chief Ellis, 1977.

33. Butler, 1974.

34. J. T. Adams, at his home, Indianapolis, Indiana, March 1976.

35. James Thomas, Forty-second National Folk Festival, Madeira School, Vienna, Virginia, August 1980.

36. Archie Edwards, 1977.

37. John Cephas, 1981.

38. Otis Rush, 1973.

39. Wild Child Butler, 1974.

40. John Work, *American Negro Songs and Spirituals* (New York: Howell, Soskin, 1940), p. 28.

41. Sam Chatmon, Smithsonian Folklife Festival, The Mall, Washington, D.C., September 1976.

Bibliography

Albertson, Chris. *Bessie.* New York: Stein & Day, 1972.

Annis, Sheldon. "I Was Born in Alabama: Bobo Jenkins." *Blues Unlimited*, no. 74 (July 1974): 18.

Autobiography: Essays Theoretical and Critical, edited by James Olney. Princeton: Princeton University Press, 1980.

Bastin, Bruce. *Crying for the Carolines.* London: Studio Vista, 1971.

Becker, Howard. *Outsiders: Studies in the Sociology of Deviance.* New York: The Free Press, 1963.

Berendt, Joachim Ernst. *Blues.* 2d ed. Munich: Nyphenburger Verlagshandlang, 1960.

Berger, Bennet. "Black Culture or Lower Class Culture." In *Soul*, edited by Lee Rainwater. New York: Trans-Action, 1970.

Blesh, Rudi. *Shining Trumpets: A History of Jazz.* New York: Knopf, 1946.

Bluestein, Gene. "The Blues as a Literary Theme." *Massachusetts Review* 8, no. 4 (Autumn 1967): 593–617.

Bradford, Perry. *Born with the Blues.* New York: Oak Publications, 1965.

Broonzy, William and Yannick Bruynoghe. *Big Bill Blues: Big Bill Broonzy's Story.* New York: Oak Publications, 1964.

Brovan, John. *Walkin to New Orleans.* Sussex, U.K.: Blues Unlimited, 1974.

Brown, Sterling A. "The Blues." *Phylon* 13, no. 4 (1952): 286–92.

Butterfield, Stephen. *Black Autobiography in America.* Amherst: University of Massachusetts Press, 1974.

Campbell, E. Simmons. "The Blues." In *The Negro in Music and Art*, edited by Lindsey Patterson. New York: Publishers Co., 1967.

Caston, Leonard. *From Blues to Pop: The Autobiography of Leonard "Baby Doo" Caston*, edited by Jeff Titon. John Edwards Memorial Foundation Special Series, no. 4. Los Angeles: JEMF, 1974.

Charters, Samuel. *The Bluesmen.* New York: Oak Publications, 1967.

———. *The Country Blues.* New York: Da Capo, 1959.

———. *The Legacy of the Blues.* London: Calder & Boyars, 1975.

———. *Robert Johnson.* New York: Oak Publications, 1973.

————. *The Roots of the Blues: An African Search*. Lawrence, Mass.: Merrimack Book Service, 1980.

————. *Sweet as the Showers of Rain: The Bluesmen Volume II*. New York: Oak Publications, 1977.

Collins, Lee. *Oh Didn't He Ramble: The Life Story of Lee Collins as Told to Mary Collins*. Edited by Frank J. Gillis and John W. Miner. Urbana: University of Illinois Press, 1974.

Cook, Bruce. *Listen to the Blues*. New York: Charles Scribner's & Sons, 1973.

Courlander, Harold. *Negro Folk Music U.S.A.* New York: Columbia University Press, 1963.

Cramer, Alex. "Johnny Shines." *Coda* 9, no. 11 (1971): 12.

Degh, Linda. *People in the Tobacco Belt: Four Lives*. National Museum of Man Mercury Series, Paper 13. Ottawa: National Museum of Canada, 1975.

Degh, Linda, and Andrew Vazsonyi. "The Memorate and the Proto-memorate." *Journal of American Folklore* 87, no. 345 (July–September 1974): 225–39.

DeMuth, Jerry. "At Home with Sleepy John Estes." *DownBeat*, November 11, 1971, pp. 9–10ff.

Dixon, Robert, and John Godrich. *Recording the Blues*. New York: Stein & Day, 1970.

Dollard, John. *Criteria for the Life History: With Analyses of Six Notable Documents*. 2d ed. New York: Peter Smith, 1949.

Dorson, Richard. "Negro Folksongs in Michigan from the Repertoire of J. D. Suggs." *Folklore and Folk Music Archives* 9, no. 1 (Fall 1966): 3–39.

Ebner, Dean. *Autobiography in Seventeenth Century England: Theology and the Self*. The Hague: Mouton, 1971.

Ellison, Ralph. *Shadow and Act*. 3d ed. New York: Vintage Books, 1972. (First edition, 1953.)

Evans, David. "Afro-American One-stringed Instruments." *Western Folklore* 29 (October 1970): 229–45.

————. *Big Road Blues: Tradition and Creativity in the Folk Blues*. Berkeley: University of California Press, 1982.

————. *Tommy Johnson*. London: Studio Vista, 1971.

Fahey, John. *Charley Patton*. London: Studio Vista, 1970.

Ferris, William. *Blues from the Delta*. London: Studio Vista, 1970; Garden City, N.Y.: Anchor Press, 1978.

————. "Interview with Lee Kizart." *Blues Unlimited*, no. 72 (May 1970): 9.

————. "Racial Repertoires Among Blues Performers." *Ethnomusicology* 14, no. 3 (September 1970): 439–49.

————. "Records and the Delta Blues Tradition." *Keystone Folklore Quarterly* 14, no. 4 (Winter 1969): 158–65.

Glassie, Henry; Edward Ives; and John Szwed. *Folksongs and Their Makers*. Bowling Green, Ohio: Bowling Green University Popular Press, 1971.

Godrich, John, and Robert Dixon. *Blues and Gospel Records 1902–1942*. London: Storyville, 1969.

Groom, Bob. *The Blues Revival*. London: Studio Vista, 1971.

Gruver, Rod. "The Autobiographical Theory Re-Examined." *John Edwards Memorial Foundation Quarterly* 6, part 3, no. 19 (Autumn 1970): 129–31.

————. "The Blues as Dramatic Monologues." *John Edwards Memorial Foundation Quarterly* 6, part 1, no. 17 (Spring 1970): 28–31.

————. "Blues Poets, Interviews and Literary Critics." *Coda* 2, no. 8 (April 1974): 12–14.

Gunn, Janet Varner. *Autobiography: Toward a Poetics of Experience.* Philadelphia: University of Pennsylvania Press, 1982.

Guralnick, Peter. *Feel Like Going Home: Portraits in Blues and Rock and Roll.* New York: Fusion Books, 1971.

———. *Lost Highway: Journeys and Arrivals of American Musicians.* Boston: David Godine, 1979.

Handy, W. C. *W. C. Handy: Father of the Blues.* 2d ed. New York: Collier Books, 1970. (First edition 1941.)

Hannerz, Ulf. *Soul Side: Inquiries into Ghetto Culture and Community.* New York: Columbia University Press, 1969.

Haralambos, Michael. *Right On. From Blues to Soul in Black America* New York: Drake Publishers, 1975.

Hughes, Langston. *The Langston Hughes Reader.* New York: George Braziller, 1958.

Hurston, Zora Neale. "Characteristics of Negro Expression." In *Negro: An Anthology,* edited by Hugh Ford. New York: F. Ungar Publishing Co., 1970. Original Editor: Nancy Cunard; New York: F. Unger Publishing Co., 1934.

———. *Jonah's Gourd Vine.* Philadelphia: J. B. Lippincott Co., 1934.

Jackson, Bruce. "Stagoloo Stories: A Bad Man Goes Gentle." *Southern Folklore Quarterly* 29, no. 2 (June 1965): 188–94.

Jarrett, Dennis. "The Singer and the Bluesman: Formulations of the Personality in the Lyrics of the Blues," *Southern Folklore Quarterly* 42, no. 1 (1978): 31–37.

Jones, Leroi. *Black Music.* New York: William Morrow, 1968.

———. *Blues People.* New York: William Morrow, 1968.

Kane, Harnett. *Queen New Orleans.* New York: William Morrow, 1949.

Keil, Charles. *Urban Blues.* Chicago: University of Chicago Press, 1966.

Kellner, Bruce. *Keep Inchin Along: Selected Writings of Carl Van Vechten About Black Art and Letters.* Westport, Conn.: Greenwood Press, 1979.

Koester, Bob. "Hoodoo Man Blues: Junior Wells' Chicago Blues Band." Delmark, DC-612.

Langness, L. L. *The Life History in Anthropological Science.* New York: Holt, Rinehart & Winston, 1965.

Leadbitter, Mike. "Big Boy Crudup." *Blues Unlimited,* no. 75 (September 1970): 18–19.

Leadbitter, Mike, and Neil Slaven. *Blues Records: 1943–1966.* New York: Oak Publications, 1968.

Leadbitter, Mike. *Delta Country Blues.* Bexhill-on-Sea: Blues Unlimited, 1968.

———. *Nothing But the Blues.* New York: Oak Publications, 1971.

——— and Eddie Shuler. *From the Bayou.* Bexhill-on-Sea: Blues Unlimited, 1969.

Lester, Julius. "Mister White Take a Break." *Sing Out* 18, no. 4 (October–November 1968).

Lightfoot, William. "Charlie Parker: A Contemporary Folk Hero." *Keystone Folklore Quarterly* 17, no. 2 (Summer 1972): 51–62.

Lomax, Alan. *Mister Jelly Roll: The Fortunes of Jelly Roll Morton, New Orleans Creole and "Inventor of Jazz."* New York: Universal Library, Grosset & Dunlap, 1950. Reprint edition: Berkeley: University of California Press, 1973.

Lomax, John, and Alan Lomax. *Negro Folksongs as Sung by Leadbelly.* New York: Macmillan Co., 1936.

Lornell, Kip, and Jim O'Neal. "Living Blues Interview: Hammie Nixon and Sleepy John Estes." *Living Blues,* no. 19 (January–February 1975): 13–19.

Lydon, Michael. *Boogie Lightning.* New York: Dial Press, 1974.

Marcus, Griel. *Mystery Train: Images of America in Rock and Roll.* New York: E. P. Dutton, 1976.

Mazzolini, Tom. "K. C. Douglas." *Living Blues*, no. 15 (Winter 1973–74): 15–19.

Merriam, Alan. *The Anthropology of Music.* Evanston: Northwestern University Press, 1964.

Merriam, Alan P., and Raymond W. Mack. "The Jazz Community." *Social Forces* 30, no. 3 (March 1960): 211–22.

Miller, Ruth. *Black American Literature.* Beverly Hills, Calif.: Glencoe Press, 1971.

Mitchell, George. *Blow My Blues Away.* Baton Rouge: Louisiana State University Press, 1971.

Murray, Albert. *The Hero and the Blues.* Columbia: University of Missouri Press, 1973.

———. *The Omni-Americans.* New York: Outerbridge & Drenstfrey, 1970.

———. *Stompin the Blues.* New York: McGraw-Hill, 1976.

Napier, Simon. *Blackwood Blues.* London: Blues Unlimited, 1968.

Neal, Larry. "The Ethos of the Blues." *The Black Scholar* 3, no. 10 (Summer 1972), 42–48.

Neff, Robert, and Anthony Connor. *Blues.* Boston: David Godine, 1975.

Odum, Howard W., and Guy B. Johnson. *The Negro and His Songs.* New York: New American Library, 1969.

———. *Negro Workaday Songs.* Chapel Hill: University of North Carolina Press, 1926.

Oliver, Paul. *Aspects of the Blues Tradition.* New York: Oak Publications, 1970.

———. *Bessie Smith.* London: Cassell, 1959.

———. *Conversations with the Blues.* London: Cassell & Co., 1965.

———. *The Meaning of the Blues.* 2d ed. New York: Collier, 1969. Original Title: *Blues Fell This Morning.* New York: Collier, 1960.

———. *Savannah Syncopators: African Retentions in the Blues.* New York: Stein & Day, 1970.

———. "Some Comments: African Influence and the Blues." *Living Blues*, no. 8 (Spring 1972): 13–17.

———. *The Story of the Blues.* New York: Chilton Book Co., 1969.

Olney, James. *Metaphors of Self: The Meaning of Autobiography.* Princeton: Princeton University Press, 1972.

Olsson, Bengt. *Memphis Blues.* London: Studio Vista, 1970.

O'Neal, Amy. "Snooky Pryor." *Living Blues*, no. 6 (Autumn 1971): 4–7.

O'Neal, Jim. "Joe Willie Wilkins." *Living Blues*, no. 11 (Winter 1972–73): 13–17.

O'Neal, Jim, and R. T. Cuniff. "Hound Dog Taylor." *Living Blues* 1, no. 4 (Winter 1970): 4–7.

O'Neal, Jim, and Bill Greensmith. "Jimmy Rogers." *Living Blues*, no. 14 (Autumn 1973): 11–20.

O'Neal, Jim, and Amy O'Neal. "Jimmy Reed." *Living Blues*, no. 25 (May–June 1975): 16–41.

O'Neal, Jim; Amy O'Neal; and Dick Shurman. "Otis Rush." *Living Blues*, no. 28 (July–August 1976): 10–28.

Osborne, Hoyle. "I Been Headed Up Ever Since: An Interview with Fred McDowell." *Sing Out* 19, no. 2 (July–August 1969): 16ff.

Oster, Harry. *Living Country Blues.* Detroit: Folklore Associates, 1969.

Ottenheimer, Harriet. "The Second Time Around: Versions and Variants in the

Life Story Narrative of Cousin Joe, New Orleans Blues Singer." *Louisiana Folklore Miscellany* 5, no. 2 (1982): 7–12.

Palmer, Robert. *Deep Blues*. New York: Viking Press, 1981.

Pearson, Barry Lee. "The Late Great Elmore James." *Keystone Folklore Quarterly* 17, no. 4 (Winter 1972): 162–72.

Perdue, Chuck. "I Swear to God It's the Truth If I Ever Told It." *Keystone Folklore Quarterly* 14, no. 1 (Spring 1969): 1–56.

Puckett, Newbell Niles. *The Magic and Folk Beliefs of the Southern Negro*. New York: Dover, 1969.

Ramsey, Frederick, Jr. *Been Here and Gone*. New Brunswick: Rutgers University Press, 1960.

———. "Leadbelly's Last Session." *High Fidelity Magazine* (November–December 1953).

Redd, Lawrence. *Rock Is Rhythm and Blues: The Impact of Mass Media*. East Lansing: Michigan State University Press, 1974.

Rooney, James. *Bossmen: Bill Monroe and Muddy Waters*. New York: Dial Press, 1971.

Rowe, Mike. *Chicago Breakdown*. London: Eddison Press, 1973; New York: Drake, 1975.

Rowe, Mike, and Mike Leadbitter. "I Was the Baby Boy." *Blues Unlimited*, no. 96 (November 1972): 4ff.

Sackheim, Eric. *The Blues Line: A Collection of Blues Lyrics*. New York: Schirmer, 1975.

Scarborough, Dorothy. "The Blues as Folksong." In *Coffee in the Gourd*, pp. 52–66. Austin: Texas Folklore Society, 1923.

Shapiro, Nat, and Nat Hentoff. *Hear Me Talkin to Ya: The Story of Jazz as Told by the Men Who Made It*. 2d ed. New York: Dover, 1966.

Shaw, Arnold. *Honkers and Shouters: The Golden Years of Rhythm and Blues*. New York: Macmillan Co., 1978.

———. *The World of Soul*. New York: Cowles Book Co., 1970.

Shurman, Dick. "Never Seen a Slide." *Blues Unlimited*, no. 72 (June 1972): 12–13.

Sidran, Ben. *Black Talk*. New York: Holt, Rinehart & Winston, 1971.

Smith, Edna. "Musical Training in Tribal West Africa." *African Music: Journal of the African Music Society* 3, no. 1 (1962): 6–10.

Stone, Albert. *Autobiographical Occasions and Original Acts*. Philadelphia: University of Pennsylvania Press, 1982.

Szwed, John. "Musical Adaptation Among Afro-Americans." *Journal of American Folklore* 82, no. 324 (April–June 1964): 112–21.

———. "Negro Music: Urban Renewal." In *Our Living Traditions: An Introduction to American Folklore*, edited by Tristram Potter Coffin. New York: Basic Books, 1968.

Titon, Jeff. "All Pretty Wimmens: JoJo Williams." *Blues Unlimited*, no. 64 (July 1969): 13–14.

———. "Autobiography and Blues Texts: A Reply to 'The Blues as Dramatic Monologues.'" *John Edwards Memorial Foundation Quarterly* 6, part 2, no. 18 (Summer 1970): 79–82.

———. *Downhome Blues Lyrics: An Anthology from the Post–World War II Era*. Boston: Twayne, 1981.

———. *Early Down Home Blues: A Musical and Cultural Analysis*. Urbana: University of Illinois Press, 1977.

————. "The Life Story." *Journal of American Folklore* 93, no. 369 (July–September 1980): 276–92.

Townley, Ray. "Bobby Bland: Blue in Name Only." *DownBeat*, September 12, 1974, p. 18.

Vechten, Carl Van. "The Black Blues." *Vanity Fair* 24, no. 6 (August 1925): 57, 86, 92.

Welding, Peter. "I Sing for the People: An Interview with Bluesman Howling Wolf." *DownBeat*, December 14, 1967, pp. 20–21.

Wells, Chauncy Westmore. "The Art of Narrative in Autobiography." *The Charles Mills Gayley Anniversary Papers: Publications in Modern Philology*, 11, pp. 57–76. Berkeley: University of California Press, 1922.

Wells, Dicky. *The Night People: As Told to Stanley Dance*. Boston: Crescendo Publishing Co., 1971.

White, Bukka. "Mississippi Blues," vol. I. Takoma Records B1001.

White, Ivey Newman. *American Negro Folksong*. Cambridge, Mass.: Harvard University Press, 1928.

Work, John Wesley. *American Negro Songs and Spirituals*. New York: Howell Soskin & Co., 1940.

Zur Heide, Karl Gert. *Deep South Piano: The Story of Little Brother Montgomery*. London: Studio Vista, 1970.

Index